The Royal Way of Death

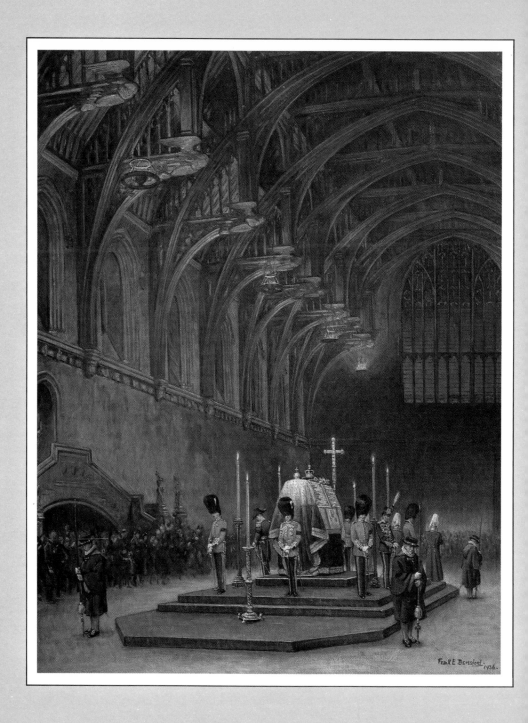

OLIVIA BLAND

The Royal Way of Death

CONSTABLE · LONDON

First published in Great Britain 1986
by Constable and Company Ltd
10 Orange Street London WC2H 7EG
Copyright © 1986 by Olivia Bland
Set in Monophoto Ehrhardt 11pt by
Servis Filmsetting Ltd, Manchester
Printed in Great Britain by
BAS Printers Ltd, Over Wallop

British Library CIP data
Bland, Olivia
The royal way of death
1. Great Britain – Kings and rulers – Death
and burial   2. Funeral rites and ceremonies –
Great Britain – History
I. Title
393'.9'0880621   GT3243

ISBN 0 09 465430 1

To Simon and our children with my love.
Long may they live!

Contents

Illustrations

Acknowledgements

I am very conscious that this book could never have been written without the help and encouragement of many people and to them all I am deeply grateful.

I offer my thanks to Her Majesty The Queen for her gracious permission to reproduce the painting, The Princes' Vigil by Frank E Beresford and for allowing me access to Ceremonial Records and newspaper cuttings in the Royal Archives.

I also thank Lord Methuen for allowing me to reproduce the Corsham Court portrait of Queen Elizabeth I.

I am very grateful to Sir Robin Mackworth-Young and Mr Oliver Everitt, past and present Librarians at Windsor and to Miss Jane Langton, Registrar of the Royal Archives and her team whose kindness and consideration were unfailing.

I would like to thank the staff of the London Library for much patient help, together with those of the National Portrait Gallery Archives, the Public Record Office, Chancery Lane and the British Library.

I extend my very grateful thanks to my colleagues at the Museum of London especially to Valerie Cumming and Davina Fennemore for years of encouragement, advice and interest and to Barington Gray for all his help with the illustrations.

A number of friends have encouraged me by their interest and provided me with information and I am grateful to them. And last, but not least, I thank my family who have wonderfully supported me and lived daily with this project for over two years.

Introduction

We all love a royal occasion. There is something in the British make-up, perhaps in the make-up of the human race, that responds to pageantry: the military band, flags, brilliant uniforms and clattering horses with jingling harnesses. British heritage is rich in such pageantry, much of it royal. As a monarchy, we have coronations and royal weddings, the State Opening of Parliament, the Trooping of the Colour and Jubilees, and we have the sombre panoply of the royal funeral.

It is today fashionable in some quarters to deride much of Britain's ceremonial life. There are those, like Mr Willie Hamilton, the Labour MP, who find it all inappropriate to modern life and an unjustifiable expense. But there are few who are not moved by a state or ceremonial royal funeral. Coronations may have little to do with the life of ordinary people, though they may enjoy the spectacle and get briefly caught up in the festive spirit of the occasion, but we have all lost loved ones. We know something of what the mourners are feeling and if we feel uplifted by the ceremonial, both religious and secular, then perhaps we may take that emotion to ourselves, on behalf of our own dead loved ones.

In the Victorian era death was overplayed with a suffocating sentimentality so that people became sated with the whole subject and its gloomy trappings. On top of this came the carnage of the First World War and by the end of it people could no longer cope with the very thought of death. Death and its trappings, mourning and elaborate funerals were pushed under the carpet and ignored. Almost alone, the royal family kept up the old traditions surrounding death. Twenty, or even ten years ago, a book on death would have been unthinkable but in the last few years there has been a sudden revival of interest in the subject. It is more openly talked about, and it is more often thought desirable to teach children about death and to include them in its rituals. A number of books about death, its traditions and ritual have come out and one college of adult education even runs a course on death.

The purpose of Christian burial, at least in the Church of England, and of the rites for the dying, is twofold: to ease, by prayer, the passing of the soul of the departed on its way to God – 'Go forth upon thy journey, christian soul . . .', as the Commendatory Prayer in the Church of England Prayer Book puts it – and to comfort those who are left behind by stressing our hopes of a life hereafter. This is all present in the royal funeral but by making of it a public spectacle, the royal family are, whether they intend it or not, inviting all of us to share in both these elements. The prayers of many in the crowd go with the body on the gun-carriage and many are uplifted and given hope by the ritual of which they seem to be a part.

But this is not all there is to it. The funeral cortège of a monarch or of a great noble in medieval times was an opportunity to demonstrate the abiding power of the ruling dynasty. All who rode or walked in the procession showed their loyalty to the dead sovereign and by inference to his successor. Gradually the emphasis changed as the monarch's position became safer and more established, but in much later times, and the funeral of Queen Victoria is an example, it took on international meaning with friendly nations and dynasties represented in the cortège. Today that aspect is almost entirely formalized with most nations who are not actually at war with one another represented at each other's funerals. Indeed they make good opportunities for the most unlikely meetings of rulers. Royal funerals have, however, always reflected the status of monarchy in the country. With this in mind, the reader of this account of funerals may compare the huge international event which was Queen Victoria's funeral with the ramshackle and slipshod ceremonial of George IV's and the tiny hole-in-the-corner funeral of Charles I when the status of monarchy in England was non-existent.

The two religious purposes of funeral ritual are shared by all the denominations of Christianity, perhaps by most religions, but they have their different ways of achieving them and lay emphasis on different aspects of the theory. Roman Catholicism lays tremendous stress on sin and the difficulties of achieving salvation. Minette, youngest daughter of Charles I and married to the brother of Louis XIV, as she lay dying in France of a horribly painful internal complaint, was upbraided by the attendant priest for asking if her agony would soon be over. She should pray for as much time and as much pain as possible to expiate her sins, was the stern reply. And she had led a relatively blameless life.

When the Hapsburg emperors of Austria-Hungary died, they were carried in procession to the doors of the Church of the Capuchin Friars in Vienna. Here the Lord Chamberlain would knock with his golden staff. In reply to the cry, 'Who asks for admittance?', he would reply, 'His Apostolic Majesty the Emperor . . .', and give a long list of important titles. 'We know him not,' would come the uncompromising reply, the doors remaining firmly shut. When the Lord Chamberlain knocked a second time and the question was put 'Who asks for admittance?', he would give another long list of titles but minor ones this time, and would receive the same reply, 'We know him not'. At a third knock, and 'Who asks for admittance?', 'Your brother Franz, a miserable sinner begs admittance' would be the answer. 'Ah, him we know'; the gates would be swung open and the late emperor buried with his forefathers within.

It is possible that the clergy play a larger part in the obsequies of an important Roman Catholic, praying round the body as it lies in state and conducting it to the church for burial. At the funeral of Princess Grace of Monaco, seen on television in 1982, it was very noticeable that the remains of the Princess were escorted in procession from the palace to the cathedral largely by priests and nuns, whereas at a Church of England royal funeral today, the clergy take over only at the church door.

When a Romanov tsar of Russia died, he lay for weeks exposed in his coffin in the fortress Cathedral of SS Peter and Paul in St Petersburg while countless thousands of his subjects shuffled past the bier, bending to kiss an icon held in the dead man's hand while Russian Orthodox priests chanted an endless litany of prayers.

At a Hindu funeral, and we have recently seen that of Mrs Indira Gandhi on television, the body is carried uncoffined and for all to see to the burning ghats where it is ritually cremated and the ashes cast upon the waters of the holy river whence they make their way to God. The Christian Protestant idea is to cast our sins at the feet of Christ and hope.

Today the royal family are almost always buried at Windsor, the Royal Burial Ground at Frogmore having, in this century, taken over from St George's Chapel itself, except for sovereigns and their consorts. Before that, Westminster Abbey housed most royal remains for the best part of three hundred years. But it was not always so. In medieval times and before, kings and queens were often buried in the nearest abbey or cathedral to their place of death or in a church associated with a saint who had special meaning for the deceased. Such a one was the Black Prince, a national hero at the time of his death in France in 1376. The Prince had a special devotion to Our Lady Undercroft in Canterbury Cathedral and planned his funeral there to the smallest details. It took four months to arrange and took on the guise of a great national event comparable to that of Nelson or the Duke of Wellington nearly five centuries later. Winchester and Worcester Cathedrals, Reading, Faversham, Waltham Abbeys all have their Royal tombs and so have many others. Richard III, killed at Bosworth Field, was buried in Leicester Abbey and his tomb later destroyed. However, since Edward the Confessor, in 1066, a number of kings and queens were buried in Westminster Abbey. One of these was Eleanor of Castile, wife of Edward I, who was embalmed and brought by easy stages from Nottingham to London, Edward later erecting a cross at each resting place along the way, the last of which is Charing Cross. But it was not until Henry VII built the magnificent chapel which bears his name that Westminster Abbey became the established burial place for royalty. Even then, Henry VIII was buried in St George's Chapel at Windsor with Queen Jane Seymour, and his two beheaded wives, Anne Boleyn and her cousin, Katharine Howard, both lie in the Church of St Peter Ad Vincula close to the spot where they died in the Tower of London. Poor Anne was not even accorded a proper coffin but was buried in an arrow case.

One of the last British kings to be buried abroad was the deposed Stuart king, James II. After an attempt to regain his throne through Ireland was thwarted by William III at the Battle of the Boyne, James and his family lived at the Palace of St Germain in France under the protection of Louis XIV. When he died in 1701, he left instructions that his body was to be buried in his parish church of St Germain en Laye. In fact this church only received part of his bowels, his embalmed body being deposited in the priory church of the English Benedictine monks in Paris and his head and brains in the Scots College in Paris. More than two and a half centuries later, another king, Edward VIII, who had also lived in France for many years following his abdication, was allowed back after his death, to be buried among his family at Windsor.

In the first hundred years of the period covered in this book, royal funerals, indeed the funerals of all the nobility and arms-bearing families, were strictly organized and controlled by the College of Arms who enforced the sumptuary legislation. These sumptuary laws regulated many aspects of life in medieval, Tudor and Stuart England including who might have a heraldic funeral, who might wear black for mourning and what that mourning might consist of. Heralds carried the hatchments of the deceased, the crested helmet, sword, gauntlets etc. whose modern counterpart are the insignia of a great or royal man which are today carried before his coffin.

As time went on, the upwardly mobile middle classes, merchants and professional people, began to infringe the sumptuary laws and arrange grand funerals for their important members. The College of Arms would exact fines, but they cheerfully paid up and continued to break the laws until in the eighteenth

Opposite: The Interior of Henry The Seventh's Chapel.

century the heralds gave up enforcing them.

Though the College of Arms arranged a royal funeral, it was the Great Wardrobe which provided everything necessary for that funeral from the coffin, pall and canopy to the clothes of all the participants. It upheld the sumptuary laws by issuing different lengths of cloth to the various ranks of persons and exact instructions as to how the garments should be made and worn. This continued until the closing of the Great Wardrobe in the nineteenth century and thereafter servants were given allowances for their mourning from the Privy Purse while persons of higher rank in the household were expected to provide their own. This continued until well into the twentieth century.

Occasionally, among our modern practices of funerals and mourning, we catch an echo from the distant past. Such an echo was to be found in the state visit of King George VI and Queen Elizabeth to France in 1938. Shortly before the four-day visit took place, the Queen's mother, the Countess of Strathmore, died and the plans for the Queen's wardrobe were thrown into disarray. For her to appear at all the events of this festive occasion in black would obviously cast a blight over the whole affair, so what was to be done? It was then fortunately remembered that up until the seventeenth century French queens wore white mourning. Mary Queen of Scots wore 'deuil blanc' as a young widow in France before she came to Scotland in 1560. The Queen was delighted with the idea and so Norman Hartnell, with a fortnight to go before the visit, transformed the entire 'trousseau' of thirty dresses into white. The result was a 'succès fou' in Paris where the French were enchanted.

Another strange link with a bygone age came in 1964 when demolition workers in Stepney came across a small lead coffin. This was taken to the London Museum where it was discovered to contain the remains of Anne Mowbray, Duchess of York who had died at Greenwich just three weeks short of her ninth birthday in 1481. Daughter of the last Mowbray Duke of Norfolk and richest heiress in the land, Anne had been married at five to the four-year-old second son of Edward IV. Her coffin was evidently removed to the Abbey of the Minoresses, known as the Minories, some twenty years after her original state funeral with a river procession, and her burial in Westminster Abbey. It had been necessary to disinter her coffin during building works at Westminster and its removal to the Minories was doubtless undertaken at the request of Anne's mother the Duchess of Norfolk who had developed close links with the Minoresses. At the time the coffin was discovered at the Minories, rough handling dislodged and badly disarranged the skeleton within. Opportunity was taken by a small team of medical and scientific experts to examine the remains which were then carefully reassembled in the fifteenth-century coffin.

On the Queen's order, the coffin was then carried to Westminster Abbey. Here a service, conducted by the Dean and in the presence of the Lord Chamberlain, was held and the Princess was reinterred in the Henry VII Chapel close to the site of her original burial place and near the alleged bones of her young husband, Richard, Duke of York, the younger of the Princes in the Tower. She was, then, the last royal person to be finally laid to rest in that ancient royal tomb house which was not yet built when the tiny Duchess died so long ago.

Queen Elizabeth I (the Corsham Court Portrait) attributed to Marcus Gheeraerts. The heavy symbolism of Father Time with his scythe over one shoulder and Death leering over the other can have given little pleasure to the sitter in spite of the Heavenly Crown to which the Prayer Book in her hand presumably helps her to aspire.

Queen Elizabeth I
'A ripe apple from the tree'

'Madame,' said Mr Secretary Robert Cecil, son of Queen Elizabeth's faithful Lord Burghley, 'to content the people, you *must* go to bed.' '*Must?*' snapped the Queen. 'The word "must" is not to be used to princes.' And she continued, 'Little man, little man,' for he was little and had a twisted spine, 'if your father had lived ye durst not have said so much; but ye know that I must die and that makes ye so presumptuous.' Elizabeth was dying, but her tongue was as sharp as ever and she was insisting upon dying on a pile of cushions on the floor of one of the withdrawing chambers of her palace at Richmond.

It was March 1603, the Queen was in her seventieth year and the forty-fifth year of her reign, and apart from smallpox in her late twenties and a number of alarming but short-lived illnesses, she had always been remarkably strong and healthy. This she herself put down to her 'exact temperance both as to wine and diet', which she used to say was 'the noblest part of physic'[1] and her active habits. All her life she had walked a great deal, briskly, 'to get up a heat',[2] hunted regularly and danced for exercise, particularly if the weather was bad. And all this she continued until a few weeks before her death.

That winter, however, she had been very low in spirits; indeed some people felt that she had never fully got over the execution in 1601 of her last and perhaps best-loved favourite, the renegade Earl of Essex.

In December 1602 her godson, Sir John Harington, came to Court and tried to cheer her by reading some of his witty verses. She smiled wanly but said: 'When thou dost feel creeping time at thy gates, these fooleries will please thee less: I am past my relish for such matters.'[3] Yet her mood was fluctuating, for a few days later she was observed dancing a coranto, and she joined in the Christmas festivities at Whitehall.

In January the Court moved to Richmond, that 'warm box to shelter [her] old age'.[4] The palace itself may have been warm, but at the time of the move the weather had turned very cold and her ladies remonstrated with the Queen for dressing in 'summer-like garments', drawing the astringent reply that they were much healthier than furs.

Throughout February Elizabeth continued to take part in affairs of state, receiving the new Venetian ambassador in all her old splendour and addressing him at length in excellent Italian. Yet about this time William Camden tells us that the Queen

> then commanded that Ring, wherewith she had joyned as it were in marriage to her Kingdom at her inauguration [her coronation ring], and she had never after taken off, to be filed off from her finger, for that it was so grown into the flesh, that it could not be drawn off. Which was taken as a sad presage as if it were portended that that marriage with her kingdome, contracted by the Ring, would be dissolved.[5]

The obvious explanation for this is that it had become painfully tight, but it had a profound effect upon the Court and all who heard about it, and people started looking towards her presumed successor, the King of Scots. At least, according to Camden, the Queen felt that this was the case, and human nature being what it is, it seems all too likely. Camden relates 'that many of the Nobility did by secret letters and messengers seeke to win favour with the Queene [King?] of Scots, that they adored him as the Sun rising and neglected her as now ready to set: (which as the feminine sex and old age are apt to suspect) she readily believed.'[6] Sir John Harington, writing to his wife on that December visit to Court, says, 'I find some less mindful of what they are soon to lose, than of what they may perchance hereafter get.'[7]

Then at the end of February came a serious blow to the Queen's morale – the death of her former lady-in-waiting, cousin and closest woman-friend, the Countess of Nottingham. In the lives of queens, close friends are few and precious, so that the loss of Lady Nottingham was undoubtedly enough seriously to undermine the failing spirits of the elderly Queen. This was almost certainly all there was to it, yet some years after her death a story was put about which, if true, would have been enough to cause a much more complete breakdown than actually occurred.

No such tale was circulated at the time, as would surely have happened in any gossip-rife court if it had any grain of truth in it, but in 1620 a story appeared in Holland to the effect that, as Lady Nottingham lay dying, she begged that the

Queen would come to see her, adding that she had something on her conscience which she must confess to her before she could die in peace. On the Queen's arrival she produced a ring which she said had been sent to her by Essex as he lay in the Tower awaiting execution with the urgent request that she should deliver it to the Queen. It was clear that Elizabeth recognized this ring as one which she had given Essex on his departure for Cadiz some years before with the pledge that whatever charges his enemies might have brought against him, or whatever actual crimes he had committed against her, if he sent her this ring she would either pardon him or at least allow him to justify himself to her in person, and indeed she had given him such a ring. But the Countess confessed, so the story went, that instead of delivering the ring immediately, she had shown it to her husband who had ordered her to hide it and say nothing to the Queen who, after several hesitations, signed Essex's death warrant. On seeing the ring, Elizabeth was seized with a passion of rage and grief, and, taking the dying Lady Nottingham by the shoulders, she shook her and, exclaiming that God might forgive her but that she never could, rushed out of the death chamber.

According to this anecdote, Elizabeth, returning to the Court, surrendered herself to despair and it is certainly true that from then until a few days before her death, she sat day and night upon cushions on the floor, having 'a persuasion that yf she once lay down she should never rise', and a great melancholy did take possession of her in her last weeks. Yet the Earl of Nottingham, more the villain of the story than his poor wife, continued close to her until the end. The tale is considered to be apocryphal. The Queen certainly visited and ministered to her old friend on her deathbed, but there was not, at the time, any suggestion of a quarrel.

Having given her spirits up to melancholy, Elizabeth quickly deteriorated physically. She could not sleep and was feverish and restless and complained of 'a heat in her breasts and dryness in her mouth and tongue',[8] and an iron band about her neck. Early in March her young kinsman, Robert Carey, of whom she was fond, arrived at Court from the North and was summoned to her presence. He found the Queen

in one of her withdrawing chambers sitting low upon her cushions. She called me to her. I kissed her hand, and told her, It was my chiefest happiness to see her in safety and health, which I wished might long continue. She took my hand and wrung it hard; and said 'No, Robin, I am *not* well!' and then discoursed to me of her indisposition, and that her heart had been sad and heavy for ten or twelve days, and in her discourse she fetched not so few as forty or fifty great sighs. I was grieved at the first to see her in such plight; for in all my lifetime before I never knew her fetch a sigh but when the Queen of Scots was beheaded. ... I used the best words I could to persuade her from this melancholy humour; but I found, by her, it was too deep rooted in her heart; and hardly to be removed.[9]

In his memoirs Carey goes on to give us a short picture of life with Elizabeth in these last days:

This was upon the Saturday night, and she gave command that the great closet should be prepared for her to go to chapel the next morning. The next day, all things being in readiness, we long expected her coming. After eleven o'clock, one of the grooms came out and bade make ready for the private closet; she would not go to the great. There we stayed long for her coming; but, at last, she had cushions laid for her in the Privy Chamber, hard by the closet door, and there she heard the service. From that day forwards she grew worse and worse.[10]

Her inner circle of courtiers had an unenviable task as she grew more cantankerous and impossible to please.

At about this time a quinsy developed in her throat. After a few days it burst and she gained some relief for a short time, but by now she seemed to have had some form of respiratory infection and soon pneumonia set in. And still she lay huddled, fully dressed, on her cushions on the floor, her ladies squatting around her. At one point she even had herself raised to her feet and remained standing, supported by her ladies, who, of course, must also stand, for fifteen hours. At last, on 21 March the Lord Admiral (Nottingham) was sent for. He came to her, knelt among her cushions and tenderly fed her with broth, but when he pleaded with her to go to bed she would take no more and rounded on him, saying that 'if he were in the habit of seeing such things in his bed as she did in hers, he would not persuade her to go there'. However, at last, Carey tells us, '... what by faire meanes, what by force he gatt her to bed'.[11]

It was, by now, obvious to all that she could not survive for she would take neither sustenance nor 'physicke'. Her mind was fixed 'wholly upon meditations and [she was] impatient of any talk unless it be with the Archbishop of Canterbury, with whom she prayed often and most devoutly.'[12]

Her Council tried to keep the news of the Queen's illness from the people for fear of unsettling them, but it got about and, during the few days when she lay dying, 'a strange silence descended on the whole city ... not a bell rang out, not a bugle sounded,'[13] wrote Father William Weston, a Catholic priest imprisoned in the Tower. The atmosphere was felt even there where the inmates listened for every sound from the outside world.

The question of the succession had never been formally settled, though all assumed that King James VI of Scotland, son of Elizabeth's old adversary and eventual victim, Mary, Queen of Scots, would succeed. But now she could do no more than call for her Council 'by signes ... and by putting her hand to her head when the King of Scottes was named to succeed her, they all knew hee was the man she desired should be after her.'[14] With that they had to be content, and Carey, though sincerely distressed at the approaching demise of his old friend and queen, arranged for horses to be stationed along the 'North Road' and laid his plans to endear himself to the new King by being the first to inform him of his succession.

Her last State duty performed, Elizabeth now gave herself up completely to making her peace with God. Robert Carey tells us that

> on the evening of the 23rd March she made signes for the Archbishop [old John Whitgift whom she had nicknamed her 'little black husband'] and her Chaplains to come to her, at which time I went in with them, and sate upon my knees full of teares to see that heavy sight. Her Majesty lay upon her back with one hand in the bed and the other without. The Bishop kneeled downe by her and examined her first of her faith and she so punctually answered all his several questions by lifting up her eyes and holding up her hand, as it was a comfort to all beholders.[15]

Manningham was afterwards told by some of the clergy that 'shee would not heare the Arch[bishop] speake of hope of hir longer lyfe, but when he prayed or spake of Heaven, and those joyes, she would hug his hand ...'[16] Carey goes on,

> After this he began to pray and all that were by did answer him. After he had continued long in prayer, 'till the old man's knees were weary, hee blessed her, and meant to rise and leave her. The Queene made a sign with her hand. My Sister Scroope [one of her ladies] knowing the meaning, told the Bishop the Queene desired he would pray still. He did so for a long halfe houre after, and then thought to leave her. The second time she made signes to have him continue in prayer. He did so for halfe an houre more, with earnest cries to God for her soul's health, which he uttered with that fervency of spirit, as the Queene to all our sight much rejoiced thereat, and gave testimony to us all of her christian and comfortable end. By this time it grew late, and everyone departed, all but her women that attended her.[17]

[25]

The Archbishop described the scene in almost identical terms.

The Queen had fallen quietly asleep and at three o'clock on the morning of the eve of Lady Day, the last day of the year by the old calendar, John Manningham, who was at Court at the time, tells us in his diary, 'hir Majestie departed this lyfe, mildly like a lambe, easily like a ripe apple from the tree ... and I doubt not but shee is amongst the royal saints in Heaven in eternal joyes.'[18] A special compartment of heaven for royalty is a nice idea and one which was very much subscribed to in the seventeenth century.

So the Queen was dead and within two hours Robin Carey was off, through driving rain, on his epic ride to inform King James of his accession to the throne of England – a ride which he completed in three days, arriving at Holyroodhouse about midnight on the third day, and which made him extremely unpopular with his peers at Court.

Meanwhile in London, King James was, that same morning, proclaimed King at Whitehall Gates, at Temple Bar and in Cheapside. Manningham tells us that 'the proclamation was heard with greate expectation and silent joye, noe great shouting. I think the sorrowe for hir Majesties departure was soe deep in many hearts they could not soe suddenly show anie great joy ...'[19] The Queen's death was indeed a great shock to the people, many of whom had known no other ruler. Unlike many monarchs she was well known to her people. Londoners saw her often as she travelled to or from functions and visited nobles and scholars in their houses all over the London area, while her progresses took her many times all over the south of England and the Midlands. On these occasions she was seen by many thousands of people and she would move among them joking and thanking them for their expressions of loyalty – the Tudor equivalent of a walkabout. She had an instinctive sympathy with her people; they felt that she had their interests at heart, and in her way she did. She believed implicitly in a rigid hierarchical pyramid with herself firmly fixed at the top and supported by her nobles and courtiers. Yet she never lost sight of the fact that the essential base on which this pyramid was founded was the common people whose loyalty was essential to its continued existence. She was always conscious that she 'reigned with [their] loves.'

As to a will, John Chamberlain tells us that the Queen '... made no will, nor gave anything away, so that they which come after shall finde a well stored jewell house and a rich wardrobe of more than two thousand gowns with all things else aunswerable.'[20]

For some days the Queen's body lay at Richmond attended only by three of her ladies, while preparations were made for her lying-in-state at Whitehall. Clapham relates that 'The Queen's body [was] left in a manner alone a day or two after her death, and meane persons had access to it.'[21] Can this be true? It seems more likely that her ladies would have guarded her remains jealously, unless the 'meane persons' were what would now be called morticians, about their business. It was the custom at the time, and for almost two hundred years after, to remove the bowels and heart from the bodies of the great and inter them separately in an urn. Indeed sometimes there was a separate procession and burial service for them; sometimes the urn was carried on top of the coffin in the funeral procession. The bodies were also embalmed. Queen Elizabeth had left orders that she was not to be embalmed or disembowelled and, according to Manningham, her wishes were respected. Elizabeth Southwell, who held a junior position at Court at the time, relates that Cecil ordered it to be done notwithstanding, but Manningham goes on that the body was simply 'wrapt up in cere cloth, and that verry ill too, through the covetousness of them that defrauded hir of the allowance of cloth was given them for the purpose.'[22] There are several strands of Court gossip detectable here.

Whatever the truth about the treatment her body received, it is certain that it would have been wrapped in 'cere cloth', a waxed linen sheet tied at the head and feet like a cracker, for this had long been the universal grave clothes for people of substance. In the middle ages the body was then dressed in rich garments and kings and queens in their coronation robes, often with costly rings on their fingers and orbs and sceptres in their hands. Edward the Confessor was dressed in such a rich robe that the grisly tale is told that when his coffin was opened in 1183, three copes for use in Westminster Abbey were made from it. By Tudor times, however, this practice had given way to a simple chemise and cere cloth and then an outer wrapping of lead, and instead of the body itself being displayed to the public, a richly dressed effigy lay on top of the coffin as it passed in procession or lay in state. A number of these effigies may still be seen in the Norman undercroft at Westminster Abbey. In Elizabeth's case, more than a month passed between her death and the funeral so it would have been impossible to have the real body on display all that time, and this became standard practice. Indeed we shall see that some later royalty lay unburied for almost three months.

But Elizabeth's effigy is not among those on show at Westminster Abbey, only a mid eighteenth-century wax one, and there are no references to it after its appearance at the funeral. It was presumed lost or destroyed until what some believe to be the very head of this effigy, carved by Maximillian Colt and painted by John de Critz, turned up in the London Museum not many years ago. An equestrian figure of Queen Elizabeth had been knocking around the Tower of London in one tableau or another for two centuries and was even at one time dressed in a suit of armour and had eventually been passed to the London

Museum. But by the end of the 1930s this figure had been dismantled and the head sat on a shelf or was used variously as a wig stand or to display Tudor jewellery. It was when it was got out for this last purpose in the late 1950s that someone at the Museum noticed a certain quality about the head and likeness to Elizabeth's tomb in Westminster Abbey. Several layers of paint were painstakingly chipped away and the original ground colour, painted with an exquisite skill and delicacy, was revealed. The head was eventually returned to the Tower, where it remains to this day and its origins will never be known for certain, but it is interesting to speculate that the head which has led such a chequered career for three and a half centuries, may have had its hour of glory as part of the effigy on the coffin of the great Queen Elizabeth herself.

At Whitehall, meanwhile, the palace was being hung with black from top to bottom. The Lord Chamberlain's accounts show details of thousands of yards of black cloth for hanging the walls, ceiling and floor of the room where the corpse was to lie and all approaches to it, as well as the chapel. There was black 'baies' for the windows, tables, chairs and stools, and black taffeta for trimming the bedstead 'whereon the corpes [was to be] first laid at Whitehall', and cloth of gold at £6 a yard was drawn up from the Great Wardrobe for some unspecified purpose, possibly for dressing the effigy. Then for the making of the coffin, which was to be lined with purple velvet, gilt nails were issued, and bullion nails for the lead in which the body was to be encased, black velvet for covering the chariot, black bits and stirrups for the chariot horses, and black drapes and black cloth, silk, ribbon and tassels for the barge which brought the corpse from Richmond.

> The Queen was brought by water to Whitehall,
> At every stroke the oars did tears let fall;
> More clung about the barge; fish under water
> Wept our their eyne of pearl, and swam blind after.
> I think the bargemen might, with easier thighs,
> Have rowed hir thither in hir people's eyes;
> For howsoever much my thoughts have scanned,
> She had come by water, had she come by land.[23]

This verse was written by one Taylor, later bargeman to Charles I, nicknamed the Water Poet. No one can say it is great poetry but it gives an idea, in its no doubt exaggerated style, of the general grief at the old Queen's passing. And so, at night, they brought her by torchlight from Richmond to Whitehall and she was installed in the black-draped Painted Chamber and lay in state, visited by day by anyone who could raise a suitably smart suit of mourning.

During this time the coffin was watched over at night by relays of her ladies, six at a time, we are told by Elizabeth Southwell, one of the maids-of-honour. Mistress Southwell goes on to tell a tale of horror that one night while she was one of the watchers, 'and being all in [their] places about the corpse, which was fast nailed up in a board coffin, with velvet, her body burst with such a crack that it splitted the wood, lead, and cere-cloth; whereupon the next day she was fain to be new trimmed up.'[24] If true, was this the result of the Queen's refusing to be 'opened' after her death? Surely such a cataclysmic event could never have been hushed up and yet, it does not appear in any of the other memoirs of the time. Mistress Southwell was a Roman Catholic and with several others sought to surround the events of Queen Elizabeth's last illness and death with ill-omens and to suggest that she had not died in a state of grace. Even at the time, people were warned against such apocrypha. John Chamberlain, writing to a friend said, '. . . no doubt but you shall heare her Majesties sickness and manner of death diversely related: for even here the papists do tell strange stories, as utterly void of truth, as of all civill honestie or humanitie.'[25] Yet her evidence, written some time after the events, was treated seriously by historians up to quite modern times, but is now discredited.

Meanwhile elaborate preparations were being made for the funeral in Westminster Abbey which was to be a bigger and grander affair than any that had gone before it. The Wardrobe accounts state that black 'baies' was issued for hanging around the West door as was cloth for musicians, clergy, vergers and bellringers. And, in the month that passed before the funeral on 28 April, many thousands of yards of various black fabrics for mourning were issued to everyone in any way concerned in the obsequies. All, except the poor men and women, are mentioned in the Wardrobe accounts individually by name, down to the merest scullion, with the amount of material allotted to him or her. There was black silk for the bargemen and 'ladies attendant on the corpse', a large quantity of black silk 'wrought well' for the chief mourner. About eighteen thousand yards in all of black was issued to well over a thousand people who were to take part in the funeral procession. Nobles, ladies and gentlemen of the royal household were supplied with a generous yardage for the making of cloaks, suits, dresses, veils and 'white heads [caps] for the attire of diverse gentlewomen', while all the lower orders, palace servants, servants of nobles etc., were supplied with four yards each of black cloth for jerkins, plus hose and hats. Then there was a number of large categories of people such as eldest sons of earls, dukes' second sons, earls' daughters to be supplied; ambassadors and their servants, poor men of Westminster and two hundred and sixty-six poor women. It must have been an immense drain on the Exchequer.

Of course, there had been no royal death for forty-five years, other than the two funerals of Mary, Queen of Scots at Fotheringay and Peterborough Cathedral, and this provided an opportunity for some change from traditional mourning which had become fixed in the Middle Ages. Until at least the middle of the sixteenth century women's mourning costume was very like a religious habit: a very long straight gown with a surcoat over it with a long train back and front, the foretrain looped over a girdle to enable the wearer to walk; a white 'Paris head' and white barbe, which was a kind of pleated bib-cum-wimple caught up to the ears and covering the chin. Over all a mantle and hood were worn by men and women alike. These were drawn right down over the face and were worn either closed like a Balaclava helmet or open in the front, and were extended behind into a 'tippet' which varied in length according to the rank of the wearer.

Dress at Queen Elizabeth's obsequies was brought right into line with the fashions of the day. Gone was the surcoat with the looped foretrain; the ladies all wore fashionable dresses over farthingales, barbes diminished to a mere bib on the front of the bodice, ruffs and white-lined wired veils were worn over their Paris heads. In the case of the grander ladies these fell right down to the ground. Only the chief mourner, the Marchionness of Northampton, wore a long train and this fashion continued until comparatively modern times. The men wore cloaks, though only the more important had hoods and tippets; most wore ordinary black trunk-hose suits and high-crowned hats with swords, the belts and scabbards of which were blacked. The clergy looked rather incongruous, wearing hats with their vestments.

So, at last, by 28 April, as King James wended his way slowly south from Scotland, the funeral of Queen Elizabeth took place. The palace of Whitehall was no great distance from Westminster Abbey, yet all London managed to see something of the procession. Stow tells us that 'the City of Westminster was surcharged with multitudes of all sorts of people, in the streets, houses, windows, leads and gutters, that came to see the obsequy.'[26] And what a sight it was: well worth a long wait. Well over a thousand people processed on foot. This was an innovation for former royal funeral processions had mostly been on horseback. There is a set of amusing contemporary drawings of the funeral procession of Anne of Cleves in 1557: there are little hooded figures on horseback, the ladies only distinguished by riding side-saddle and the train bearers to the chief mourner clutching the train rather precariously from their horses some distance behind.

This procession was headed by six Knights Marshals' men 'to make the way' with their gold staves, followed by the poor men and the two hundred and sixty-six poor women walking four by four in black gowns and white wired out veils. These poor people or alms men and women were a relic of the medieval tradition of bedesmen – poor men or women who prayed for the soul of the deceased in return for his charity and walked in the funeral procession carrying their rosaries. With the Reformation this practice became unacceptable, but alms were still distributed and poor people remained a feature of grand funeral processions. At Elizabeth's death, money was distributed to the poor of Greenwich, where the Queen was born, and Richmond, where she died, as well as Westminster and probably it was the Westminster contingent of these beneficiaries who took part in the procession. Next came servants of gentlemen, esquires and knights, porters, trumpeters, and Rose Pursuivant at Arms in hooded cloak, his tabard over it, worn sideways with the short sleeves back and front. These were followed by two sergeants-at-arms, the Standard of the Dragon, and then two 'Queries' leading a horse caparisoned in blue velvet to the hocks, emblazoned with the royal arms, bearing a side-saddle and nodding feathers on its head. After this came the lowest ranks of servants – Children of the Almondry, Woodyard, Scullery, Pastry, Scalding House and Larder. 'Child' was a rank of worker and had nothing to do with age. The next grade were 'Gromes', which covered such posts as 'Maker of Spice Bags', Coopers, Cart Takers and 'Wyne' and Wheat Porters. After officers of the 'Lord Maior' and servants of noblemen and 'Embassadors', 'Gromes' of the Chamber and more trumpeters, came Blewmantle Officer of Arms, another sergeant-at-arms and then the Standard of the Greyhound. And so on through Yeomen of all the aforementioned departments and more – the Counting House, the Butterie, the Tallow Chandlerie, interspersed with more heralds, standards, horses, and Children and Gentlemen of the Chappell.

The next grade up were the clerks and sergeants of all the departments of the Household; 'Chief Clarke of the Wardrop', Clark of the Green Cloth and so on through chaplains, secretaries, 'Doctors of Phisick', aldermen of London and the Recorder, the Queen's solicitor, attorney and sergeant. Then 'Mr of the Revells' and of the 'Tents' and on to the Great Officers of State; the Lord Chief Justice of England, 'Controller' and Treasurer of the Household, Chancellor of the Exchequer, bishops and faithful little Sir Robert Cecil, the late Queen's Principal Secretary, to mention but a few. The French Ambassador was the only one, apart from the chief mourner, to wear a train, carried by a bare-headed train-bearer.

The most important part of the cortège was now approaching. The Great Embroidered Banner of England was borne by the Earl of Pembroke and Lord Howard of Effingham, the Helm and Crest by Ralph Brooke, York Herald of

Arms, the Target by Chester Herald, the Sword by Norroy King of Arms, and the Coat by Clarenceaux King of Arms. These were the 'hatchments' or achievements of the dead sovereign and in early times would have been buried with the deceased for use in the after life, but by this time they were merely carried in the procession.

And here at last was the 'Chariott drawn by four grey horses trapped in black velvet, upon which Chairett stood the coffin covered with purple velvett and upon that the Representation'. This was the effigy of the dead Queen and was apparently so lifelike that Stow tells us that 'when [the multitude] beheld her statue or picture lying upon the coffin set forth in royal [Parliamentary] robes, having a crown upon the head thereof, and a ball and sceptre in either hand, there was such a general sighing and groaning and weeping as the like hath not been seen or known in the memory of man'.[27] Over the 'charrett' was held a fringed canopy, and twelve banners tracing the Queen's ancestry were carried alongside.

Now came the richly caparisoned Palfrey of Estate led by the Earl of Worcester. This again was a relic of medieval practices when the dead king's charger was ridden up the nave of Westminster Abbey at his requiem mass and symbolically offered up at the door of the choir. This was a perk of the Church. In this case two esquires were in attendance to lead it away as the procession entered the Abbey. This was followed by a Gentleman Usher of the Privy Chamber and Garter King-of-Arms and then the chief mourner, the Marchionness of Northampton, premier noblewoman of England. Her black silk gown was 'richly wrought' and her widely wired out veil combined with a mantle sweeping to the ground and into a long train. She was supported on either side by two important officers of state, the Lord Treasurer, Lord Buckhurst, and the recently widowed Lord Admiral, the Earl of Nottingham. Her train was borne by two countesses.

Groups of ladies of the aristocracy and maids-of-honour followed after, and Sir Walter Ralegh, Captain of the Guard, looking rakish with his tippet flung over his shoulder, and his guard, marching in ranks of five with their halberds reversed, brought up the rear of this amazing cortège. Considering the distance, it seems likely that those at the head of the procession were well installed in the Abbey before the coffin had left the palace.

Little is known of the burial service except that the Bishop of Chichester, the late Queen's Almoner, preached a fulsome eulogy and all her chief officers broke their staves in the traditional manner across their knees and threw them into the open grave as the coffin was lowered into the vault in King Henry VII's Chapel, symbolizing the fact that their duties were now at an end.

Elizabeth now lay with her sister Mary; divided by religion in life, in death they were united and the inscription on the monument raised to them both by James I

The monument, by Maximilian Colt, in Henry VII's Chapel, Westminster Abbey to Princesses Sophia and Mary, infant daughters of James I.

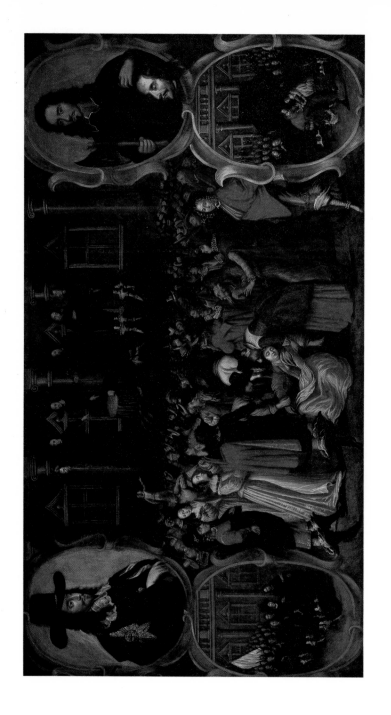

The Execution of Charles I, attributed to Weesop.
This colourful interpretation of the scene owes much to the artist's imagination.

Funeral of Elizabeth I showing the Chief Mourner and her attendants.

three years later reads, in translation from the Latin: 'Companions in rule and in the urn, we, the sisters Elizabeth and Mary sleep here in the hope of resurrection.' The fine full-length recumbent marble figure by Maximillian Colt is thought to be a good likeness, possibly even taken from the deathmask. The colouring was by Nicholas Hilliard, the miniaturist, and gilding by John de Critz I. Unfortunately both the colouring and gilding have long since vanished, but it remains a fine tomb. Though James stipulated that it was not to cost more than £600, Dean Stanley, writing in 1869, tells us that the eventual cost was £965, 'besides stonework'.[28] James I was more generous to the memory of the predecessor he had never met than was Elizabeth to her sister Mary who, dying with Calais on her heart and buried by the Catholic rite, remained without tomb or memorial. Indeed, during the whole of Elizabeth's reign her coffin lay under a pile of rubble. All that may be seen of her is a crude plaster head displayed in the Treasury which may or may not be that of her funeral effigy. James did, however, build an even grander and more expensive tomb for his mother, Mary, Queen of Scots. He had her moved to the Abbey from Peterborough Cathedral where she had been buried after her execution at Fotheringay, and she rests in the opposite aisle to Elizabeth in the Henry VII Chapel.

Evidently Elizabeth's tomb made a great impression at the time, and depictions of it were hung in 'every London and most country churches' where 'each loyal subject created a mournful monument for her in his heart'.[29] One such depiction, at St Saviour's, Southwark, bore the lines which summed up the general feeling in splendidly effusive doggerel:

St Peter's Church at Westminster
Her sacred body doth inter;
Her glorious soul with angels sings,
Her deeds have patterns been for kings,
Her love in every heart hath room:
This only shadows forth her tomb.

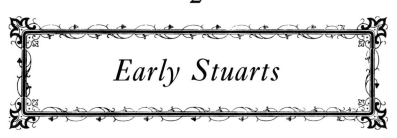

2

Early Stuarts

When James VI and I and his queen, Anne of Denmark, reached London some time after the funeral of Queen Elizabeth, they brought with them Henry, soon to be made Prince of Wales, Elizabeth, named after her godmother, the old Queen of England and Charles, a delicate child, born in 1600. But they left two little graves behind them in Scotland. The Lady Margaret, born in 1598 lived only two years and then was borne to Linlithgow in a tiny leaden 'kist', and little more than a year later she was followed by Duke Robert who lived no more than a few weeks. A black velvet 'mort cloth and a chest of oaken timber to lay [him] in after his death' were paid for by the Lords High Treasurers of Scotland. Like their elders, the bodies of royal children were embalmed and then elaborately dressed. Lady Margaret's grave clothes called for '10 quarters of wool, 6 of lining, 6 of crimson taffeta @ £8 the ell and 8 ells of florence ribbon'.[1]

As in ordinary families, the deaths of royal children were frequent in the seventeenth century and help us to discern prevailing attitudes. Death stalked constantly about among old and young alike and was treated reverently and formally, but briskly, and when all was over it was dismissed from the mind until next time. Frequently in letters of those days one reads that so and so 'hath recently lost his wife', or daughter, or quite likely both, baldly stated without any such comment as 'so tragic' or 'it is taking him a long time to get over it' as might be said today. One guesses that mothers simply tucked their dead babies away at the backs of their hearts and went stoutly on with the business of living and probably of producing more babies. Thus when the two infants, Lady Margaret and Duke Robert, had died, their obsequies were carried out with all the formality due to their rank. Mourning was issued, to the remaining royal children as well as to the Court, and the dead children lay under black palls attended by nobles for some days while their funerals were arranged. They were carried in procession with one of their brothers or sister as chief mourner in a hood and train, and buried in a royal vault. And when all the formalities were over, James and Anne put it firmly out of their minds and, soon after, departed for England.

James was an earnest and intellectual man, but awkward, reserved and a homosexual. His sense of humour, if any, was ponderous and often misplaced, and he was not known for tact or delicacy. He also hated anything to do with death. So it is unlikely that he and his queen derived much comfort from each other and it is hardly surprising that Anne, lacking a strong mind or beliefs, turned from him and immersed herself in the frivolities of Court masques and gossip, her personality growing chillier and her tongue sharper all the time.

For a time after their arrival in England all went well. There were no more deaths, but neither were there any births. Then in 1605 Princess Mary was born, to be followed the next year by Sophia, and Anne must have felt herself overtaken by a nightmarish repetition of the last few years of their lives in Scotland. Princess Sophia lived only three days and then a black draped barge brought her from Greenwich to Westminster Abbey where she was buried in a black marble tomb in the shape of a cradle containing a plump and healthy looking baby, in King Henry VII's Chapel close to the tomb of Queen Elizabeth. Perhaps by now the King's horror of obsequies was getting the better of him for he gave orders that she was to be buried 'as cheaply as possible, without any solemnity or funeral'. The King is described as taking her death 'as a wise man should'.[2] Nevertheless, someone (could it have been the King himself?) devised a sweetly poignant inscription for the cradle grave. The little princess is described as '. . . a Royal Rosebud plucked by fate . . . to flower again in Christ's own Rosegarden'.[3]

The following year Princess Mary died aged two and a half, described by her father as 'a most beautiful infant'. As she lay dying she is reputed to have repeated, 'I go, I go – Away I go,' and again, 'I go, I go.'[4] She is buried next to her sister and commemorated by a stiff little figure in a black dress lying on one elbow, a lion at her feet, and looking far older and worldly wise than her two and a half years. For some time afterwards James was wont to say, with heavy and tortuously theological wit, that he 'would not pray to the Virgin Mary, but . . . for the Virgin Mary'.[5]

The year 1612 dawned bright and hopeful for the royal family. The Prince of Wales was eighteen; a handsome, lusty, extrovert youth, adored by the people, among whom he was frequently to be seen. Feelers had been put out in several directions to arrange an advantageous marriage for the Prince – should it be the daughter of the King of Spain or of the Duke of Savoy, the sister of the King of France, or could they find a Protestant princess? Henry pronounced himself willing to fall in with his father's wishes, only saying rather wistfully, 'Your Majesty may think that my part, which is to be in love with any of them, is not yet at hand.'[6] But for the time being these negotiations were left in abeyance while a marriage was arranged between his sister, the pretty sixteen-year-old Princess Elizabeth and the young Palsgrave Frederick, the Elector Palatine.

It is true that Henry was not well. Whereas he had been a notable athlete, excelling at all equestrian sports as well as dancing, 'leaping' and especially tennis which he would play hour after hour, and being 'of a somewhat full, round face, and very pleasant disposition, his visage began to appear somewhat paler, longer, and thinner than before, he himself being more sad and retired than usual'.[7] He began to suffer from giddiness, nose bleeds and lassitude, and it is now thought that he may have developed tuberculosis, or possibly porphyria like his grandmother, Mary, Queen of Scots, which was to pass on into the Hanoverian dynasty. Yet he never complained and no one much noticed, being entirely taken up with Elizabeth's forthcoming marriage, so that well into the autumn he was allowed to continue his after-supper swims in the Thames at Richmond and long river-side walks in the moonlight 'to heare the trumpets sound an echo, which many suspected, because of the dew then falling, did him small good'.[8]

At the beginning of October King James had the body of his mother transferred from Peterborough Cathedral and installed, with a third funeral, in the handsome new tomb he had had prepared for her in the south aisle of King Henry VII's Chapel at Westminster, where it became a place of pilgrimage to devout Scots who treated her bones almost as those of a saint. However the final entombment of a grand-mother none of them had known had no power to dampen the spirits of the young royals as they embarked on the festivities surrounding the arrival of the Prince Palatine and the betrothal of this dark, handsome youth and the fair Elizabeth. The two young people were in love and romance and merrymaking were in the air, not sickness and death. Henry played his part nobly for several weeks, attending banquets and putting himself out to entertain his attractive young brother-in-law-to-be in spite of his failing health. His household were beginning to notice his increasing weakness and his 'dead, sunk eyes.'[9] Nevertheless, he played cards with Frederick, rode with him and played tennis with him, culminating in a match of epic proportions on Saturday, 24 October. It was one of the last things he did. The next day he went to chapel at St James's and was forced to listen to a sermon on a text from Job: 'Man that is born of woman is of few days and full of trouble. He cometh forth like a flower, and is cut down; he fleeth also as a shadow and continueth not.'[10] Prince Henry could struggle no more against his affliction; that day, after dinner, he took to his bed and never left it again.

His illness lasted twelve days and is described day by day in unrelenting detail by Cornwallis. Every remedy known to seventeenth-century physicians was tried, from 'sharpe, tarte cordials and cooling juleps and . . . gellies', through bleedings, 'purgations' and 'glysters' (enemas), to freshly killed pigeons applied to his shaven head, 'a cocke, cloven by the backe . . . to the soles of his feet',[11] spirits and quintessences. Finally, as a last resort, the Queen sent to the Tower of London for Sir Walter Ralegh's cordial, a secret remedy which that gentleman, at that time a prisoner in the Tower, swore would be efficacious 'unless in the case of poison'.[12] This naturally gave rise to rumours of poisoning when the Prince failed to respond.

Sir Walter Ralegh concocted his 'great cordial' in a laboratory he was allowed to fit up in the Tower of London during his 12-year imprisonment there. Only fragments of his original formula survive, but it appears to have consisted of some 40 roots, seeds, herbs and spices, some of which were probably brought by Ralegh from South America, distilled in wine and then combined with an incredible mixture of tinctures of Bezoar stone, red coral, pearls dissolved in 'oyle of Vitreoll & oyle of Sulphure', 'Eastern Bole', 'Terra Sigillata', hartshorn, ambergris, musk and sugar. A veritable witch's brew. In the case of Prince Henry the remedy gave temporary relief by inducing a great sweat, but the effect was not lasting.

All the most eminent physicians and 'chirurgeons' of the day were called in and squabbled over the dying boy whose violent pains and fever, and finally convulsions, daily increased. Yet it was not until the eleventh day that they admitted the possibility of death and summoned the Archbishop of Canterbury to give what spiritual comfort he could to the, by now, delirious prince.

Although, by the seventeenth century, there had been some advance in medicine, and more particularly in surgery, doctors still clung to the medieval theory of 'humours'. The four chief humours of the body were blood, phlegm, choler and melancholy or black choler. Sickness was caused by an imbalance of these humours and some of them had to be drawn off to restore the balance; hence the endless succession of purges, emetics, cuppings and bleedings imposed by physicians of the Stuart period, and this treatment did not go out of use until well into the nineteenth century.

The behaviour of the King and Queen was, even at the time, thought odd. After visiting the sickroom on the eighth day of the Prince's illness, with the rest of the royal family and 'divers others of the Court', they went their separate ways, Anne to Somerset House and James to Theobalds, his country seat, twelve miles from London, 'there to expect the doleful event'.[13] To us it seems unbelievably heartless for parents to abandon their dying son, but then we are accustomed to the idea of royalty enjoying a cosy family life with their children constantly around them. It was not so in the seventeenth century and Prince Henry had been brought up in a separate establishment since babyhood. He would have been virtually a stranger to his parents. Besides, though they did not know what the Prince's fever was (it is now thought to have been typhoid), the doctors were warning of 'contagion' and their responsibilities to the state would not allow the King and Queen willingly to expose themselves to danger. Princess Elizabeth, who was devoted to her glamorous brother, tried several times to get in to see him. She disguised herself and paid £1 to a coachman and two footmen of Prince Charles's household who tried to smuggle her in, but each time she was discovered and turned away. She must have been distraught at hearing afterwards that Henry's dying words were said to have been, 'Where is my deare sister?'[14]

And so, on the 6 November, after several convulsions the 'horrible violence of which caused his backbone, shoulders, armes and tongue . . . [to] disjoyntingly divide themselves', and several false alarms 'at which there arose wonderfull great shouting, weeping and crying in the chamber, court, and adjoyning street, which was so great . . . that they brought him againe',[15] Henry, Prince of Wales, died. And Cornwallis 'lifted up [his] minde to a higher watch tower, remembering that his soul now resteth in heaven where all cares, troubles, sores, sickness, crosses and afflictions shall no more annoy him; where the feares, jarres, jealousies, discontents, mutinies, uproars and dissensions of state shall never vex him . . .'[16]

On the other hand, in this world, 'jealouses and dissensions' were very much still around. At once everyone started apportioning blame; the doctors blamed each other, the Court murmured of poison administered by means of a bunch of grapes, a 'venemously scented pair of gloves', by a servant of the Earl of Somerset. Even the King came in for his share of the blame and for a time it was said to be the general belief (certainly false) that James had connived at the poisoning of his own son by his favourite, the Earl of Rochester, to whom the Prince was known to be antagonistic.

In fact, for a short time, the King appeared much affected by grief. He came up from Theobalds to the Kensington house of Sir Walter Cope, 'not brooking well the sight of any of his own houses',[17] and here he received the condolences of the young Prince Charles, now heir to the throne, the Princess Elizabeth and her betrothed, the three young people coming all together in one coach to visit him. Later he received all members of the Council and then, complaining that 'the winde blew thorough the walles' so that he 'could not lie warme in [his] bed'[18], returned to Theobalds bearing young Frederick with him for some hunting. The grief of Anne, alone at Somerset House, is unrecorded.

It is to be hoped that Frederick found consolation in hunting with the King, for his marriage was 'by this late accident retarded because yt wold be thought absurd that forrain ambassadors coming to condole the Prince's death shold find ... feasting and dauncing: so that it is deferred till May day'.[19] James might not like to dwell on death himself, but he did not wish to be misunderstood abroad. Mourning was decreed until 24 March and the 'fiancing' of Elizabeth and Frederick, celebrated on 27 December, took place in deepest black.

While preparations for the funeral, set for Monday 7 December, were going on, there occurred what Chamberlain describes as 'a very ridiculous accident' but sounds more like a cruel hoax.

A very handsome young fellow much about [the Prince's] age and not altogether unlike him, came stark naked to St James whiles they were at supper sayeing he was the Princes ghost come from heaven with a message to the King: but by no manner of examination could they get any more out of him, or who set him to worke: some say he is simple, others mad. He belongs to one of the Chauncerie. All the penance they gave him was two or three lashes, (which he endured as yt seemed without sense) and keeping him naked as he was all night and the next day in the porters lodge where thousands came to see him: the King sent to have him dismissed without more ado or enquirie.[20]

Meanwhile, at St James's, the body of the said Prince being 'bowelled, embalmed, and closed up in lead, there were foure chambers hung with blackes'.[21] Cornwallis goes on to give us an accurate picture of how things were arranged at the death of a royal personage, and it seems likely that, with minor alterations for the rank or age of the deceased and place of death, this became the regular drill. The 'blackes' were hung as follows:

the guard chamber and the presence chamber with blacke cloth, the privy chamber with finer cloth, and that which was his highness's bed-chamber with blacke velvet; in the midst whereof was set up a canopy of black velvet valanced and fringed; under which, upon tressles, the coffin, with the body of the prince was placed; covered with a large pall of black velvet, and adorned with scuchions of his armes. Upon the head of which coffin was layde a cushion of blacke velvet, and his highness's cap and coronet set thereon, as also his robes of estate, sword and rod of gold; and so it remayned (being daily and nightly watched) until two or three dayes before his highness's funeral. In which time, every day, both morning and evening, prayers were said in his presence, or privy chamber, by his chaplaines, and his gentlemen and cheife officers attendant thereat.[22]

There then ensued proceedings which are not explained by Cornwallis but which, it seems possible, were intended to represent a slow progress out of this world into the next. On the Thursday before the funeral the Prince's body was moved from his bedchamber to the privy chamber, on Friday from there into the presence chamber and on Saturday to the guard chamber. Here a procession was formed of all the Prince's officers and chief officers and the coffin was carried into the chapel where it was placed under a canopy in the choir. A service was read by the Bishop of Lichfield and gentlemen and children of the Chapel Royal 'sung divers excellent anthems, together with the organs and other winde instruments, which likewise was performed the day following, being Sunday'.[23]

On Monday the funeral took place, and what a gathering it was. A procession numbering over two thousand people took part, taking four hours to marshal and quite putting the funeral of Queen Elizabeth in the shade. The reason for this is that, whereas at Elizabeth's funeral there was only one royal household involved, the funeral of the Prince of Wales involved not only his own household, but that of the King, of the Queen, of his brother, Prince Charles, and even of the Elector Palatine, by now one of the family. And all had to be provided with 'blackes'.

Headed by 140 'poor men in gownes', the procession wended its way, to the sound of trumpets, fifes and drums, from St James's to Westminster Abbey via Charing Cross. Bearing in mind that there was no Trafalgar Square in those days, this is exactly the route that is taken to this day. They were all there: nobles and gentlemen, heralds, horses, 'covered with scuchions, cheiffrons and plumes', and all the household servants from chaplains and apothecaries to children of the woodyard and scalding house, multiplied several times. The Prince's hatchments were carried by Officers of Armes, and then came the open chariot bearing the coffin under its canopy and the effigy lying upon it robed in purple velvet and ermine, his cap and coronet on his head and his gold rod in his hand. At his feet sat the devoted Sir David Murray, his Master of the Wardrobe, who had been with him since Scottish days, hooded and cloaked.

Then came the tiny, dignified figure of the 12-year-old Prince Charles, the chief mourner, almost staggering under the weight of his great black cloak and train for which eighteen yards had been issued by the Great Wardrobe.[24] He was supported by the Lord Privy Seal and the Duke of Lennox, and after his train bearer came brother-in-law-to-be Frederick. Several more groups of nobles and 'strangers attendant on Count Palatine', the Guard, various marshals and the multitude passed into the Abbey where Henry was laid to rest in a new vault at the feet of his grandmother, so newly installed there, and in which many of his family would later lie.

Prince Henry's household remained together, presumably tying up the loose ends, until the end of December, and were then dismissed at a short service with the moving exhortation to 'Go in peace, and live as those who have lost such a master; and those that serve a master whom they cannot lose.'[25]

Whether Henry would have been a better king than Charles, and would therefore have averted the Civil War and changed the course of all subsequent history is still argued over by historians. He had all Charles's belief in the Divine Right of Kings, but he had charm and an altogether lighter touch, and much is forgiven those who have charm. On the other hand his almost medieval desire for glory could have plunged the country into potentially disastrous and certainly expensive foreign wars.

The next to go was the Queen, Anne of Denmark, in 1619. She and James, the once devoted couple, had long since drifted apart, Anne living mostly at Denmark House, as Somerset House had been renamed in her honour, or Greenwich. As well as her frivolity and shrewishness, her religion was a cause of friction between her and James and they often quarrelled when they met. Anne, once a Protestant princess, had been converted to Roman Catholicism long ago in Scotland. She held to this resolutely enough, refusing to take the Anglican communion at her coronation, yet at the same time annoying her priests by continuing to attend Church of England services. She seemed to take a perverse pleasure in upsetting both parties.

However, in the last few months of her life the royal relations were patched up and as her always poor health deteriorated and dropsy developed, James visited her dutifully twice a week until the middle of February when she seemed to be on the mend and he took himself off to Newmarket. Anne herself seemed unaware of the approach of death; she continued to sit on the religious fence and refused to make a will. She was reputed to own 'a world of brave jewels' and her daughter Elizabeth, now the mother of the first three of her fourteen children and soon to become briefly Queen of Bohemia, had expected to inherit some of them. This was not to be and none of the usual bequests were made. Indeed she died intestate and a large quantity of jewellery and money were stolen by two of her servants, the rest of her estate passing to Prince Charles, who was with her when she died. As to her faith, she died without receiving the last rites of the Roman church and may or may not have made some sort of recantation to the Archbishop of Canterbury who, determined that she should die in the Anglican faith, visited her the day before she

Anne of Denmark by an unknown engraver. This engraving was circulated at the time of the Queen's death and includes the King's astronomical verses.

died. He reported her to have responded to his urging with 'I renounce the mediation of saints and my own merits, and only rely on my Saviour Christ, who has redeemed my soul by His blood'.[26] It does not sound like Anne even on her deathbed, and may well have been broadcast by way of Protestant propaganda.

By the time the Queen died on 2 March, King James was himself ill at Theobalds and shortly afterwards became so dangerously ill that for eight days it seemed that he too might die. But he recovered and spent his convalescence writing a poem to her memory. It is a verse very much in the Renaissance idiom, alluding to a comet which was visible at the time and extolling the virtues of royalty in general rather than those of his late lamented queen:

> Thee to invite the great God sent his star,
> Whose friends and nearest kin good princes are
> Who, though they run the race of men and die
> Death serves but to refine their majesty.
> So did my Queen from hence her court remove
> And left off earth to be enthroned above.
> She's changed, not dead, for sure no good prince dies,
> But, as the sun, sets, only for to rise.[27]

'The King was ernest to have [the funeral] hastened',[28] but for ten weeks Queen Anne lay in state while money was with some difficulty raised for it, an effigy was made, the head of which may still be seen at Westminster Abbey, and her ladies bickered over precedence in the funeral procession.

Over in Germany, Anne's daughter, Elizabeth, appears to have been stricken with more than disappointment over her mother's jewels. Her old governess, Lady Harington, who was on a visit to her, delayed her departure for England in order to console her in her grief and missed her granddaughter's wedding. No doubt her sorrow was genuine as was her concern over her father's illness, but she was much comforted by receiving several outfits of the latest French mourning sent to her from Paris.

James, on the other hand, by now well known for his horror of the trappings of death, quickly cast off all black and on his return to London on the first of June, to an enthusiastic reception, rode through the City dressed entirely in pale blue. What did foreign ambassadors think, and report to their princes, when they came to offer their condolences?

When the funeral at last took place on 13 May, it was, says Chamberlain, 'a drawling, tedious sight', not the dramatic masque-like affair the Queen might have planned for herself. She had died at Hampton Court, and, if the whole company walked all the way from there to Westminster, it would certainly account for them 'laggering all along even tired with the length of the way and the weight of their clothes, every Lady having 12 yardes of broade cloth about her and the countesses sixteen'. There were, this time, two hundred and eighty poor women besides 'an army of meane fellows that were servants to the Lordes and others of the traine, and though the number of Lordes and Ladies were very great, yet ... altogether they made but a poore shew which perhaps was because they were apparrelled all alike ...'.[29] The chief mourner, who must always be a woman at the funeral of a woman, was the Countess of Arundell, possibly representing the Princess Elizabeth. Kings did not attend the obsequies of their inferiors, even their queens, and James was not present but a departure from tradition was the Prince of Wales riding just in front of the hearse. And the event did not pass without a disaster in the crowd, 'as is commonly seen in such assemblies, a younge man beeing killed outright by the falling of a stone from Northampton House ... thrust out by mischance and carelessness, of those above'.[30]

The solemnities in the Abbey, at which the Archbishop of Canterbury preached, continued until after six o'clock, and then there was an unaccountable delay of several weeks before Anne of Denmark was modestly interred under the floor of a chapel in the north-east corner of Henry VII Chapel which was later to become conspicuous for the tombs of the first Duke of Buckingham and his Duchess.

James himself died almost exactly six years later in March 1625. For some time he had been suffering from gout and an intermittent fever accompanied by vomiting and pain, possibly once again porphyria rearing its ugly head in the royal family. Although only fifty-eight, he seemed a much older man and in the last year or two he had been gradually abdicating his responsibilities to his son Charles and most of his time was spent at Royston, at Newmarket or at his favourite Theobalds where he was still able to watch the hunting and hawking from a litter. When he had first come to England James had been received at Theobalds by its then owner, Secretary Robert Cecil, soon to be created Marquis of Salisbury, and was so thrilled with the house that he made Cecil exchange it for the, by then, rather ramshackle Hatfield. Now it sheltered his old age, and it was here in early March that he was seized by a violent attack of influenza or tertian ague. So fevered did he become that he could only obtain relief by bathing his hands in cold water and drinking pints of small beer. He was treated by his doctors and had improved enough to contemplate moving to Hampton Court when his favourite, Buckingham, and his mother unaccountably decided to take a hand in his cure. They

[45]

obtained some medicine and a plaster from a Dr Remington of Essex and administered these to the King in the absence of his physicians. The resulting bout of fever was fearsome and the doctors justifiably furious, but the two shut them out of the King's bedchamber and continued their treatment. Small wonder then that the usual rumours of poison were widely believed although the post-mortem by the royal surgeons, who would have loved to accuse Buckingham and the outside doctor, showed no signs of anything untoward.

By now James was gravely ill and realized that he was dying. He was perfectly lucid, however, and sent for Prince Charles with whom he had a long conversation, so private that the Court was ordered several rooms distant. On 24 March he made public profession of his faith and received Holy Communion at the hands of John Williams, Bishop of Lincoln. Later that day he suffered a stroke and, after lingering for three days, conscious, though speechless, died on 27 March.

That morning Charles I was proclaimed at the gates of Theobalds and some days later the body of his father was carried to London in a 'convoy ... well accompanied by all the nobilitie about the towne, the pensioners, officers and household servants, besides the Lord Maior and aldermen. The shew would have been solemne but that it was marred by fowle weather, so that there was nothing to be seen but coaches and torch.'[31]

For five weeks he lay at Denmark House in the Strand, once the home of his queen, surrounded by six splendid silver candlesticks brought by Charles from Spain on one of his courting trips. Meanwhile the Court was in a nervous ferment as to their future. The Countess of Bedford relaid the current gossip to a friend:

> What the King's resolucion is yett for his owne and his father's servants, he hath not declared farder than the wight staves which are to remain as they wear; but for the greene cloth, and other inferior officers both of the household and chamber, itt is thought he will imploye his owne and dismisse his father's, because he hath caused the latter to be all removed to Denmark House to attend the body, and lodged the former about himselfe at Whitehall.[32]

Presumably this unsettled period has to be endured by courtiers at the death of the sovereign to this day.

The funeral was arranged with unusual dispatch considering its size, taking place less than six weeks after the King's death. This was probably because the new King wished to get on with his marriage to Princess Henrietta Maria of France, and indeed the proxy wedding took place even before the funeral.

Funerals seemed to be getting bigger all the time, and this time 'blacks' were issued to over nine thousand people and 'the whole charge [was] said to arise to above £50,000'.[33] How could the Exchequer afford such an outlay, and especially with a wedding in the offing? Chamberlain described the funeral as 'the greatest . . . that was ever known in England . . . [and] the herse likewise beeing the fairest and best fashioned that heth ben seen, wherein Inigo Jones, the surveyor did his part'.[34] King Charles himself was chief mourner, a morbidly familiar role to him by now, following on foot from Denmark House to Westminster Abbey. All the same Chamberlain found it 'a confused and disorderley' affair and it was five o'clock before they were all in the Abbey. Then the Bishop of London preached for two hours, rather ineptly likening the late King to King Solomon, and at last King James was lowered into the vault under the central tomb of Henry VII and his queen.

James I was not a great or inspiring king and in their hearts his people did not much mourn him, but the conventions were observed and the funeral sermon and eulogies from Oxford and Cambridge 'and other choise witts' were published and circulated with the astrological theme still to the fore:

Can a King die and we no Comet see?
Tell me, Astrologers, how can this be.[35]

The Divine Right of Kings was still firmly in place, but 24 years and a civil war were to make a great difference. There were to be no eulogies at the death of the next king.

At first fortune favoured Charles I and his queen. After a difficult start to marriage, Henrietta Maria fell deeply in love with her husband and he with her, remaining faithful to her to the end, a phenomenon almost unheard of among seventeenth-century monarchs, and by 1640 the royal nurseries contained five children. But this period had not been without grief and disappointment to the couple. Their first-born, Charles, Duke of Cornwall, born prematurely in 1629 lived only just long enough to be baptized. The disaster was blamed variously on a dogfight between two huge hounds which had frightened the Queen, a jolting on landing from her barge at Greenwich and uphill walking. Baby Charles was followed to the grave in 1639 by little Princess Catherine, the youngest of the family who also died on the day of her birth, and in 1640 by Princess Anne aged three. Anne's birth had been a difficult one and she was delicate and consumptive from the start, but sweet and affectionate and lived long enough to win the love of her family who mourned her sincerely when she died. She was a bright, intelligent child, for when she was dying she is reported by one of the royal rockers to have said: 'I am not able to say my long Prayer [the Lord's Prayer] but I will say my short one, "Lighten mine eyes, O Lord, lest I sleep the sleep of death". This done, the little lamb gave up the ghost.'[36]

All three were buried with suitable pomp in Westminster Abbey and each time the royal family and Court went into black for some weeks.

Gradually the clouds gathered over Charles I's reign and events drag slowly and painfully through the years of the Civil War to the triumph of the Roundheads, the King's imprisonment and trial on a charge of high treason and murder. All this is well-known history and beyond the scope of this book. It is after his conviction that we take up the story once more.

It was on Saturday, 27 January 1649, after a trial lasting a week before the Lords and Commons of England, a court whose authority he persistently denied, that King Charles I was sentenced to death by 'the severing of his head from his body'. He had been a prisoner for two years and Parliament was all-powerful. Soldiers were everywhere, even in the King's bedroom and it was they who were his chief enemies. As he passed among them on his way to and from the trial in Westminster Hall, many of them swore at him, blew tobacco smoke in his face and even spat upon him, whereas the common people in the crowd were often heard lamenting and calling out, 'God bless your Majesty', risking the wrath of the soldiery.

All this Charles bore with the utmost patience and dignity, merely remarking to those nearest him as he rose to leave the hall having been refused the right to address the court after the sentence had been pronounced: 'I am not suffered to speak – expect what justice other people will have!'[37]

After the trial the King was carried in a closed sedan, closely guarded, from Whitehall to St James's Palace where he was lodged in his usual bedchamber. They were already building the scaffold outside the Banqueting House and even the stern Commissioners thought it unseemly that the King should be within earshot of the hammering. With him went his only remaining attendant, Thomas Herbert, who ministered to his every earthly need, and William Juxon, Bishop of London, who did the same for his spiritual comfort. By now the King knew that his end was very near and almost all his remaining time was spent with the Bishop, in prayer and meditation on the scriptures, politely declining all visits except a messenger from Holland bearing a 'sorrowing letter' from the Prince of Wales. His dogs, Gypsy, a greyhound, and a spaniel, Rogue, had been with the King throughout his tribulations, but now he felt they were a distraction, and had them removed.

There was one visit, however, that he could not avoid, painful as it was bound to be. This was the parting with two of his children. Henrietta Maria was safely in

France with the youngest, Henrietta, whom her father had never seen, the Prince of Wales and the Duke of York were in Holland, as was Mary, now married to the Prince of Orange. But thirteen-year-old Elizabeth, a plain and serious girl, and eight-year-old Henry, Duke of Gloucester, were in London where they had spent the whole period of the Civil War in custody. At this time they were at Syon House in the care of the Earl of Northumberland, and on the day before his death they received a summons to take leave of their father at St James's. The children had seen their father once or twice in the last few years, but Elizabeth could well remember the days before the war when they were a happy family of brothers and sisters and, in spite of royal protocol, often in the company of their parents.

It was a tearful parting on both sides; the King 'kissing his children had such pretty and pertinent answers'.[38] Herbert tells us that 'the Princess being the elder, was the most sensible of her Royal Father's Condition, as appeared by her sorrowful Look and excessive weeping; and her little Brother seeing his sister weep, he took the like Impression, though by reason of his tender Age he could not have the like Apprehension.'[39] But the meeting is perhaps most poignantly described by Elizabeth herself. The King had said to her 'But sweetheart, thou wilt forget what I tell thee,' to which she had replied, 'shedding abundance of tears', that she would write down all he said. And so, that night, she did. Through the stilted seventeenth-century English comes clearly the awful solemnity of the occasion, the tenderness of a father who was at the same time still very much King and Defender of the Faith. We see two frightened children and yet there is just a flash of pride in the importance of what she is recording and in herself as the big sister. It is headed, 'What the King said to me on the 29th of January, 1648–9, the last time I had the happiness to see him':

He told me he was glad I was come, and although he had not time to say much, yet somewhat he had to say to me, which he could not to another, or leave in writing, because he feared their cruelty was such, as they would not have permitted him to write to me. He wished me not to grieve and torment myself for him, for that would be a glorious death that he would die – it being for the laws and liberties of this land, and for maintaining the true Protestant religion. He bade me read Bishop Andrew's sermons, Hooker's Ecclesiastical Polity, and Bishop Laud's book against Fisher, which would ground me against Popery. He told me he had forgiven all his enemies, and hoped God would forgive them also; and commanded us, and all the rest of my brothers and sisters, to forgive them. He bid me tell my mother that his thoughts never strayed from her, and that his love should be the same to the last. Withal, he commanded me and my brother to be obedient to her, and bid me send his blessing to the rest of my brothers and sisters, with commendation to all his friends. So, after he had given me his blessing, I took my leave.

There followed a postscript:

Farther, he commanded us all to forgive these people, but never trust them; for they had been most false to him and to those that gave them power, and he feared also to their own souls; and he desired me not to grieve for him, for he should die a martyr, and that he doubted not but that the Lord would settle his throne upon his son, and that we should all be happier than we could have expected to have been if he had lived; with many other things, which at present I cannot remember. Elizabeth.

And here Elizabeth added yet another postscript, evidently after consulting her brother:

Then taking my brother Gloucester upon his knee, he said, 'Sweetheart, now they will cut off thy father's head.' Upon which the child looked very steadfastly upon him. 'Heed, my child, what I say; they will cut off my head, and perhaps make thee a king. But, mark what I say, you must not be a king, so long as your brothers Charles and James do live. For they will cut off your brothers' heads, when they can catch them, and cut off thy head too at the last. And therefore, I charge you, do not be made a king by them.' At which the child, sighing deeply, replied, 'I will be torn in pieces first.' And these words coming so unexpectedly from so young a child, rejoiced my father exceedingly. And His Majesty spoke to him of the welfare of his soul, and to keep his religion, commanding him to fear God, and He would provide for him. All of which the young child earnestly promised.[40]

It is a very poignant little document and it is as well that she wrote it down so promptly, for Elizabeth was, herself, not long for this world. Bystanders seeing the children leave St James's Palace predicted that she would die of grief and within a few days it was put about that she had actually done so. But, in fact it was to be the following year that she died, still a prisoner at Carisbrooke Castle, of a wasting disease, possibly cancer brought on by the trauma of these events. So the King took his leave of his children, giving them his blessing, his remaining jewels, mostly broken Georges and Garters. He kept only the George which he wore, and all wept so lamentably 'as moved others to Pity that formerly were hardhearted'.[41]

Time was now running out for King Charles. Tuesday, 30 January dawned bitter cold, with a rigid black frost and little wind. But two hours before dawn the King was awake and preparing himself. He had slept soundly for some four hours – it was Herbert on a pallet at his side whose sleep was troubled – but now he wanted to be sure of being ready when the call came. He dressed with his usual care, saying to Herbert, 'Let me have a Shirt on more than ordinary, by reason the season is so sharp as probably may make me shake, which some Observers will imagine proceeds from fear. I would have no such Imputation. I fear not Death! Death is not terrible to me. I bless my God I am prepared.'[42]

To Herbert the King entrusted his parting words and gifts to his children: his own, personally annotated Bible to the Prince of Wales; his large silver ring, which incorporated a sun dial and a slide rule in its design, to the Duke of York; and various stiff books of sermons to the others; and then the good Bishop Juxon arrived and together they 'went to prayer'. When the Bishop read the 27th Chapter of St Matthew's Gospel which relates the Passion of Our Lord, the King asked him if he had specially chosen that passage, 'being so applicable to his present Condition' but was told that it happened to be the proper reading for the day. He concluded with 'a chearfull Submission to the Will and Pleasure of the Almighty'[43] just as the clock on St James's Palace struck ten and Colonel Hacker, the officer placed in charge of him, knocked on the door and summoned the King to Whitehall.

Charles rose at once and, giving into Herbert's hands his silver bedside clock which he bade him keep in his memory, put on his hat, took up his cane and set out across the Park between the lines of waiting troops. He walked fast, faster than the soldiers who marched behind and before and the slow beat of the drum that set the pace. As best he could above the continuous rolling of the drums, the King conversed cheerfully with the Bishop on his right and a Colonel Tomlinson, who shared guard duties with Hacker, on his left. And so they came to Whitehall and passed into the Palace.

In Whitehall itself a vast crowd had been gathering since dawn. The street right back to Charing Cross was full, as well as every window and rooftop. But this was not the jovial crowd which generally came together to view an execution. They shuffled their feet and blew on their fingers in the biting cold, but where were the ribald jokes and laughter? This multitude was half ashamed of being there and glanced furtively at the black-hung scaffold built out from Inigo Jones's Banqueting House. And when a cry went up from the rooftops that the King was on his way there was a murmur of prayer that spread even into the ranks of soldiers drawn up there.

Now, however, there was an unexpected delay. The King was conducted to his own bed-chamber and here the Bishop celebrated Holy Communion, after which Charles rose cheerfully saying, 'Now let the rogues come. I have heartily forgiven them and am prepared for all I am to undergo.'[44] But no rogues came. The King rested awhile and prayed and talked with Herbert and Juxon. Herbert was ordered to find a white satin nightcap from the closet. A meal was brought which Charles at first refused, wishing the Sacrament to be his last earthly food, but the kindly Bishop persuaded him saying, 'Sire, Your Majesty has long been fasting; it is cold; perhaps on the scaffold some faintness . . .' 'You are right,'[45] said the King and took a little bread and a glass of claret. But the interminable wait (nearly four hours while the Commissioners argued and delayed over signing the death warrant) was preying on the nerves of all concerned. Indeed it finally broke the nerve of Herbert who fled, pressing the satin nightcap into Juxon's hands and promising to wait at the end of the Banqueting House to help him with their master's body.

At last, at about two o'clock, the call came – Colonel Hacker once more knocking at the door with the death warrant in his hand, and the King was escorted through the rooms and galleries of the Palace where, behind the soldiers, 'abundance of men and women crowded in'[46] and he heard them pray for him, now unrebuked by the soldiers. Down the length of the Banqueting House he came and out through an enlarged window on to the black draped scaffold, with the same indifference as he would have entered Whitehall on a masque night.[47] Those of the crowd who were in high windows or on rooftops could see what took place on the scaffold, but those on the ground, most of whom had by now waited six hours or more in the biting cold, could see no more than the heads and shoulders of the protagonists for the black drapery hung waist high all round the scaffold. Many contemporary prints and pictures of the scene are at fault here, omitting the black hangings in the interest of depicting the scene.

Waiting on the scaffold was a small crowd of people – several soldiers on guard, two or three shorthand writers to record the event and two sinister figures, masked and heavily disguised; these were the common hangman, Richard Brandon, and his assistant, Ralph Jones. Before them was the block, no more than eight inches high, and to either side of it, staples had been driven into the floor with which to fasten down the King if he should resist. They had seriously misjudged his character if they thought Charles would put up any struggle. He glanced at them with a disdainful smile, merely asking if a higher block could not be procured. The only sign of anxiety he showed was when someone's flapping cloak brushed against the blade of the axe and he burst out, 'Take heed of the axe! Take heed of the axe!' And again, 'Hurt not the axe that may hurt me.'[48] In the well-known words of the Puritan poet, Andrew Marvell:

> He nothing common did, nor mean,
> Upon that memorable scene;
> But with his keener eye
> The axe's edge did try ...

Unfolding a small piece of paper he was carrying, and speaking from headings, the King now made his last speech from the scaffold. It was a vindication of his politics and course of action and ended thus:

> Sirs, it was for the liberties of the people that I am come here. If I would have assented to an arbitrary sway, to have all things changed according to the power of the sword, I needed not to have come hither; and therefore I tell you (and I pray God it be not laid to your charge) that I am the martyr of the people. I die a Christian according to the profession of the Church of England, as I found it left me by my father.[49]

Unfortunately his words were heard by almost no one in the crowds, such was the press of soldiers on horseback between them and the scaffold, but the speech was recorded by the shorthand writers and by Colonel Tomlinson who was at the King's side.

Now the King took off his coat and diamond-studded George, which he handed to Juxon with the word, 'Remember.'[50] He then replaced his cloak and put on the white satin nightcap and with Juxon's help, tucked his long hair into it. 'I have on my side a just cause, and a merciful God,' he said, turning to the bishop, who answered, 'Yes sire, there is but one stage more which, though turbulent and troublesome is yet a very short one; and consider, it will carry you a great way, even from earth to heaven.'[51] 'I go,' replied the King, 'from a corruptible to an incorruptible crown, where no disturbance can take place.'[52]

Turning to the headsman, the King now gave his last instructions: 'I shall say a short prayer, and when I hold out my hands thus – strike.'[53] After a moment or two he knelt down and laid his head upon the block. The executioner bent down to tuck in a stray lock of hair and the King, thinking he was going to strike, called out, 'Stay for the sign.' Now comes one of the supremely ironic remarks of all time, coming from one who is on the point of murdering his king: 'I shall wait for it, sir, with the good pleasure of Your Majesty'![54] A moment more, the hands went out, for an instant the great axe hung high in the air. A single sickening thud was heard; the masked figure bent and then the crowds below saw him rise, holding up by the hair the severed head.

Philip Henry was a Westminster schoolboy and was in the crowd to witness the historic scene. Long afterwards he recorded that 'at the instant [of the blow] I remember well there was such a groan by the thousands then present as I never heard before and desire I may never hear again.'[55] It was the sole occasion in history when the English murdered their king and it was as if every man asked himself what he had done.

Now there was a surge forward and some, nearest the scaffold, tried to climb upon it, dipping handkerchiefs in the blood and searching for pieces of hair and other gruesome mementoes.[56] But the authorities had feared an organized demonstration and the mounted troops had their orders. They charged simultaneously from the direction of Charing Cross and from Westminster, squeezing the multitude between them and scattering them, every man for himself.

Poor 'lamenting' Herbert re-emerged and, with Bishop Juxon, took charge of the body which, he says, 'was immediately coffin'd, covered with a black Velvet-Pall' and taken to the 'Back-Stairs' to be embalmed and the head reunited with it. It was then removed to St James's where 'A doleful spectacle',[57] it was for several days on view to a strictly limited public, decently covered in black velvet but without all the usual trappings of state.

'Where to bury the King was the last Duty remaining.'[58] Herbert and the Bishop would have buried him with the rest of his family and former kings in King Henry VII Chapel, but this was refused by 'those that were then in power',[59] who feared its becoming a place of pilgrimage and dissent. So they had to think again and soon lighted upon St George's Chapel at Windsor, the home of Charles's beloved Order of the Garter, and permission was granted for a simple burial there on 6 February. Herbert relates that the corpse was carried to Windsor in a 'Hearse covered with black Velvet, drawn by Six Horses also covered with black; after which, Four Coaches followed ... in which were about a Dozen Gentlemen and others, most of them being such as had waited on his Majesty at Carisbrooke-Castle and other places ... all of them being in black'.[60] It was a meagre procession indeed compared with those of his forebears. No mourning was issued and no Court mourning decreed, though many put themselves into black. This was not remarkable enough to draw censure upon them as, in any case, black, grey and dark brown were predominant in the days of the Puritan Commonwealth. In Holland the late King's sister, Elizabeth of Bohemia and his daughter Mary, Princess of Orange, plunged their Courts into deepest mourning. Likewise, Queen Henrietta Maria who was living at the Louvre in Paris naturally put herself and her suite into mourning when she finally received the news of the execution, as did the Prince of Wales and the Duke of York. But the rulers of a number of European countries, including Holland and France, maintained an ambiguous attitude. They sent condolences to the bereaved family but kept a weather eye on the new masters in England and ordered no mourning for themselves and their courts.

When the cortège arrived at Windsor there was some delay. The governor had been warned, but otherwise no preparations seem to have been made. The coffin was first carried into the Deanery and deposited on a long oak table which may be seen there to this day, and then moved to the King's own bedroom while Herbert and his friends went off to the Chapel to decide upon the most suitable spot for the burial. They had just 'pitcht upon the Vault where King Edward IV is interr'd being in the North-side of the Choire',[61] when there suddenly arrived a group of noblemen headed by the Duke of Richmond who had been authorized by Parliament to arrange the burial, and they took the decision upon themselves. 'One of those Lords beating gently upon the Pavement with his Staff perceived a hollow sound, and ordering the Stones and Earth thereunder to be removed, discovered a descent into a Vault, where two coffins were laid ... the one very large of antique form, the other little ...'[62] They had discovered the tomb of King Henry VIII and Queen Jane Seymour, and there it was decided to bury King Charles.

A lead inscription was quickly made and fixed to the coffin. In capital letters it said simply, KING CHARLES 1648 (this is by the old calendar which ran from Lady Day, 25 March). And then, on the shoulders of some 'Gentlemen that were of some Quality in Mourning' and followed by the governor and a little procession of lords, the King was carried to the Chapel. Herbert tells us that, as they went, 'the sky was serene and clear, but presently it began to snow, and fell so fast, as by that time they came to the West-end of the Royal Chapel, the black Velvet-Pall was all white (the colour of Innocency) being thick covered with Snow. So went the White King to his Grave, in the 48th Year of his Age, and the 22nd Year and 10th Month of his Reign.'[63]

However the King's tormentors had one last turn of the screw in store. In the Chapel Bishop Juxon stood ready to read the Burial Service according to the Book of Common Prayer, when the Puritan Governor of the Castle stepped forward and forbade him to do so on the grounds that this book had been proscribed by Parliament, and no argument would move him. According to Fuller: 'The Bishop of London stood weeping by, to tender that his service which might not be accepted. Then was [the coffin] deposited in silence and sorrow in the vacant place in the vault (the hearse-cloth being cast in after it) about 3 of the afternoon; and the Lords that night, though late, returned to London'.[64] A bleak end to a violent chapter of our English history.

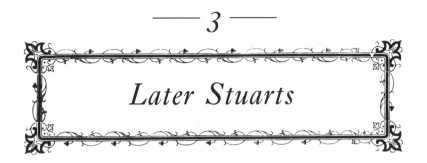

3

Later Stuarts

The Commonwealth lasted over eleven years, but time caught up with Oliver Cromwell, Lord Protector of Great Britain, and on 3 September 1658, His Highness, as he was by now styled, succumbed to a particularly virulent attack of malaria at Whitehall on the anniversary of two of his greatest triumphs – the battles of Dunbar and Worcester. Strictly, Cromwell's death is outside the scope of this book, yet there are some points about his obsequies which seem worth mentioning. They were performed in all respects like those of a king, and played a major part in the development of the tradition of royal funerals as we know them today.

Cromwell never became king in his lifetime, though in the last months of his life there were rumours of a coronation in the offing, but his ritual lying-in-state at Somerset House was certainly made to look like that of a king. This took place from 18 October to 10 November, and crowns were very much in evidence. It was said that some weeks previously his body had been secretly buried in Westminster Abbey, which may have been due to a bungled embalming, as was said at the time, or alternatively it could have been fear that someone might steal the body. To snatch the body of the Protector himself would have been a great coup for the monarchists.

A lifesize wax effigy of the Lord Protector lay upon a, by now, empty coffin on a catafalque in the black-hung Somerset House. It was robed in purple and ermine, a sceptre in one hand and an orb in the other, a purple cap on its head and, no mistaking it, an imperial crown standing behind it. Halfway through this public display the effigy was stood up and the crown actually placed upon the head, where it remained until some days before the state funeral. The funeral itself was a grand military affair, as befitted the great commander, though the ordering of it was in the hands of the Heralds Office. The cost was reputed to have been some

£100,000, more than double that of James I on which it was modelled. Thirty thousand yards of black cloth for mourning was issued, but, an innovation, the streets were closely lined with troops of the New Model Army in their buff uniforms with black mourning facings, their buttons blacked and colours draped with cypress, the forerunner of crape. From this grew a tradition which lasts, with variations, to this day.

However, the grand funeral was not the end for Oliver Cromwell. At the Restoration, Charles II had the bodies of Cromwell and two other regicides exhumed, dragged through the streets to Tyburn, hanged, beheaded and the heads stuck up on poles on Westminster Hall while the bodies were flung into a common pit at Tyburn. The skull remained, rotting, on its spike until late in the reign of James II (i.e. some seventeen or eighteen years), when it was blown down in a violent storm. It was picked up by a passing soldier, who, realizing what it was, took it home under his cloak. His daughter sold it and it came down by devious routes to its present resting place at Sidney Sussex College, Cambridge, Cromwell's own college.

So much for the Lord Protector. His son Richard's 'reign' was short and undistinguished and in May 1660 a delegation from England invited Charles II to reclaim his throne. On 29 May, the King's thirtieth birthday, he rode into London to scenes of wild jubilation, accompanied by his brothers James, Duke of York and Henry, Duke of Gloucester. 'And all this without one drop of blood,'[1] as John Evelyn recorded in his diary.

Young Henry was at this time a graceful young man of almost twenty. He had an eager, pleasing manner and showed promise of certain ability and ambition. His personality resembled, to some extent, that of his brother the King, who was very fond of him. Yet the difficult years of his youth had left their mark on his character. The childhood years of imprisonment followed by transportation at the age of twelve to a luxurious life at the French court, had left him somewhat spoilt and arrogant, but then how could it have been otherwise?

At any rate, in that glorious summer of 1660 everyone was disposed to turn a blind eye to any royal shortcomings. The royal family was gathering to celebrate the glorious Restoration. The Queen Mother was to come over from France, bringing with her fifteen-year-old Princess Henrietta Anne, Charles's beloved Minette, who had not seen England since, as a two-year-old she was smuggled out of the country at the height of the Civil War. And Mary, the Princess Royal, now at twenty-nine, the widowed Princess of Orange, was also expected. Festivity and celebration were the order of the day.

But before any of the royal visitors could arrive, 'the mirth and entertainments of that time raised [the young Duke of Gloucester's] blood so high, that he took the small-pox'.[2] For a week or so he was very ill, but on 11 September he was pronounced out of danger and the Duke of York set off to meet his mother and sisters. Alas, the improvement did not hold; there was a sudden relapse, and on the evening of 13 September he died 'by the great negligence of the doctors',[3] as Pepys was at pains to confide to his diary. He 'died much lamented by all, but most particularly by the King, who was never in his whole life seen so much troubled as he was on that occasion'.[4] Two days later Pepys announced, prosaically, between a visit to his landlord and to his parents, that he had 'bespoke mourning for [him]self for the death of the Duke of Gloucester'. As a man living close to Whitehall and the court, Pepys felt able to adopt mourning, though as a member neither of the nobility nor of a royal household, it looks slightly like social climbing. Mrs Pepys had some trouble with hers, the tailor having failed her, which was an embarrassment as they were dining out. In a few days mourning was 'the mode of all the ladies in towne'. The King was observed 'in purple mourning for his brother'.[5] Purple was a mourning colour reserved exclusively for kings, at least during full mourning. It was thought improper for sovereigns to be seen to be too closely touched by death.

Eight days after his death, the Prince's body, the second Prince Henry to die in less than fifty years, was brought by water from Somerset House to Westminster Abbey for a private burial, unusually quickly owing to the smallpox. Pepys encountered the waterborne cortège at about 8 o'clock in the evening and the burial took place about midnight in the Stuart vault in the Henry VII Chapel. Torchlight funerals were becoming the custom among the great, and the torches were then extinguished at the graveside.

A private funeral for a member of the royal family was much frowned upon by the poor of London who otherwise stood a chance, albeit a slim one, of being chosen to walk in the procession and consequently provided with a warm set of black clothes. Each time there was a grand funeral a certain number of London churches were invited to provide about twelve poor men or women each (according to the sex of the deceased) to walk in the procession, and there was fierce competition between parishes to win this benefit for some of their poor. The state papers of the seventeenth century are peppered with pleas from parish clerks and clergymen, as being 'one of the poorest parishes in London' to be allowed to provide some of the necessary almsmen or women.

A few days after Henry's funeral there arrived on their delayed visit, Henrietta Maria and 'Minette' from France and Princess Mary from Holland. Mary's husband, William, had died of smallpox some ten years previously only days before the birth of their son, William, who was one day to become King William III of England.

Even without the death of her younger brother, Mary was not in good form during this visit. She was inordinately incensed at the recent marriage of her brother James to her former maid-of-honour, Anne Hyde. Also she was not strong and had complained ever since her arrival in London of 'an oppression of her chest caused by the smoke of the city'.[6] She was, however, pleased at the Restoration of Charles, not least because it removed a heavy drain on her purse; she had gone into debt and pawned jewellery to support her brothers. She had been good to her exiled brothers and they were fond of her in spite of her difficult manner.

At all events, the festivities leading up to this first Christmas of the reinstated monarchy were at their height and mourning for the Duke of Gloucester was 'partly laid aside',[7] when the 'Court was thrown into great alarm by a report that the Princess Royal, who had been indisposed for several days, was seriously and even dangerously ill, and that her disorder was pronounced to be small-pox'.[8] At once the machinery of seventeenth-century Court medicine swung into action. Beer was prescribed which 'caused the disappearance of the eruption and a fainting fit ensued',[9] and relief was only achieved by the reappearance of the eruption. The doctors were terrified. They had been severely blamed for not bleeding the Duke of Gloucester and so now they erred in the other direction and 'bled the princess too profusely'.[10] At one point there was a temporary improvement, and the medical men decided it was only measles, but it was not sustained and it soon became obvious that she was sinking.

While the doctors fought for her body, another battle was going on for the Princess's soul. Henrietta Maria tried to get to her daughter in hopes of a deathbed conversion to Catholicism, but King Charles had had experience before of his mother's proselytizing activities within the family and he firmly removed her and Minette, under cover of fear of infection, from Whitehall to St James's and the Queen Mother had to be content with sending one of her French physicians to her daughter. But it was all to no avail and on Christmas Eve, conscious to the last and willing her young son to the care of her brother, Mary gave up the fight and 'the Lord took her to Himself'.[11] She was twenty-nine and had been a widow for ten years.

Bishop Burnet, who had something sour to say about most people, states that the Princess Royal 'was not much lamented', though he did give it to her, grudgingly, that she had 'kept a decent court' in her widowhood and 'supported her brothers very liberally'.[12] However, the gossipy Venetian resident described 'the intense grief of the whole Court and especially of the King, who loved her most tenderly'. Strict mourning was instantly resumed and he wrote pointedly to his government that 'the foreign ministers have followed suit and [he had] incurred an additional expense of £23 sterling'.[13] He went on to say that the Queen Mother, in her grief, had decided to return to France, taking the young Princess Henrietta Anne, soon to be married to the loathesome Duc d'Orleans, younger brother of Louis XIV, with her.

In Holland, Mary's beloved aunt, Elizabeth of Bohemia, with whom she had so often shared her homesickness, received the news with despair, and took it upon herself to break the news to the now orphaned ten-year-old William. Herself in floods of tears, she took the undemonstrative boy in her arms and, perhaps infected by her grief, he appeared to bystanders to feel his loss 'more acutely than might have been expected from a child of his age'.[14]

Charles II evidently did not believe in prolonged obsequies. Mary was at once embalmed and brought in a black-lined barge from Whitehall to Somerset House, it being inauspicious for a body to remain in a royal residence. There, in the rooms scarcely dismantled of their black hangings for the Duke of Gloucester, Mary lay in state for a mere five days and then, at 9 o'clock at night was conveyed upriver to Westminster and privately interred alongside her brother. The habit of female mourners for deceased women seems to have lapsed since Queen Anne of Denmark's death, and the Duke of York was chief mourner to his elder sister.

King Charles paid for mourning for all her attendants and agreed to pay for their keep for ten weeks after her death, but not everyone behaved so well. The Countess of Chesterfield, who was of the Princess's household, almost before her mistress was cold, had taken a position with the Duchess of York, who had once been her junior in Holland, 'and,' wrote Lord Craven to Elizabeth of Bohemia, 'waits more on the Duchess than I ever saw her do on her mistress'.[15] And not content with that, she insisted, as of right, on keeping the Princess's wardrobe for herself and refused to give up some valuables in her charge until her legacy of £400 was paid. Two months later Lord Craven wrote that the Princess was 'as much forgotten . . . as if she had never been'.[16] Life at that gay Restoration Court must go on, which is not to say that death had finished with it, far from it.

In the early summer of 1661 there arrived in England Elizabeth of Bohemia herself, that same enchanting Princess whose wedding to the Elector Palatine had been postponed by the death of her brother Henry, Prince of Wales, nearly fifty years before. She had never been back in all that time and life had dealt variously with her. Within a few years of marriage, her husband had become King of Bohemia but kept his throne no more than a few months which earned Elizabeth the title of the Winter Queen. Soon afterwards they lost their German state too, and she spent all the intervening years in Holland where she brought up a large tribe of children in increasingly straitened circumstances. In this country she was chiefly known, except by the very old, as the mother of Prince Rupert of the Rhine, of whom more later. Like Mary of Orange, she had been kind to Charles and his brothers during their exile in Holland and now the King's chickens were coming home to roost.

Charles was not deliberately neglectful, but there was so much to do and so many amusements more alluring than a sixty-five-year-old aunt, however fond he had once been of her. And so, when she arrived in London, no provision had been made for her, and her old friend Lord Craven was obliged to put her up at his house in Drury Lane. She found the Court already once more in mourning for the infant Duke of Cambridge, first son of the Duke and Duchess of York. Neverthless, in July the King did take her to the theatre and listened patiently to her tales of woe. During the winter she moved into Leicester House, in what is now Leicester Square, but the move was too much for her and she went down with bronchitis. Charles visited her and begged her to move to Whitehall where she could be comfortably nursed back to health. Possibly he was ashamed to have a Princess of Great Britain die in a rented house. But the invitation came too late and on 12 February 1662 she died.

Elizabeth's funeral was easy to arrange; they had only to pull out of a file the arrangements for that of the Princess of Orange. Their circumstances were precisely the same: eldest daughter of the King of England. To the modern way of thinking, it seems odd that Mary, at least, was not transported back to Holland to be buried with her husband and the royal house of Orange, but she was interred in England among her own family. Elizabeth's case – that, virtually, of a displaced person – was somewhat different and it made sense to follow her own instructions that her body should be interred 'amongst those of her ancestors, and close to that of her elder brother, Prince Henry'.[17]

As in Mary's case, the funeral was held five days after her death and, with the exception of her own servants, was made up of the same people. But this time, in memory of her position as Queen, a royal crown was borne by heralds before the coffin. Faithful Lord Craven, who mourned her sincerely, preceded her and the tall figure of her son, Prince Rupert, came behind as chief mourner. And so, according to John Evelyn, 'This night was buried in Westminster the Queene of Bohemia after all her sorrows and afflictions being come to die in her Nephews armes the King'.[18]

Anne Hyde, Duchess of York, paid dearly for her presumption in marrying above her station. She bore James eight children, of whom only the two eldest daughters, Mary and Anne, survived infancy. Six little coffins filled up the spaces in the Stuart vault. Some, and not only princes, lay in state in the Painted Chamber at Whitehall and were buried with great heraldic ceremony, while others were interred quite privately 'without Officers of Arms or any solemnity'.[19] It is hard to find the criterion for who among the royal babies rated what degree of ceremony. Then in 1671, Anne herself died after several years of ill health, probably of a gynaecological nature. The Venetian Resident reported her death, 'to the distress of the Duke her husband'.[20] Never a beauty, Anne had, of late, put on a great deal of weight and James no longer even pretended to be faithful to her, but she remained a major influence in his life, particularly in matters of religion. She was widely believed to have been instrumental in bringing him to the Roman faith and this made her very unpopular in the country. As she lay dying, the Anglican Bishop of Worcester, Dr Blandford, went in to her to try to persuade her to recant at the last minute, but he found the Queen, Portuguese Catherine of Braganza, sitting with her and, Burnet tells us, 'he had not the presence of mind to begin prayers which would probably have driven the Queen out of the room, but that not being done, she pretended kindness and would not leave her. The most he could manage was, "I hope that you continue still in the truth?" ... she repeated the word, "Truth! Truth!" often. A few minutes afterwards she expired.'[21] In fact her own priest had already been with her and she died 'fortified by the full rites of the Roman Catholic Church'.

The Duchess may have been unpopular in her lifetime, but at her death the formalities were scrupulously observed. James may have been sincerely sorry; at any rate he kept to his chamber, 'admitting no visitants' for several days and then emerged to receive condolences along with the King and Queen. Everyone was back in black and once more the Venetian Resident, always with an eye to the main chance, 'followed the example of [his] colleagues in putting on mourning and trust[ed] to [their] Excellencies for relief for this fresh expense.'[22]

Exactly a week after her death the Duchess joined her babies in Westminster Abbey. For one day she lay in the Painted Chamber, now definitely established as the proper place for this function, and that night was

most solemnly attended to the Abbey by her own, the King's, the Queen's and the Duke's servants, all the nobility and gentry, and many members of the Parliament House, all in their blacks, guarded by two companies of foot and finally interred in the Royal Vault of King Henry VII's chapel, the ceremonies performed by the Bishop of Rochester as Dean of the Cathedral.[23]

Barely was Anne cold, when the Duke 'opened negotiations for a fresh marriage'. He now had no son and so 'he must marry in accordance with the King's wishes, the Queen offering no promise of posterity'.[24] And in 1673 he married Mary Beatrice of Modena, another Catholic princess, and more princes and princesses were born and joined their half brothers and sisters in the vault. The cot death of one, the infant Duke of Cambridge was blamed on the mismanagement of his wet and dry nurses – a nasty situation for them.

A sideways glimpse of the different attitudes to death in the family in seventeenth and late nineteenth-century England is caught in this description, by Edgar Sheppard, a Victorian historian, of the death, at nine months, of Princess Katharine Laura, eldest daughter of James and Mary Beatrice in 1675. He tells us, with horror, that

> Whatever might be the grief of the youthful mother for the loss of her infant she was compelled to dry her tears, and appear in public very soon after this afflicting event; for Evelyn mentions in his Diary a magnificent ball, which was given by the Duchess of York . . . at St James's barely two months after the loss of her child.[25]

Evelyn, in contrast, does not think it necessary to mention the death of the child in connection with the ball. In all, of the fifteen children born to James by his two wives, eleven – six sons and five daughters – died in infancy.

In the later years of the reign of Charles II and in his immediate circle was a man admired and respected by all classes of Englishmen. This was Prince Rupert of the Rhine, son of Elizabeth of Bohemia, and he filled a role very much like that of Earl Mountbatten of Burma almost three hundred years later. Rupert was the son of an English princess and a German prince, and had dedicated his life to England and specifically to the cause of the Stuart monarchy. He had been a dashing commander on land in the Civil War and later at sea, and had been one of the early builders of the British Empire, particularly in West Africa and, as Governor of the Hudson's Bay Company, sowed the seeds of the British Dominion of Canada. He was also a notable scientist, with a number of useful inventions to his name.

In later life Prince Rupert, a bachelor, though no celibate, made his home at Windsor Castle, of which he was Governor and Constable from 1668. However, as a Privy Councillor and a man with a number of London-based commitments, he still maintained his house in Spring Garden, Whitehall, and it was here that he came towards the end of November 1682. His old head and leg wounds were troubling him and he had a slight fever, but on the evening of his arrival in London he went to the theatre and intended to preside at a meeting of the General Court of the Hudson's Bay Company to be held at his house the next day. The meeting took place, but Rupert was, by then, not well enough to attend it. Pleurisy had developed and 'an intermitting feavor', for which the old scientist refused to be bled, and four days later, 29 November, shortly before his sixty-third birthday, Prince Rupert of the Rhine, Duke of Cumberland, was dead.

The report of the post-mortem makes interesting reading.

Prince Rupert's body being opened, three strange things were found in him. The first was a stone in his kidneys bigger than a great nut which lay so that it would have stopped the passage of his urine, but what is strange, there was a hole in it, through which the water passed so freely that he in his whole life was never troubled with any pain of the stone. Another was that in the skin that covers the brain grew a bone and in his heart another.[26]

In his will he left everything to his two natural children, Dudley Bard and Ruperta Hughes, and to his mistress, Margaret Hughes, and his executor was the Earl of Craven who had been so devoted to his mother. To his servants he left all the money owed him by the King. Let us hope that the debt was paid! In the course of his duties, Craven found an iron chest, the Prince's petty cash, in which were 1,694 guineas, the money received for such minutely accounted items as 'an old blind mare – £1.0.0' and a pack of hounds at £120.[27]

It is said that King Charles had lately been somewhat at odds with the Prince who had possibly overplayed the role of elder statesman to his younger cousin, and that Charles ordered the funeral arrangements with rather an ill grace.

Ill grace or no, the funeral, when it took place on the night of 6 December, was all that it should have been for a prince closely related to the King and hero of many legendary land and sea battles. But first there was the lying-in-state in the Painted Chamber at Whitehall. There is a description of the lying-in-state at Somerset House of the great Duke of Albemarle in 1670 which, though he was not royal, is worth quoting fully for the insight it gives us into how it was done in the second half of the seventeenth century. The layout for Prince Rupert at Whitehall and for subsequent royals for a long time to come would almost certainly have been identical:

The Three Rooms at Somerset House were furnished in manner following: The First Room was hung with Bays from top to bottom, adorned with Escucheons, and furnished with Sconces, and Wax-Candles unlighted; and

Formes placed about it, covered with Bays.

The Second was hung with Cloath, adorned with Escucheons, and furnished with Sconces and Candles, unlighted, the Forms about it covered with Cloath; at the upper end, a Haute-pass floored with Bays, a Canopy of Black Velvet, the vallance Fringed, the Pendant within half a yard of the Ground; a Majesty-Escucheon of Taffeta, a Black Velvet Chair with Arms, and a Footstool.

The Third Room was hung with Velvet, floored with Bays, adorned with Escucheons, and Black Sconces, with White Wax Tapers, and at the upper end upon a Haute-pass, a Bed of State of Black Velvet was placed with Black Plumes at the Four corners of the Tester; at the Head a Majesty-Escucheon, and another in the midst of the Tester. Upon the Bed was placed a Coffin covered with a fine Holland-Sheet of Eight bredths, and Eights ells long, and over that, a Pall of Black Velvet of Eight bredths and Eight yards long, and thereupon the Effigies of the Duke . . . [in armour, wearing his coronet and robes, and the Garter.]

About Five foot distant from the Bed, was a Rail covered with Black velvet and close to the inside of the Rail, were placed on both sides, the Bannerols, three Banners, and a Guydon, and at the Foot, the Standard, and Great Banner; between these on the Sides, were also placed Twelve Black Stands, with as many Silver Candlesticks, with large White Wax Tapers in them.

At the Bed's Feet, was a little Table covered with a Carpet of Black Velvet, and thereupon were placed the Coat of Arms, Sword, Target, Helm and Crest, Gauntlets, and Spurs. Between the Standard and the great Banner, hung a Crystal Branch with Twelve Sockets, and therein as many Tapers of Wax.

In this Room . . . the Tapers were continually burning when it was exposed to sight, which was every day (except Sunday) during the space of about three weeks. 40 Gentlemen, 20 a day were on duty, 4 in the first Room, 6 in the second, 10 in the third, 5 on each side of the rail of the Bed of State with their backs to the wall.[28]

The King and the Duke of York were represented at the funeral, but royalty did not then, and on the whole do not to this day, attend funerals themselves for any but the closest family. As well as all the usual nobles and officials and Rupert's own household, those who took part in the procession to the Abbey reflected the pursuits of the Prince. There were soldiers, sailors, watermen and tennis players, a gunsmith and a huntsman. Faithful Lord Craven, now seventy-six, was chief mourner. The service was at 8 o'clock at night and lasted till midnight and then the old war-horse was laid to rest in the Henry VII Chapel, fittingly among the bones of the royal family he had identified with and served all his life.

The Court went into mourning. 'Three weeks [the King was] in purple and plain linen and three weeks in black cloth'[29] and then Rupert of the Rhine, holder of countless honours, was forgotten.

That King Charles II 'took an unconscionable time a-dying' is one of those useless pieces of historical information that everyone knows, wrongly, as it happens. In fact his last illness took from Monday morning to Friday at noon, but it doubtless seemed an eternity to the King and to his attendants crowded round the deathbed.

Charles's last day of active life was Sunday, 1 February 1685. John Evelyn was at Whitehall that day and was scandalized at what he saw that evening. 'I can never forget,' he tells us,

> the inexpressible luxury and profaneness, gaming and all manner of dissoluteness and as it were total forgetfulness of God [it being Sunday evening] which this day se'night I was witness of, the King sitting and toying with his concubines, Portsmouth, Cleveland and Mazarin etc. [his mistresses, Louise de Kerouaille, Barbara Villiers and Hortense Mancini] a French boy singing love songs in that glorious gallery, whilst about twenty of the great courtiers and other dissolute persons were at Basset round a large table, a bank of at least 2000 in gold before them . . . Six days after was all dust.[30]

The King had dined heartily that night, but unusually included two goose eggs in his menu which may have accounted for the restless night he passed. Thomas Bruce, as Gentleman-in-Waiting, and Harry Killigrew, as Groom of the Bedchamber, shared his room as was the custom. After undressing the King and attending him to his private closet where they stood around joking with him as he 'eased himself', Bruce holding the candle and Killigrew the paper, they closed the bedroom door with a brass handle on the inside and settled down for the night. But the King, who always slept like the dead, tossed and muttered all night and Bruce, on his truckle, found sleep impossible. By the fitful, flaring light of the Scotch coal fire, a whole pack of Charles's spaniels wandered restlessly about, stretching and yawning, and a dozen or so pendulum clocks chimed the quarters. Bruce was going out of waiting the next day and decided that he would have to catch up on his sleep then.

When the King woke and got up, he felt very ill and went through to his closet in search of some 'King's Drops'. His countenance, when one of his gentlemen met him in his dressing-room, was pale as ashes. Two of his doctors were waiting to attend him, having been previously summoned to dress one of his heels which had, for some time, plagued him with a painful sore. These two were hastily summoned and, with Will Chiffinch, Page of the Backstairs, persuaded the King back to his bedchamber where it became apparent that his speech was affected. Then, while he was being shaved, 'with his knees against the window',[31] he was seized with a violent convulsion and fell back with a terrible cry into the arms of Bruce. Help, of a seventeenth-century sort, was at hand in the person of Sir Edmund King, one of the surgeons attending him, who, happening to have his lancet in his pocket, 'blooded the King'. In doing so he was, quite literally, taking his own life in his hands as the law stated that no one might bleed the sovereign without the consent of his chief ministers, the penalty of disobedience being death. This consent could not immediately be obtained as the ministers were not at hand, but the doctors alleged that Charles would die if he were not bled. King therefore took the risk and went ahead, drawing off sixteen ounces of blood from the King's right arm, which mercifully was pronounced to have been a success. At any rate, after about two hours, during which time the doctors worked on him with everything they had, the King's speech returned and thereafter he was mostly conscious and perfectly lucid to the last.

Charles II is usually thought of as having had a stroke, indeed a series of strokes, or what was at that time more vaguely described as an 'apoplexy'. Yet he was never paralysed and, after the first couple of hours, was never without speech, two classic symptoms of a stroke. The cause of death is therefore still considered something of a mystery, though from time to time, medical historians and journalists pick at the problem. It is even suggested that he may have slowly poisoned himself through his scientific experiments which included much work with mercury. Whatever the cause, it seems likely that the actual cause of death was kidney failure, possibly a form of Bright's disease.

At any rate, by the time the King came out of his first 'apoplexy', everyone had been alerted. The Duke of York came from St James's so hot foot that he arrived wearing one shoe and one slipper, and the Queen was summoned from her apartments. Indeed everyone who was anyone was summoned and crowded into the stuffy bedchamber. Catherine of Braganza, Charles's delightful but childless queen, was seized with a fit of hysterical grief at the sight of her husband in such a state and, fainting, had to be carried away. He must have been a ghastly sight, 'his eyeballs turned up that none but the whites were seen',[32] for the Princess Anne, daughter of the Duke of York, was not allowed to visit her uncle. As she was pregnant, it was feared that the sight might induce a miscarriage.

'The Duchess of Portsmouth swooned in the chamber, and was carried out for air; Nelly [Gwyn] roared to a disturbance, and was led out and lay roaring behind the door.'³³ The Duchess of Portsmouth, however, regained her cool to the extent of

> sending many strong boxes to the French Ambassadors . . . And the second day (. . . the chamber being kept dark) she came and went of the inside of the bed, and sat down on't, and taking the King's hand in her's, felt his two great diamond rings; and thinking herself alone, asked him what he did with them on, and said she would take them off, and did it at the same time, and looking up, saw the Duke [of York] on the other side, stedfastly looking on her, at which she blushed much, and held them towards him and said 'Here, Sir, will you take them?' 'No, Madam' said he, 'they are as safe in your hands as mine. I will not touch them till I see how things go.' But since the King's death she has forgot to restore them . . .³⁴

The King, having come out of his first fit, might have recovered if the medical profession could have left him to rest quietly and regain his strength. He was, after all, only fifty-four years old. But it was not to be; throughout Monday and the following night they bled him and purged him, administered tinctures of white vitriol in peony water, juleps of prepared pearls, sneezing powders of white hellebore root, emetics of orange, infusions of metals in white wine, blistering agents, spirits of sal ammoniac in antidotal milk water to mention but a very few of their remedies. Peruvian bark, oriental bezoar stone from the stomach of an eastern goat, spirits of human skull, and every herb and spice known to man were tried. His head was shaved and red-hot irons and plasters applied to his scalp and to the soles of his feet. Frequent applications of cantharides made his urine scalding, which then had to be counteracted with bland emulsions. Everything known to seventeenth-century man was tried and, to quote Antonia Fraser, 'all had one thing in common: they were extremely painful to the patient.'³⁵

On Tuesday the King seemed better, indeed he was pronounced out of danger and the bells of London rang and the people rejoiced. But the doctors only redoubled their efforts. The patient was forbidden to speak and the remnants of his famous wit flashed through as he remarked that such a dictum would have killed Harry Killigrew, a noted chatterbox. He, however, suffered this treatment as he did all the others with resigned patience. Broths and possets were given to keep up his strength, but purges, enemas, emetics, cuppings and bleedings continued to drain it away. Though the improvement was sustained through Wednesday, by Thursday he had relapsed and was obviously dying.

[69]

The bishops and chaplains now moved centre-stage. Since the onset of the King's illness they had been saying the prayers for the sick in both the Chapels royal, relieving each other every quarter hour through the day and night. Now they were summoned to the bedside and began the services for the dying. But their presence and their prayers failed to give the desired comfort to the King, who remained restless and he refused to take the Sacrament.

About this time Barillon, the French ambassador, went to visit Louise, Duchess of Portsmouth whom he found overcome by grief and worry. She confided to him that 'at the bottom of his heart the King is a Catholic'.[36] She urged him to find the Duke of York, himself a Catholic, and remind him of his duty to his dying brother. It is descriptive of the religious mood in England at that time that, even with the King so near death, Louise literally feared for her life if her involvement should become known. Barillon repeated what he had just been told to the Duke who had, that morning, been besought by the Queen to 'take advantage of any opportunity that offers' to bring him to a state of grace according to the Catholic faith. She attested that he had long desired conversion to Catholicism but, as King of a Protestant kingdom had resolutely put all such thoughts from him. The Duke agreed that he had been 'thinking of nothing else', but still hesitated. It was not until Barillon came to him with Louise's plea that he roused himself, saying, 'You are right, there is no time to lose: I would risk everything than not do my duty on this occasion.' Going to the King's bedside, he found him still resolutely refusing the Sacrament which the bishops were urging upon him. Bending down, James whispered something inaudible to the surrounding clerics in his brother's ear to which the King replied, 'Yes, with all my heart.'[37]

So far so good, but the next part of the secret plot was more difficult: how to clear out the hovering bishops and how to find a Catholic priest. There were in the palace of Whitehall two groups of Catholic priests, those of the Queen's suite who were Portuguese and those of the Duchess of York who were Italian. Neither spoke nor understood English, also it was thought undesirable, for their own sakes, to involve openly the Queen or the Duchess in the plot. The Duke had just decided to send to the Venetian resident for one of his chaplains, when someone discovered among the Queen's priests one Father John Huddleston. Long ago, in the dangerous days after the battle of Worcester, when Charles was a fugitive fleeing for his life, Huddleston had helped the young king in his escape and as they lay hidden for several days, had talked to him of his faith. Charles had liked the priest and had listened with interest to what he had to say, and it is possible that his interest in Roman Catholicism stems from that time. His presence at Whitehall as the King lay dying, seemed like divine intervention. An educated, yet simple and plain-speaking man, he was just what was needed at this critical moment. The only problem was that the good father was not carrying with him, on his social visit to the Queen's chaplains, the elements of the sacrament, though he did have a phial of holy oil for anointing the dying. So a Portuguese priest was dispatched in search of these elements while Huddleston was dressed up in the wig and cassock of an Anglican clergyman. Thus disguised, he was smuggled up the backstairs and into the King's dressing-room while the Duke of York cleared the bedchamber of its crowd of onlookers by the simple expedient of loudly announcing that the King wished everyone except the Earls of Bath and Feversham (well known Protestants to allay suspicion) to leave the chamber. Father Huddleston was then brought in by a secret door beside the bed and the King, seeing him cried out: 'You that saved my body is now come to save my soul.'[38] The priest then proceeded through the Roman rite of confession and absolution, the King answering and declaring his sins in a strong voice, ending with, 'Into Thy Hands, Sweet Jesus, I commend my soul. Mercy, Sweet Jesus, Mercy.' When Huddleston asked him if he would receive the sacrament of holy communion, the Portuguese priest having secretly arrived with the host, Charles replied, 'If I am worth, fail not to let me have it,' and struggled to rise to a 'better posture' to receive it, but was calmed by the priest assuring him that 'Almighty God, who sees into the heart would accept his good intention.'[39] Bishop Burnet recounts that the 'hostie' stuck in his throat and the Earl of Feversham stuck his head out of the chamber and called for a glass of water from the company who had assembled there, wondering what had been going on for the last half hour.

The Catholic rites of communion and extreme unction over, and the prayers for the dying recited, Father Huddleston slipped away as he had come, by a back way, and the company was allowed back into the room. All saw at once that the King was calmer, and so he continued through that Thursday night and into the next day: calm and perfectly clear in his mind. It was at this time that he begged pardon of his attendants that he was 'so long a-dying'. The medical men, by now numbering fourteen, continued with the last desperate measures of their profession; powdered Goa stone was administered, and later 'the Oriental Bezoar stone, from its normal habitat in the stomach of an Eastern goat, was transferred to its last resting place in that of the King'.[40] Even that by now old-fashioned remedy, Ralegh's cordial, was tried, but the King grew steadily weaker. The waiting bishops begged him many times to receive the sacrament which they had ready in an adjoining room, but Charles always refused them, on the pretext that he was too weak.

About midnight Queen Catherine came to take her leave of the husband who had always been good to her, if not faithful. She was so overcome with grief that she several times fainted and was finally persuaded by her physicians to stay in her room, from whence she sent a message to the dying King asking his pardon if she had ever offended him. 'Alas, poor woman,' replied the King, 'she beg my pardon! I beg hers with all my heart.'[41] Catherine had always adored Charles and it was to her unending grief that she was never able to give him a legitimate heir.

Now Charles bade farewell to his natural children, embracing each of them, blessing them and putting them into the care of his brother, especially Burford, Nell Gwyn's high-spirited son, whose education he begged the Duke to oversee, saying that he would 'be spoiled else'. Only the eldest, Monmouth, exiled abroad, was not there, and no one dared to mention his name. 'He desired [James] to be well to Portsmouth, and not let poor Nelly starve.'[42] At some time in the early hours, as the innumerable palace clocks chimed out the slowly passing quarters, he gave his keys to James and wished him a long and prosperous reign, embracing his weeping brother affectionately.

About 6 o'clock he asked for the curtains to be opened, 'that [he might] once more see the day',[43] and reminded his attendants that it was the day to wind up the eight-day clock in his room. At about seven his breathing began to fail and he struggled to sit up. The watching vultures, his physicians, swooped upon him and bled him of twelve ounces and administered their strongest heart stimulants, but to no avail. By ten o'clock he was in a coma and, shortly before noon on Friday, 6 February, quietly and with no further convulsions, 'it pleased God to call him to himself'.[44]

Great were the general expressions of grief. Although it was Friday, every church in London was thronged with weeping people and 'there was scarce a servant maid betwixt White Chapell and Westminster who was not in black crape . . . upon this occasion'. The Earl Marshal published a proclamation to the effect that

> all persons concerned [should] put themselves into the deepest mourning that is possible: (Long Cloaks onlie excepted), And that as well all Lords, as Privy Councillors, and Officers of His Late Majesty's Household do cover their coaches and chairs and clothe their Livery Servants with black cloth; and that none presume to use any varnished or bullion nails to be seen on their coaches or chairs: except HM, the Queen Consort, Queen Dowager and their Royal Highnesses.[45]

King James was proclaimed that afternoon and the Council and others, including John Evelyn, repaired to his bedchamber where he and the Queen were resting after their ordeal. James had just risen and received them 'in his undress'. Mary was still in bed but 'put her hand out seeming much afflicted'. They then went to offer condolences to the Queen Dowager who received them in her bedchamber. About a month later Evelyn describes Catherine receiving

> Envoyes and Great Persons to condole the Death of the late King: [she] received them on a bed of mourning, the whole chamber seiling and floore hung with black, tapers lighted; so as nothing could be more lugubrious and solemn: The Queene Consort sat out under a state on a black foot cloth, to entertain the circle as the Queen use to do, and that very decently.[46]

In England the mourning bed was just coming into fashion from the continent, though Catherine, as a former Portuguese princess, was probably familiar with the practice. There are a number of these great mourning beds, dating from the late seventeenth and eighteenth centuries, still to be seen in some of the English stately homes, but for the best description of their use we must go to France. Princess Elizabeth Charlotte (Liselotte) was the granddaughter of Elizabeth (Stuart) Queen of Bohemia and, in her voluminous correspondence, leaves us this description of her own experience in such a bed at the death of her husband (who was no great loss to her), the brother of Louis XIV, in 1701:

> I had to receive the ceremonial visit of the King and Queen of England [James II and Mary of Modena, by then exiled in France] wearing the strangest apparel: a white linen band across my forehead, about it a cap which tied under my chin like a veil, over the cap les cornettes, and over them a piece of linen that was fastened to the shoulders like a mourning coat, with a train seven ells long. I was dressed in a coat of black cloth with very long sleeves; ermine two hands wide, bordered the cuffs. There was more ermine of the same width down the front of the coat from throat to floor, and a girdel of black crape reaching to the ground in front and a train of ermine, seven ells long.
>
> In this get-up, with the train arranged to show the ermine, I was placed on a black bed in an entirely blackened room. Even the parquet was covered and the windows hung with crape. A great candelabra with twelve candles was lit, and there were ten or twelve candles burning on the chimneypiece ...[47]

It is probable that Catherine of Braganza presented a similar picture but with more concession to current fashion.

[73]

In his diary, Evelyn noted that on 14 February, 'The King was [that night] very obscurely buried in a vault under Hen: 7th Chapell in W'minster, without any manner of pomp, and soone forgotten after all this vanity.' This was said to be on account of 'His late Majesty dying in, and his present Majesty professing, a different religion to that of his people . . .'[48] Evelyn may have been confused by the fact of the funeral following so soon after death, or by its taking place at night which was a comparatively new custom in this country. In fact everything that should have been done at the death of a monarch was done, the pattern being the funeral of 'His Royal Grandfather King James'. First the King lay in state for some days in the Painted Chamber at Whitehall, the leaden coffin by Sir Christopher Wren surmounted by a standing effigy, still to be seen at Westminster Abbey, whose twisted and deeply lined face reflects the suffering of his last illness. An imperial crown of tin gilt and a cap of crimson velvet turned up with ermine were on his head. The Lord Chamberlain's papers give all the instructions: what grade and shade of hangings to be hung where, what lights where, what material was to be issued to whom and for what purpose and even how many dishes those who attended the body in twelve-hour shifts, 'to take care that no Crowds or undecent company of people be admitted',[49] could claim at dinner and supper. All the usual mourning was ordered, but there were one or two strict provisos: the late King's mistresses might put themselves into mourning but not their servants, and, while he was about it, the Lord Chamberlain sent a pithy note ordering that the late King's hangings from Greenwich, 'now in the possession of the Duchess of Portsmouth',[50] were to be returned forthwith to HM Wardrobe.

On the night of 14 March the funeral took place with the usual heraldic procession to Westminster, but being at night, was called a 'private funeral'. The coffin was carried under a fringed canopy to the solemn beat of muted drums and the eerie light of hundreds of flambeaux. James II and his Queen attended – it was a quite new departure for ladies to be present at the funeral of a man – and Prince George of Denmark, the stolid husband of the Princess Anne, was chief mourner. The 'depositum plate' on the coffin dated King Charles's reign from his father's execution rather than from the Restoration.

No concessions were made to Charles's 'dying in a different religion'. Archbishop Ken firmly read the Anglican burial service, the Great Officers broke their staves and Charles II was laid to rest in the south-east corner of the Henry VII Chapel, where he remained unmarked until the badly corroded coffin was

Opposite: The wax effigy of Charles II, now to be seen in the Museum at Westminster Abbey, which originally stood upon the coffin at his lying-in-state at Whitehall and lay on it in the funeral procession.

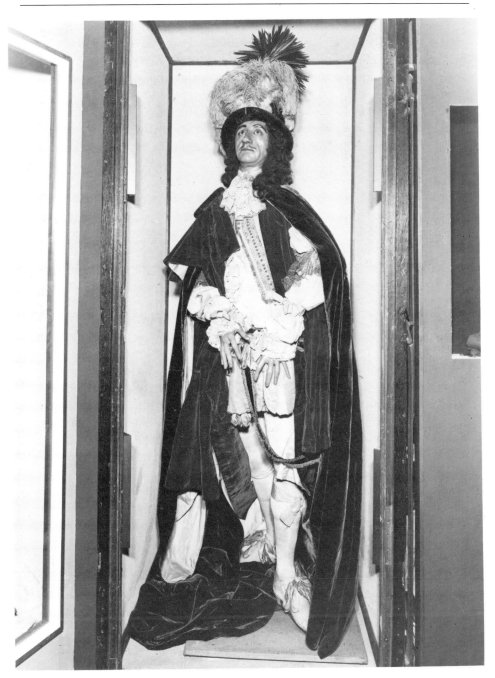

discovered while heating was being installed in 1867. When last seen in 1977, it was in no better state and the royal remains were clearly visible. The Stuarts lie tightly packed in that south vault underneath their ancestress, Mary, Queen of Scots, and none but she have any memorial other than a name on a square paving stone in the floor.

King Charles was succeeded by his brother, James, but his reign was cut short after three years. The country would not accept a Catholic King and a Catholic succession, for James had, by now, a living son, and at last the Glorious Revolution of 1688 ushered in the joint reign of his eldest daughter, Mary, and her husband, William, Prince of Orange.

William and Mary were an oddly assorted couple; she tall, graceful and beautiful and he small, stunted and asthmatic. She was emotional, lighthearted and extrovert while he was cold, formal, withdrawn and a notorious homosexual. Nevertheless, Mary adored him and he, in so far as his chilly personality would allow, was fond of her. Mary had been heartbroken at leaving Holland where she had spent twelve happy years, and had at first pined for their home at Het Loo which she was never to see again. But hers was a buoyant personality and she soon settled once more in England, especially enjoying making a home for William at Kensington House which they had bought as a healthier abode for an asthmatic than Whitehall.

On the morning of 21 December 1694, while Londoners prepared for Christmas and a black frost held the Thames in an icy grip, Queen Mary got up in her bedchamber at Kensington, feeling far from well. She had been very tired lately and earlier in the month had been laid low for several days with what was feared to be smallpox. It was raging in London that autumn and Mary had never had it. However, it proved to be a false alarm and the Queen was soon herself again. This time, however, though she said nothing to alarm her attendants or the King, Mary knew that something was seriously wrong. She locked herself up in her little closet and went through all her private papers, burning some and putting the rest in order, and when this was done she took a dose of quinine, went quietly to bed and never left it again. By the next day it was obvious that it was smallpox and a panic-stricken fear gripped the King. Both his parents had died of it – his mother was that Princess Mary who died on a visit to her brother Charles II soon after the Restoration – and he had a terrible dread of the disease. Now it was to take his wife too and William went quite to pieces. His icy reserve left him and he intermittently sobbed hysterically and fainted. Several times his gentlemen had to carry him from the bedroom and lay him on a camp bed which had been put up in an ante-room.

[76]

The news of the Queen's illness spread fast, and soon the Court were tip-toeing about with frightened faces as they whispered the latest bulletins to each other. And it was the same in the streets of London, for Mary was a popular queen and English too, and they did not want to be left with foreign William. There was a gloomy portent for the superstitious as well, and most people were superstitious in the seventeenth century. One of the lions at the Tower had died and the last time that had happened had been at the death of King Charles.

On Christmas Day hopes rose as congregations all over the country prayed for the Queen. Mary was feeling better and the spots had disappeared. After all it had been measles, they said. But that evening she was worse again and when her doctors examined her, they found that, far from disappearing, the spots had 'turned in on themselves', and their faces were very grave. Nine of them, under the celebrated Dr Radcliffe, went to work on the poor Queen, employing most of the remedies that had so signally failed to cure Charles II, so that we may imagine what sufferings were piled upon those of the smallpox.

William was frantic. Bishop Burnet, now Bishop of Salisbury, had an audience with him about this time and

> he burst out into tears; and cried out, that there was no hope of the Queen; and that, from being the happiest, he was now going to be the miserablest creature upon earth. He said, during the whole course of their marriage, he had never known one single fault in her; there was a worth in her, that nobody knew besides himself.[51]

The Archbishop of Canterbury spent two whole days standing at the Queen's bedside. He tried gently to make known to her that she should be prepared for death and

> she presently apprehended his drift, but showed no fear or disorder upon it. She said, she thanked God she had always carred in her mind, that nothing was to be left to the last hour; she had nothing then to do, but to look up to God, and submit to His will.[52]

She then received the sacrament along with all the bishops who were present, but, Burnet tells us, 'not without some concern, that she should not be able to swallow the bread, yet it went down easily.'[53]

The Queen put a small 'scrutoire' of letters, saved from her last turnout, into William's hands, but by now she seemed to be deliberately removing herself from

The Death of Mary II: an imagined scene by a Dutch engraver, Pieter Percoy.

the emotions of this world. 'She avoided giving herself or him the tenderness, which a final parting might have raised in them both.'[54] At this last hour their roles were reversed and it was the once emotional Mary who waved her husband away. She was too weak to take his passionate outpourings. Nothing now seemed to do her any good but prayer, and mercifully the nine doctors had at last given up and left her in peace. She was, by then, 'Upon the Wing', according to Burnet, and so, in an atmosphere of prayer, sometimes awake, sometimes dozing, she lived on until about one o'clock on the morning of 28 December when, 'after two or three small strugglings of Nature without such agonies as are usual',[55] Queen Mary died. She was only thirty-two and in the sixth year of her reign.

William was overcome. He fainted dead away and was carried to his own room where he remained for days in a state of complete collapse, refusing to see anyone.

And indeed, a desolation seemed to have come over the whole nation, as if the frost which held the ground and the water in its icy grip had also numbed the hearts and minds of the people. Their grief also united them with William, of whom they had not previously thought much.

The Archbishop was as much needed as ever to minister to William, who, at one time, seemed about to join his wife, and turned his mind to religion. He came to be on such intimate terms with the King that he even dared to broach the subject of Betty Villiers whose affair with William had been the cause of much scandal at Court and much pain to Mary, and William promised to have done with her.

The two Houses of Parliament met and sent condolences to William before voting money for the obsequies, and the Earl Marshal ordered mourning for all entitled to wear it. Mary's body was embalmed and her heart, in a purple velvet box within an urn was placed next to that of Charles II on a shelf in the vault at Westminster. This was the usual custom at the death of an important personage and continued into the nineteenth century so that every vault has shelves as crowded with urns as the space below is with coffins.

Meanwhile, as William mourned and the Court ordered their blacks, the most senior member of the late Queen's household, her Mistress of the Stole, the Duchess of Devonshire, was feathering her own nest. It was a fairly well established tradition that senior courtiers were entitled to the perk of many of the furnishings of their master's or mistress's private rooms. But the Duchess did not wait to be invited; she had the contents of Queen Mary's apartments listed and removed within days of her death. When the King came out of his shock he was enraged and ordered them all to be restored. The Duchess resisted and an unseemly wrangle went on for some time.

For a time the Queen lay at Kensington, where the Withdrawing Room was draped in black, and was then moved to Whitehall for the more formal lying-in-state. This time they seem to have reverted to the old habit of long-drawn-out obsequies, for Mary's lying-in-state was not until 21 February and the funeral not until 5 March, 'a few ghastly flakes of snow [falling] on the black plumes of the funeral car'.[56] Celia Fiennes, on one of her many journeys, was an eyewitness of both and, though the scene is now familiar, her description seems worth recording.

The Queen dying before the King he omitted no ceremony of respect to her memory and remains which lay in state in Whitehall in a bed of purple velvet all open, the canopy the same with rich gold fring, the middle being the armes of England curiously painted and gilt, the head piece embroider'd richly with a crown and cyphers of her name, a cusheon of purple velvet at the head on which was the Imperiall Crown and Scepter and Globe, and at the feete another such a cusheon with the Sword and Gauntlets, on the corps which was rowled in lead, and over it a coffin cover'd with purple velvet with the crown, and gilt its moldings very curious; a pall on all of a very rich tissue of gold and silver, ruffled round about with purple velvet which hung down on the ground, which was a halfe pace railed as the manner of the princes beds are; this in a room hung with purple velvet, full of large wax tapers, and at the 4 corners of the bed stood 4 of the Ladyes of the Bed Chamber – Countesses – with vailes; these were at several tymes relieved by others of the same.

The anty chamber hung with purple cloth, and there attended four of the Maids of Honnour, all in vailes, and the gentlemen of the Bed Chamber; pages [in] another roome all in black, the staires all below the same. The Queen dyeing while the Parliament sate, the King gave mourning to them [500 members] and cloakes, which attended thus; the Speaker having his traine bore up, then the Lord Major the same, and attended by the Aldermen and officers of the Household, then the Guards, then the Gentleman Master of the Horse led the Queens led horse cover'd up with purple velvet; next came the open chariot made as the bed was, the cannopy the same all purple velvet, a high arch'd teister ruffled, with the rich fring and pall, which was supported by six of the first Dukes of the Realme that were not in office; this chariot was drawn by the Queens own 6 horses covered up with purple velvet and at the head and feete was laid the emblems of her dignity, the Crown and Scepter on a cushion at the head, and Globe and the Sword and Gauntlets at the feete; after which the first mourner walked being supported by these Lords, the Lord President of the Councill and the Lord Privy Seale, she having a vaile over her face, and her traine of 6 yards length being bore up by the next Dutches assisted by four young ladyes; after which two and two the Ladies followed and likewise, all on foote on black cloth strained on boards, from Whitehall to Westminster Abby where was a sermon, in which tyme the body of the Queen was reposed in a masulium [mausoleum, on which a robin which had flown in from outside had perched] in form of a bed with black velvet and silver fringe round, and hanging in arches, and at the four corners was tapers and in the middle a bason supported by cupids or cherubims shoulders, in which was one entire great lamp burning the whole tyme.

Then after the service of burial which is done with solemn and mourning musick and singing, the sound of a drum unbraced [the anthem, specially composed by Purcell, and featuring repeated, muffled strokes of the timpani, was 'Thou knowest, Lord, the secrets of our hearts; shut not thy merciful ears unto our prayers, but spare us Lord most Holy'], the breaking of all the white staves of those that were the officers of the Queen, and flinging in the keys of the rest of the offices devoted by that badge into the tomb; they seale it up and soe returne in same order they went. There is allwayes a High Steward made for all solemnityes of the Kings and Queens, and he is only soe for that day, and he goes just before the led horse. The pages also lead all the horses that draws the chariot, and the Yeaumen of the Guard walks on each side, and the Gentlemen Pensioners, the guards on horseback being set in ranke on each side all the way. This is the manner of publick funeralls but if it be Kings then the ladyes attend not.[57]

One particular point of interest is highlighted by Bishop Burnet; all members of Parliament walked in the procession and in Westminster Abbey 'places were prepared for both houses to sit in form. This could never happen before since the sovereign's death had always dissolved our parliaments ...'[58] In this case of a double sovereignty, Parliament continued to sit. All had therefore to be supplied with mourning, and indeed, Evelyn noted in his diary on 5 March, 'Was the Queen's funeral infinitely expensive ...'[59]

Soon after Mary's death, William was reconciled with Princess Anne who, in spite of a quarrel which had remained unhealed at Mary's death, had sincerely grieved over the loss of her sister. The King invited her to visit him at Kensington and they remained on good terms thereafter. Her petty quarrel with Anne was the only fault anyone could find with Mary, and this she stuck to stubbornly right up to her death.

In the United Provinces, the news of the death of their Prince's consort was greeted with general sorrow. Mary, who had loved the Dutch, had been much loved in return. There was much speculation as to whether, with Mary dead, William could survive as King, and the States General offered him their support. In France, on the other hand, now the home of Mary's deposed father, her death was welcomed and was seen by many as an opportunity for reinstating James with French help. Fortunately neither hope nor fear was justified and William kept a firm grip on his throne. James, meanwhile, shocked many even at his own Court, by refusing to allow mourning to be worn for his daughter.

William was now a very eligible widower and offers soon came flowing in from Europe. But the King would have none of them. Though he soon got over the shock, and once again busied himself with the affairs of his two countries, he never remarried.

The great sorrow of Queen Mary's life had been that she was never able to have a child. After two miscarriages early in her marriage, she and William appear to have given up hope. Her sister, Anne, however, wrestled bravely on to provide an heir for England. Altogether she gave birth seventeen times and almost all were stillbirths or infants who lived only a few hours. But soon after Mary came to the throne, Anne had a son, William, Duke of Gloucester, and this child was a great comfort to the childless King and Queen. Even after the rift with Anne, her son had often stayed with his uncle and aunt at Kensington where he modelled himself on the 'Soldier King'. As he grew up it became evident that he was very delicate, with a head too big for his body (he is now thought to have had hydrocephalus), but he was soldier mad and William and Mary encouraged this by giving him swords and drums and allowing him to drill a tiny army of small boys in Kensington Gardens. After Mary's death this relationship continued, although the King was often away. He supervised his education and had just given him Queen Mary's apartments at Kensington when, following his eleventh birthday party on 25 July 1700, the little Duke fell ill, possibly yet another case of smallpox. The doctors did their worst, but his frail body could not withstand their onslaughts and five days later the last Protestant hope of the Stuart dynasty was dead.

London was sincere in its mourning for Anne's only child and crammed into Whitehall for the lying-in-state in such numbers that the Lord Chamberlain had to make a ruling that only those in full mourning would be admitted. As no one below the rank of gentry was allowed to wear mourning, this ruled out all but the the politest of society. The private funeral, on the night of 9 August, was a gloomy affair by the light of guttering torches held by a guard of honour who lined the route from Whitehall to Westminster Abbey.

In 1701 it was King James's turn to die. Still an exile in France, his obsequies, at Saint Germain en Laye, are outside the scope of this book. Suffice it to say that, whereas James had refused to put himself or his suite into mourning for his daughter, William, with commendable restraint, refrained from returning the insult and ordered partial mourning, as for a relation, the nobility not to put their servants into mourning. Louis XIV now recognized James's son as King and Jacobite intrigue for 'the King over the water' was strengthened.

During much of 1701 King William was in indifferent health. He was only fifty-one and his chronic asthma had for some time been better, but now it was his legs that were giving cause for concern. Both were very swollen, with a pale, soft swelling, and the treatment of his doctors only made it worse. They bandaged them tightly which, not surprisingly, merely sent the swelling up higher and must have been intensely painful. He spent the summer in Holland where, in spite of his legs, he spent much of his time hunting. Needless to say, his Dutch doctors and

English doctors gave quite different advice. The King tried all their remedies but it was obvious that he had little faith in their prescriptions. The fact that he had conquered his asthma to a great extent probably says more for his active and outdoor way of life and his almost modern diet, quite sparing and containing a lot of fruit, than for his doctors' purgings and cuppings.

The journey back to England in October exhausted him and he was forced to spend some days in bed. But within a few days of reaching Hampton Court he was out again, 'I did not think one could recover so soon,'[60] he said, and this he continued to do all through the winter. His legs were now so bad that he could hardly walk and riding must have been agony. It was not surprising, therefore, that when, on 20 February, his new mare, Sorrel, stumbled on a molehill while he was riding near Hampton Court, he was thrown heavily and broke his collar bone. Incidentally, this incident is the origin of the Jacobite toast to 'the wee gentleman in black velvet', the mole. But what is a broken collar bone to a soldier? The King would have nothing made of it beyond putting his arm in a sling, and returned to Kensington that night. The jolting carriage ride must have been acutely painful. It was business as usual for more than a week, although by then it was found that the break had not mended and that the hand and arm were very swollen. He insisted upon continuing as usual until 2 March, when he caught a chill. Sitting by an open window, he had fallen asleep in the sun, but by the time he woke the sun had gone in and he was chilled to the marrow. The doctors now moved in with their whole armoury, but he refused all they prescribed. By 4 March he was in a high fever and could keep nothing down, and the doctors were obviously despairing, for Sir Walter Ralegh's cordial, that last resort of the hopeless, was forced upon the poor tired King. Even yet he might have pulled through, but he was weary of life. Even before his accident he had confided in Albemarle and Portland that he felt so weak that he did not expect to live another summer.

Still the King struggled with affairs of state, sending messages to Parliament from his sickbed about the union of England and Scotland which was his dearest wish. But he was sinking fast. His worn out lungs were failing him and he struggled for breath. He said goodbye to his friends, 'and called for the Earl of Portland [Hans Willem Bentinck who had come with him from Holland so long ago], but before he came, his voice quite failed, so he took him by the hand, and carried it to his heart with great tenderness.'[61] Almost immediately afterwards, as the Archbishop read the Commendatory Prayer, between 7 and 8 o'clock on the morning of Sunday, 8 March 1702, 'shutting his eyes he expired with 2 or 3 soft gasps.'[62] And when they undressed him they found on a ribbon round his neck a little gold ring that he had given Mary long ago in Holland, with a lock of her hair in

The Deathbed of William III, by a Dutch engraver, P van den Berge.

it; a private demonstration of devotion by an undemonstrative man.

Except for his faithful Dutchmen who were prostrated with grief, there was very little lamentation for a king still felt by most Englishmen to be a foreigner. Grief was swallowed up in a wild surge of enthusiasm for Anne, a truly English queen. Queen Anne herself was caught up in this wave of popular feeling and made no attempt to prolong the obsequies. Everything was done correctly but no more than decently. The funeral took place at midnight on 12 April and mourning, in English silk rather than Italian crape, to appease the English weavers, was cut to a minimum. Anne herself was in black for her father with purple trimmings for William, but mourning ceased altogether after the coronation on 23 April.

Queen Anne was neither beautiful nor clever, but her heart was all for her people and during her twelve years on the throne she worked conscientiously at government. Her reign is remembered for the Act of Union with Scotland and for the great victories of Blenheim and Oudenarde, and Anne herself for her passionate friendship and final quarrel with Sarah, Duchess of Marlborough, the

Mrs Freeman of their famous correspondence.

Anne was passionately devoted to her stolid husband, Prince George of Denmark and 'had been throughout the whole of her married life a pattern of domestic affection'.[63] When, in the last years of his life, he was ill with dropsy and asthma, she sat up with him night after night and 'proffered to her sick consort those patient services which are generally supposed only to be the deeds of females in the humbler walks of life.'[64] When he died on 28 October 1708 aged fifty-five, her grief was said to be insupportable, and she sank into an almost Victoria-like stupor of mourning. She kept the Prince's private rooms just as he had them and often sat there all alone with his carpentry tools and books around her. For six months she lived in complete seclusion except to go to chapel where no one dared be seen with so much as a coloured handkerchief and the Queen herself was shrouded in black and purple.

At last the prayer which must have tormented the poor Queen for so many years, that she might be the happy mother of children, was dropped from the liturgy, and when Parliament was so ill-advised as to present an address to the Queen, who was now forty-four and in very poor health, 'That Your Majesty would not so far indulge your just grief, as to decline the thoughts of a second marriage,' she replied curtly that 'The subject of this Address is of such a nature, that I am pursuaded you do not expect a particular answer.'[65] No one could imagine that the Protestant succession still depended on Queen Anne, and Parliament was much laughed at for their idiocy.

On 13 November Prince George was buried in Westminster Abbey, 'after the same manner as King Charles the 2nd, which was privately, at 12 at night'.[66] His coffin was the largest anyone remembered seeing, for George had been a large and heavy man, but Anne's own was to be even larger – almost square.

Queen Anne had lost her prop and stay, her confidant, and the sole object of her care and devotion. She was now truly alone. But instead of being allowed to mourn in peace, the Queen was plagued by the Duchess of Marlborough who carried on a most insensitive campaign of asserting her rights and claims to the friendship of the Queen over those of her new favourite, Abigail Masham. She must have driven Anne almost mad, but she got her deserts and, after a final dramatic row, the Queen freed herself once and for all of the domination of this termagant Duchess.

The Court of Queen Anne had always been a dull one. Now it sank into a positive 'slough of despond'. Jonathan Swift gives us a picture of how it was:

August 8 [1711]. There was a drawing room today at Court but so few company that the Queen sent for us into her bedchamber where we made our bows and stood, about 20 of us, round the room, while she looked at us round with her fan in her mouth and once a minute said about three words to some that were nearest her, and then she was told dinner was ready and went out.[67]

The boredom of those compelled by their positions to attend regularly at Court must have been intense. But the Queen did have one pleasure, and a highly unlikely one. Almost to the end of her life she enjoyed hunting, and there are descriptions of her going flat out across country in a specially designed chariot, as she drove thirty or forty miles after a stag, staying out until four in the afternoon.

It is quite beyond the scope of this book to analyse the ailments Queen Anne suffered and died from. At various times her malady has been described as syphilis and porphyria, which her great-great-grandmother, Mary, Queen of Scots suffered from, but these diagnoses do not stand up to modern medical scrutiny. Lady Mary Wortley Montagu put it neatly enough when she wrote, 'the Queen died suddenly, worn out with a complication of distempers.'[68] And we may be sure that her doctors tortured her poor weary, bloated body with all the battery with which we have become so familiar, culminating, as always, in Sir Walter Ralegh's cordial. She was at least spared the constant bleedings, however, as it was known that the Queen much preferred to be 'cupped'. And she was luckier than some as the final crisis lasted no more than three days. The account of the Queen's last illness and death in the Gazette is brief:

This day [Sunday, 1 August 1714] at half an Hour past Seven in the Morning, died our late most Gracious Sovereign Queen Anne, in the Fiftieth Year of her Age, and the Thirteenth of Her Reign; a Princess of exemplary Piety and Virtue. Her Majesty complained on Thursday last of a Pain in Her Head: The next Day she was seized with Convulsion Fits, and for some time lost the use of Her Speech and Senses, which tho' She afterwards recovered upon the Application of proper Remedies, She continued in a very weak and languishing Condition till She expired.[69]

At once the dead Queen's ladies began to behave in a manner which also has become familiar: 'Lady Masham, Mrs Hill and Danvers are cried out upon for their behaviour; though they roared and cried enough whilst there was life, but as soon as there was none they took care of themselves . . .'[70]

Opposite: An engraving commemorating the death of Queen Anne, by Grainger after Wale, and circulated at the time.

Queen
ANNE.

Ascended the Throne March 8 1702 — Died Aug.t 1 1714.

For three weeks the Queen's body lay at Kensington where she had died, though the day after her death the 'Bowells [were] taken, to Henry VII Chapel in Her late Majesty's coaches and put in a vault' which the Dean was instructed to have opened. Then, the night before the funeral, a hearse covered in purple velvet, conveyed the coffin to Westminster where, by means of a specially constructed wooden bridge from Palace Yard, it was borne into the Prince's Chamber where it lay in state, for by now the Palace of Whitehall and its Painted Chamber had been destroyed in the great fire of 1689.

The interment took place on the night of 24 August. Being private, there were no poor men and women in the procession, but it was, nonetheless, well attended and must have been a noble sight. The vast coffin was carried, under its canopy, by fourteen carpenters, in loose black coats and caps, and escorted by three dukes on either side as pall bearers. The Duchess of Somerset, in a 'vaile' of thirty yards of crape, was chief mourner, supported by two more dukes, her husband and the Duke of Richmond. Fourteen countesses, in twenty-six-yard veils, followed, but conspicuous by their absence were the Duke of Marlborough and his disgraced Duchess. 'At the entrance within the Church [the cortège was met by] the Dean and Prebends attended by the Choir in their habits all having wax tapers in their Hands.'[71]

And so, in little more than a century, the proud Stuart dynasty, so far as the throne of Great Britain was concerned, faded into history and the crown passed into the foreign hands of the Electoral House of Hanover in the person of His Most Gracious Majesty King George I.

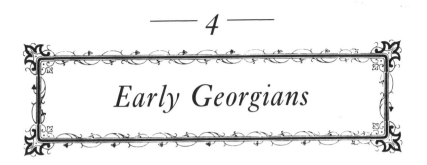

4

Early Georgians

The Stuart period had been one of revolution in more than one sense. Not only had there been the violent revolution of the Civil War and later the bloodless 'Glorious Revolution' of 1688 which brought William and Mary to the throne. There was also an almost imperceptible revolution working its way in the minds of the men and women of the period. This, very broadly, was a humanist movement: a growing confidence in man's achievements and potential, allied to a strong interest in science. By and large rulers did not subscribe to this new thinking, and rightly, from their point of view, for it was this line of thought which ultimately and in its most extreme form led to such violent upheavals as the American War of Independence and the French Revolution. Charles II was certainly interested; he founded the Royal Society and was a good amateur scientist himself.

With William and Mary came an increased interchange of ideas with the continent, William being very much a European in thought; but the reign of Queen Anne called a halt to these developments by providing an intensely conservative climate at the top. Anne completely lacked intelligence herself and gave no encouragement to the great minds of her day. Then George I was an elderly man, fifty-four, by the time he succeeded to the throne of Great Britain; no innovator himself, he was a European, and his arrival in 1714 with a large suite opened up England again to continental trains of thought. He also brought with him his son George Augustus and his attractive and highly intelligent daughter-in-law, Caroline of Anspach, who was interested in all the latest philosophical thinking and surrounded herself with the most modern minds. So, by the time her husband came to the throne in 1727, England had been brought to the brink of the Age of Reason.

Parallel with these philosophical developments, medicine and surgery were making progress, and so by the time of the first royal death of the Hanoverian era, a new attitude to death was noticeable.

In the seventeenth century people lived in daily expectation of death. John Evelyn never so much as recovered from a cold without writing in his diary that God, in His mercy had seen fit to restore him to health, and this was not uncommon, neither was it a mere figure of speech. To most people God was a real presence in their lives. Eighteenth-century people, at any rate in high society, were less religious and, with improvements in medicine and surgery, began to expect to live and to blame their doctors rather than God if they did not. Here also Caroline's influence was felt as she was among the first to adopt the Turkish habit of inoculation against smallpox, introduced to England by Lady Mary Wortley Montagu for her children. We read more of people 'expiring' than of 'God taking them to Himself', and there was an almost imperceptible shift of emphasis away from the departed and on to those who remained behind, with more and more elaborate funerals and the emergence of undertakers to make all the arrangements and furnish the procession with plumed hearses and mutes with weepers (funeral attendants with long scarves trailing from their hats), draped wands and trays of plumes.

Of course royal funerals had always been elaborate, and the College of Arms, the Lord Chamberlain's Office and the Great Wardrobe continued to handle most of the arrangements. Nevertheless, by 1751, an undertaker had gained a toe-hold in the business of royal obsequies, as we shall see later.

George I and his Queen need not detain us. George's wife, Sophia Dorothea, never came to England, having been divorced and imprisoned in one of his castles in Hanover, following an illicit love affair many years before. She died, still a prisoner, in 1726 and her husband allowed no one to go into mourning or take any notice of the event. Seven months later, in June 1727, he himself died on his way to Hanover, which he had always preferred to England, and was buried in Hanover. Oddly enough, he died in the same room of the same castle at Osnabrück in which he had been born sixty-seven years before.

That put George Augustus on the throne as George II and he and Caroline reigned happily enough for ten years except that they could not get on with their eldest son, Frederick Louis, Prince of Wales. The feud was total and was only resolved by the Prince's own death in 1751. Not getting on with their heirs was the hallmark of the Hanoverian monarchs; from George I, who had abominated George Augustus, to George III and the Prince Regent, there was a complete lack of harmony, so much so that rival courts were set up and the government and aristocracy split between the two camps.

George II was a difficult, irascible man. He had mistresses, as was usual for

[90]

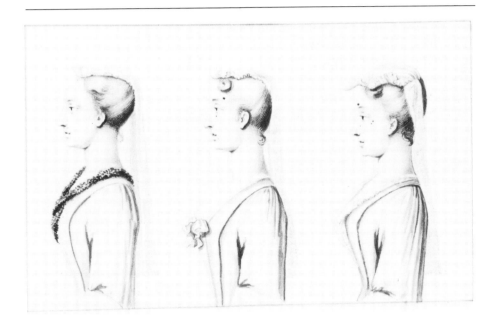

Fashion plate – 'First days of mourning' – for George I, by Bernard Lens.

princes in those days, but, though he did not often show it, indeed he constantly bullied and snubbed her, he adored Caroline and relied upon her for companion-ship and advice. She understood him and provided him with the stable background he required.

'Sunday 20 – At 11 o'clock this Night, died of a Mortification of ye Bowels, her Majesty Wilhelmina Dorothea Caroline, Queen Consort of Great Britain etc. aged 54 Years, 8 Months, and 20 Days,'[1] announced the *Gentleman's Magazine* for November 1737 – no discreet euphemisms for the eighteenth-century press. It is a simple and brief announcement, but the reality had been anything but brief; it had been twelve days of pain and horror for the poor Queen and her family.

On 9 November Queen Caroline was taken suddenly ill, with what she called the cholic, at her new library in St James's Park. She hurried home to St James's Palace, dosed herself with 'Daffy's Elixir' and went to bed. But she got up again in the afternoon to attend a drawing-room, fearing that the King would complain at her absence; he was always impatient of illness and up to now the Queen had usually managed to hide her many ailments from him. Almost at once she went up to her old friend, Lord Hervey, Vice Chamberlain of her Household, saying, 'Is it not intolerable at my age to be plagued with a new distemper? Here is this nasty cholic that I had at Hampton Court come again.'² Hervey thought she looked dreadfully ill and persuaded her to go at once to bed, where her condition rapidly declined with terrible pain and vomiting continuing day after day. The King, her unmarried daughters, Amelia (sometimes called Emily), Caroline, Louisa and Mary were constantly with her, as well as her physicians who administered 'snake root' and other stimulants, but nothing brought relief.

The Queen's suffering cannot have been much helped by her family either. Princess Caroline alternated between weeping and having copious nose-bleeds and the King between covering her face and hands with tears and kisses and snapping at her. In his undoubted distress and anxiety, what Lord Hervey described as 'the natural brusquerie of his temper' asserted itself. When, one morning, after a sleepless night of torment, the Queen lay resting, her eyes fixed vaguely at some point in space, 'Mon Dieu!' he exclaimed. 'What are you looking at? How can you stare like that? You look like a calf that has just had its throat cut.'³ A mixture of brutality and tenderness which must have been most exhausting. Hervey says that he hardly ever went into her room without snubbing her for something, and that 'he was always capable of using those worst whom he loved best'.⁴

The Prince of Wales may have hoped for a deathbed rapprochement with his mother, but it was not to be. When he tried to visit her, the King flew into a rage and cried:

This is like one of the scoundrel's tricks; it is just of a piece with his kneeling down in the dirt before the mob to kiss her hand at the coach door when she came from Hampton Court to see the Princess, though he had not spoken one word to her during her whole visit. I always hated the rascal, but now I hate him worse than ever. He wants to come and insult his poor dying mother; but she shall not see him . . .⁵

The Queen wondered that 'the Griff', as he was nicknamed, had not asked to see her, saying tartly, 'but sooner or later I am sure one shall be plagued with some message of that sort, because he will think it will have a good air in the world to ask to see me; and perhaps hopes I shall be fool enough to let him come, and give him the pleasure of seeing my last breath go out of my body . . .'⁶ A strange relationship indeed.

It was not until the Queen's illness had gone on for some days that, entirely against her wishes, the King sent for the surgeon, Ranby, and divulged the probable real cause of his wife's trouble. Fourteen years previously, after the birth of her youngest daughter, Caroline had suffered an 'umbilical rupture', and this had now 'mortified'. For some reason the Queen was terribly ashamed of this 'making her person distasteful to the King'[7] and fought against having it revealed. Or perhaps she was just frightened, and with good cause, for there followed the most horrifying series of operations, cuttings and probings and dressings, sometimes several times a day, and of course, quite without any anaesthetics, as the surgeons fought to prevent the spread of infection. Yet somehow through it all, Caroline retained the shreds of her well-known sense of humour, or at any rate, of the ridiculous. She had to ask Ranby to stay his hand till she could stop laughing when his wig caught fire from a candle as he was bending over her to operate.

But it was all to no avail and slowly the Queen grew weaker. It was now obvious that she must die and it was spoken of openly. Taking off the ruby ring the King had put on her finger at her coronation, and putting it on his, she said, 'This is the last thing I have to give you – naked I came to you and naked I go from you. I had everything I ever possessed from you, and to you whatever I have I return. My will you will find a very short one: I give all I have to you.'[8] She urged him to marry again. 'Non, j'aurai des maitresses,' sobbed the distracted King. 'Ah! Mon Dieu! Cela n'empêche pas,'[9] was her wry rejoinder.

The Queen was attended, towards the end, by Archbishop Potter who prayed with her but, for some reason, she resisted all offers of the sacrament. Was it that she did not feel able to receive it without being reconciled with her son, or just that she was not a religious person? The matter was much speculated upon around the palace and the Wales faction, both before and after her death, put about spiteful epitaphs like Chesterfield's: 'And unforgiving, unforgiven dies!'[10] However, the Archbishop silenced the Court gossips by saying firmly that 'Her Majesty was in a heavenly disposition.'[11]

On the twelfth day of her illness, Sunday, 20 November, the exhausted Queen asked one of her doctors how long he thought her agony could go on. 'Je crois que votre Majesté sera bientôt soulagée' was the welcome reply, to which she responded, 'Tant mieux.'[12] Indeed, soon afterwards, a rattle began in her throat; the Queen said calmly, 'I have now got an asthma. Open the window,' adding, as she clasped the King's hand, the one word, 'Pray,' and before Princess Emily could read more than ten words of a prayer, her suffering was at an end. Princess Caroline snatched up a looking glass and held it to her lips, but there was no mist upon it and she cried out, 'Tis over!'

The King was quite inconsolable. He wept and lamented and went on and on about Caroline's virtues and perfections (and his own, it must be added) to anyone

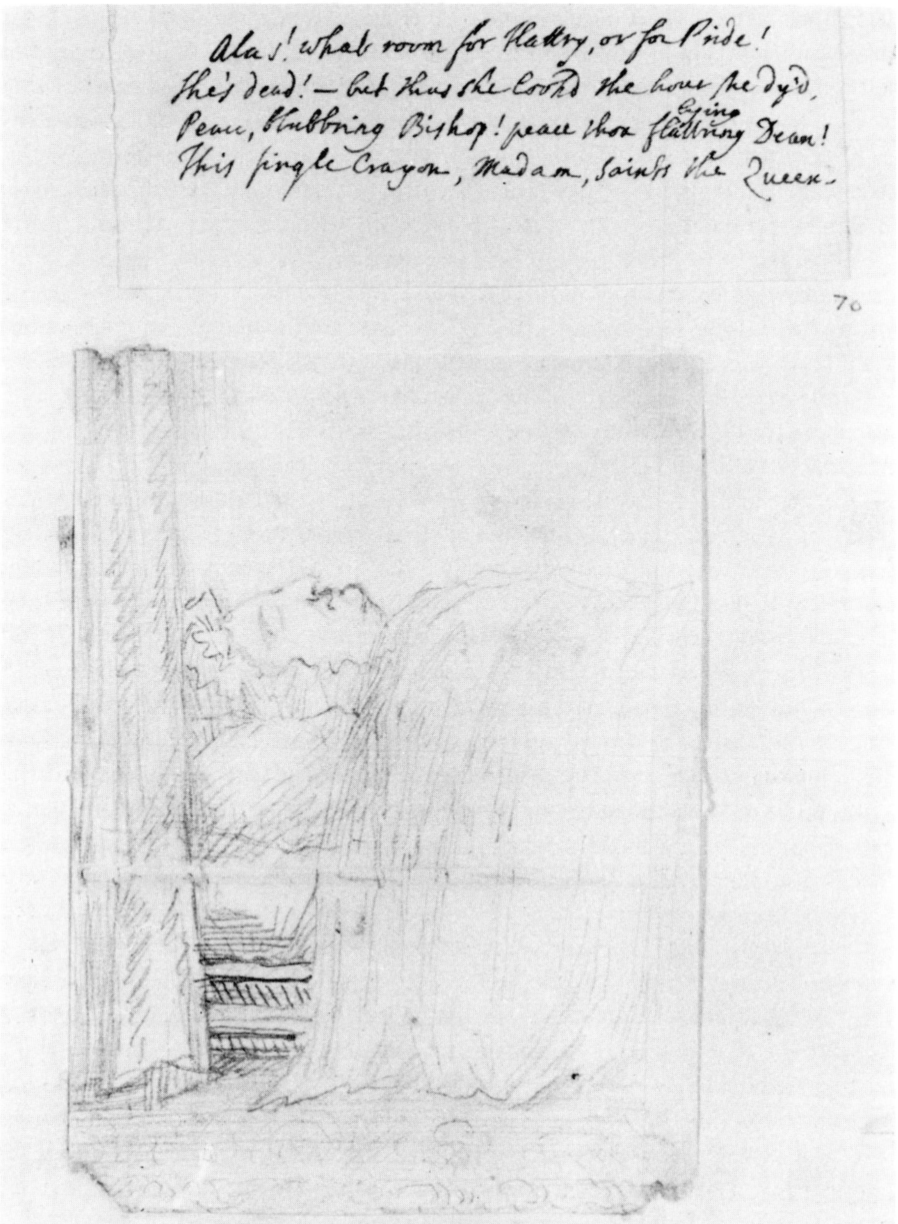

Alas! what room for flattry, or for Pride!
She's dead! — but thus she look'd the hour she dy'd.
Peace, stubbning Bishop! peace thou flattring Dean!
This single Crayon, Madam, saints the Queen.

70

69

[94]

who would listen. 'Jesus, how tiresome he is,'[13] groaned Princess Emily to Lord Hervey, as he regaled them with his bravery on the field of battle. Matters of state were neglected for weeks, but he did attend scrupulously to the Queen's affairs. Her will leaving everything to him, turned out to have very little in it but debts, for she was generous to a fault. The King took all these debts upon himself and continued the pensions and payments to all her many lame ducks, saying, 'I will have no one the poorer for her death but myself.'[14] Caroline was widely mourned by all classes of society.

Someone told the King that one of the Hanoverian suite had a portrait of the Queen which was considered a very good likeness. One morning, while he was still in bed, he sent for this portrait to be brought to him in his bedroom, telling its owner to 'Put it upon that chair at the foot of my bed, and leave me until I ring.' For two hours he lay gazing at the picture and then, at last, quite calm, he rang for it to be taken away. 'I never yet saw a woman fit to buckle her shoe,'[15] he told its owner.

General mourning for the whole of Society was announced in the *London Gazette*, with detailed instructions as to what people were to wear. But some time was allowed for mourners to fit themselves out with all that was necessary. The first order stated that mourning would commence on 27 November, but the date was subsequently changed to 4 December which gave them a full fortnight to put themselves into 'deepest mourning, long cloaks only excepted'. Instructions went out for ladies to wear 'black bombazines [i.e. matt fabric], plain Cambrick Linnen, Crape Hoods, Shamoy Shoes and Gloves, and crape Fans; and for their Undress, dark Norwich Crape'. Not even shoes or gloves might be shiny. Men were to wear 'black cloth without Buttons on the Sleeves or Pockets, plain Cambrick Cravats and Weepers, Shamoy shoes and gloves, Crape Hatbands and black Sword and Bucklers',[16] for undress, dark grey frocks. Military officers were to appear before the King in red faced with black and an interesting, rather pretty detail for the servants of the Officers of the Royal Household was that they were to wear black with shoulder knots of 'Ribbands' of the colour of their liveries. Of course coaches and chairs were to be dull black all over with never a bullion nail or a coat of arms to be seen.

After three months mourning was slightly relieved. Men might wear fringed hats and in undress, frocks of a lighter grey, while ladies might wear silk and some trimmings, white gloves, shoes and jewellery, but, oddly enough, no diamonds. In undress they might wear white or grey lustring, tabby or damask. A further six

Opposite: Queen Caroline on her death bed. A pencil sketch, probably drawn on the spot by Dorothy, Countess of Burlington and surmounted by a verse by Pope.

weeks and men, though they continued in black, could have coloured ribbons, fans and tippets. The whole period of mourning lasted six months.

Princess Amelia was to be chief mourner at the funeral, fixed for the night of 17 December, and the minutest of instructions governed her dress and that of the ladies attending her. They were all to have all-enveloping veils, the Princess's to contain, 'from the gathering of the neck to the end of the Train, seven yards in length and to come down to the Feet before. The Head [cap] to be in the same Crape'.[17] The train bearers, two duchesses, were to have one yard less in length and one foot off the ground in front, ladies of the bedchamber, five and a half yards and one and a half feet off the ground in front, while maids-of-honour to the late Queen should have five-yard trains, two feet off the ground in front and women of the bedchamber, just crape hoods.

For almost a month the body of Queen Caroline lay in its coffin in her own bedchamber at St James's Palace, watched over by her ladies and frequently visited by the grieving King. Then the night before the funeral a short service was held here, conducted by the Archbishop of Canterbury and attended by the King and the Princesses. This was the King's farewell to his Queen, for he would not be attending the funeral and, immediately afterwards, the coffin was carried in torchlight procession to Westminster to be laid in the Prince's Chamber until the following evening.

The funeral, in accordance with the Queen's request, was a simple one. A new vault, for the use of this family, had been opened near the tomb of Henry VII and the procession, headed by the choir and clergy, lighted tapers in their hands, wended its way there to the singing of the Psalm, *Domine refugium*. After the committal prayers, Garter King-of-Arms proclaimed Caroline's style and titles and the choir sang an anthem specially composed by Handel for the occasion: 'The Ways of Zion do mourn and she is in bitterness: all her people sigh and hang down their heads to the ground. How are the mighty fallen! . . . When the ear heard her, then it blessed her: and when the eye saw her, it gave witness of her . . . Her body is buried in peace, but her name liveth for evermore.'[18] A hundred and sixty-four years later, the same anthem was sung in Westminster Abbey at the memorial service for Queen Victoria.

As at the funeral of Anne of Denmark, the coffin was not lowered into the vault during the service. It remained under its canopy in the chapel while the mourners retired and later, with a short private service, was placed in a large stone sarcophagus, of which more will be heard later, in the chamber below.

Gradually the King took up the threads of life again, but he missed Caroline dreadfully and was, for some time, prey to morbid fancies to do with 'the material aspect' of death. There is an extraordinary story in a letter from Lord Wentworth to his father, Lord Strafford:

> Saturday night, between one and two o'clock, the King waked out of a dream very uneasy, and ordered the vault, where the Queen is, to be broken open immediately, and have the coffin also opened; and went in a hackney chair through the Horse Guards to Westminster Abbey, and back again to bed. I think it is the strangest thing that could be.[19]

Many bereaved people probably suffer from such nightmares, but few carry it so far, even if they had the means to do so.

Two of the King's daughters married and left him; Amelia and Caroline stayed on, the old maids of the family, playing cards with their father of an evening. His ministers encouraged him to take up with his mistresses again, feeling themselves on surer ground, as to influence, with them than with the Princesses. 'I'll bring Madame Walmoden over,' declared Sir Robert Walpole to Lord Hervey, 'and I'll have nothing to do with your girls: I was for the wife against the mistress, but I will be for the mistress against the daughters.'[20] At last King George took up the reins of government once more: he continued his regular visits to Hanover, he went campaigning and won glory on the field of Dettingen, but he never married again.

The delicate Princess Caroline, who her mother had not expected to survive her by more than a year or so, in fact lived another twenty years, though in increasingly ill health and living a very retired life. She had a passion for Lord Hervey, a married man, and when he died in 1755 she followed soon afterwards. 'Her whole income was dispensed between generosity and charity and till her death, by shutting up the current discovered the source, the jails of London did not suspect that the best support of their wretched inhabitants was issued from the Palace.'[21]

But it was 'Poor Fred', the despised Prince of Wales who was the next to go. He had had pleurisy in the winter of 1751 but recovered and by March was well enough to go to the House of Lords, and

> from thence to Carlton House, very hot, where he unrobed and put on a light unaired frock and waistcoat, went to Kew, walked in a bitter day, came home tired, and laid down for three hours, upon a couch in a very cold room at Carlton House, that opens into the garden ... The Prince relapsed that night, has had three physicians ever since and has never been supposed out of danger till [20 March].[22]

That night he was considered well enough for cards to be played in his ante-room, but suddenly, at about 9 or 10 o'clock, the Prince was seized with a violent fit of coughing. His doctors looked at one another, saying, 'Here is something I do not like,' Frederick pressed his hand to his stomach, crying, 'Je sens la mort!'[23] and before the Princess, his wife, could get from the foot of the bed to the head, he was gone. Or, as the *Gentleman's Magazine* put it, 'he complained of a sudden pain, and an offensive smell, and immediately threw himself backwards and expired.'[24] The post-mortem pronounced that he had died 'by the breaking of an imposthume between the pericardium and the diaphragm, which threw the matter contained in it upon the substance of the lungs'.[25] And it was rumoured that this was caused by a blow from a tennis ball some years before.

> Here lies Fred,
> Who was alive and is dead:
> Had it been his brother,
> Still better than another;
> Had it been his sister,
> No one would have missed her;
> Had it been the whole generation,
> Still better for the nation:
> But since 'tis only Fred,
> Who was alive and is dead,
> There's no more to be said.[26]

Such was the cruel and cynical verdict of the broadsheet writers of the London streets. It is impossible to imagine a journalist of even the most scurrilous gutter press putting about such stuff on the death of any royal person today. It is thought to come from the pen of a Jacobite, the reference to the brother being 'Butcher Cumberland', villain, from the Jacobite point of view, of the 1745 rebellion. Indeed one version ran 'Had it been the Butcher . . .'

Augusta, the widowed Princess of Wales, was dreadfully shocked. She had sat up with her husband night after night throughout his illness although she was heavily pregnant with their ninth child, so we may presume that she was at least fond of him, and added to this were two worries. What would be her position now, *vis à vis* the King with whom, ever since her arrival in this country, they had been on such bad terms? And what was to be done about the Prince's crippling debts, for it was widely said that, like his mother, he was generous to a fault, but without her brains? The first problem was quickly solved; the King, who appeared much

The Effigies of His late Royal Highness Frederick Prince of Wales

March 1750. Aged 45.

Obit. 20

Nixon Del. et Sculp.

Memento Mori

An engraved Memento Mori card on the death of Frederick, Prince of Wales.

shocked himself, at once sent kind messages to the Princess and within a day or two they were 'grown as fond as if they had never been of different parties'.[27] The young family were speedily taken under the King's wing and young Prince George, at that time eleven years old, was soon proclaimed Prince of Wales. The debts were a problem more difficult to solve, but with the King's support the Princess had less cause to worry and most of them were never paid. Sadly, the new, patched-up relationship did not last and the violent animosity that followed lasted for the rest of the reign.

The funeral took place on the night of Saturday, 13 April, quietly and with a somewhat meagre procession. Contrary to what might have been expected, the chief mourner was not Prince George, but the Duke of Somerset and there was no anthem, just 'Two drums beating a dead march, during the service',[28] and then 'poor Fred' was laid to rest close to the mother who had spurned him in life, his 'white staff officers' throwing their broken staves into the vault.

One small point of possible interest to some is that this appears to be the first occasion at which an undertaker was used at a royal funeral. There is a bill for £43 9s. 6d. from a Mr Harcourt who, among other things, laid out the corpse, provided the coffin, winding sheet etc., 'two wooden urns covered with lead and lined with silk for ye Bowells' and 'six men to move the Body under the canopy'.[29] By no means all of this was paid, it being considered that some of the services mentioned had been provided by the Great Wardrobe and others.

At this funeral the Committee of Lords appointed to arrange everything, found it necessary, from past experience, to issue an order to the effect that 'the Pall, Sheet, Cushions with all Blacks and Utensils whatsoever' used in the ceremony should be put into the custody of 'His Majesty's removing Wardrobe'[30] until it could be decided legally who should have them. This was to prevent the repetition of a most unseemly dispute which had arisen at former funerals between the Dean and Prebendaries of the Abbey and the King's heralds and Pursuivants at Arms. And another rumpus that was stamped out at a later funeral was the attempt by the mob to break into the Prince's Chamber at Westminster to steal 'the silver Chandelier Candlesticks, Canopy etc.'[31] after the procession had left it. Troops were ordered to remain and guard the door at the bottom of the stairs leading to the Prince's Chamber. This was hardly surprising as the candles themselves would have been worth a fortune to the poor. £763 10s. 0d.[32] was spent on 'waxlights' for the Abbey, the House of Lords and the Prince's Chamber at the funeral of the Prince of Wales, and the astronomic sum of £1969 12s. 10d.[33] at that of Queen Caroline. Did the price of candles plummet in the fourteen years between the two funerals, or was the Prince of Wales's funeral meanly lit by comparison?

A somewhat irreverent ink sketch of George II in his later years by George Townshend, later 4th Viscount and 1st Marquis, a frequenter of the Court in the 1750s.

King George II's death at Kensington Palace on 26 October 1760 had about it all the attributes of vulgar farce. The last British King to lead troops on the field of battle was not allowed the dignified death of the ageing military hero. He died in the lavatory and his death is described, briefly and with typical neatness, by Horace Walpole in a letter to a friend, as ever on the lookout for good gossip.

[101]

He went to bed well last night; rose at six this morning as usual, looked, I suppose, if all his money was in his purse, and called for his chocolate. A little after seven, he went into the water closet – the German valet de chambre heard a noise louder than royal wind, listened, heard something like a groan, ran in, and found the hero of Oudenarde and Dettingen on the floor, with a gash on his right temple, by falling against a bureau – he tried to speak, could not, and expired.[34]

Not for him protracted agony at the hands of his doctors. At the post-mortem it was found that 'the great ventricle of the heart had burst. What an enviable death,'[35] says Walpole. He was gone before even Princess Emily, his surviving unmarried daughter, could be summoned from her apartments nearby.

Walpole was not given to showing emotion on anyone's account, but, indeed, it seems likely that King George was very little mourned. He had become more and more pompous and irascible of late, indeed downright bad tempered with all those who came into contact with him, and most people were delighted to see a young and personable grandson of the late King ascend the throne as King George III. 'The young King, you may trust me, who am not apt to be enamoured with royalty, gives all the indication imaginable of being amiable. His person is tall, and full of dignity; his manner is graceful and obliging...'[36] With a young bachelor king on the throne, life at Court looked like being changed very much for the better, madness and blindness being well out of sight, more than a half century ahead.

The funeral was arranged, with unusual speed, for the night of 11 November. Again Horace Walpole's gossipy account is much the most readable record of the event and worth quoting in full, though the scene will not be new to the reader.

Do you know, I had the curiosity to go to the burying t'other night; I had never seen a royal funeral; nay, I walked as a rag of quality, which I found would be, and so it was, the easiest way of seeing it. It is absolutely a noble sight. The Prince's Chamber, hung with purple, and a quantity of silver lamps, the coffin under a canopy of purple velvet, and six vast chandeliers of silver on high stands, had a very good effect. The Ambassador from Tripoli and his son were carried to see that chamber. The procession through a line of foot-guards, every seventh man bearing a torch, the horse-guards lining the outside, their officers with drawn sabres and crape sashes on horseback, the drums muffled, the fifes, bells tolling, and minute guns, all this was very solemn. But the charm was the entrance of the Abbey, where we were received by the Dean and Chapter in rich copes, the choir and almsmen all bearing torches; the whole Abbey so illuminated, that one saw it to greater advantage than by day; the tombs, long aisles, and fretted roof, all appearing distinctly, and with the happiest chiaroscuro...

I had been in dread of being coupled with some boy of ten years old – but the heralds were not very accurate, and I walked with George Grenville, taller and older enough to keep me in countenance. When we came to the chapel of Henry the Seventh, all solemnity and decorum ceased – no order was observed, people sat or stood where they could or would, the yeomen of the guard were crying out for help, oppressed by the immense weight of the coffin, the Bishop read sadly, and blundered in the prayers, the fine chapter, 'Man that is born of a woman', was chanted, not read, and the anthem, besides being unmeasurably tedious, would have served as well for a nuptial. The real serious part was the figure of the Duke of Cumberland, heightened by a thousand melancholy circumstances. He had a dark brown adonis [wig], and a cloak of black cloth, with a train of five yards. Attending the funeral of a father, how little reason so ever he had to love him, could not be pleasant. His leg extremely bad, yet forced to stand upon it near two hours, his face bloated and distorted with his late paralytic stroke, which has affected too, one of his eyes, and placed over the mouth of the vault, into which, in all probability, he must himself so soon descend – think how unpleasant a situation! He bore it all with a firm and unaffected countenance. This grave scene was fully contrasted by the burlesque Duke of Newcastle. He fell into a fit of crying the moment he came into the chapel, and flung himself back in a stall, the Archbishop hovering over him with a smelling-bottle – but in two minutes his curiosity got the better of his hypocricy, and he ran about the chapel with his glass to spy who was or was not there, spying with one hand, and mopping his eyes with t'other. Then returned the fear of catching cold, and the Duke of Cumberland, who was sinking with heat, felt himself weighed down, and turning round, found it was the Duke of Newcastle standing upon his train to avoid the chill of the marble. It was very theatric to look down into the vault, where the coffin lay, attended by mourners with lights. Clavering, the Groom of the Bedchamber, refused to sit up with the body, and dismissed by the King's order.[37]

Sir Horace did not know it, but he had just witnessed the last of our sovereigns to be buried in Westminster Abbey.

Another thing that Walpole does not mention, and probably did not know, was what happened when the coffin was lowered into the vault. It is a touching footnote to the love of King George II and his Queen Caroline. The King had left orders that his coffin was to be placed in the stone sarcophagus which already held that of Queen Caroline, and that a side board of each coffin was to be removed, that their bones might lie together, as in a double bed. It was his last act of devotion to his wife and characteristic of the man who was always so brusque to her in life, that he should make such a romantic gesture twenty-three years too late for her to enjoy it. When the vault was opened in 1837 the two planks were still to be seen, propped up against the wall of the vault.

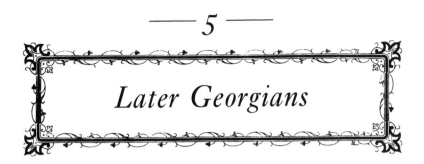

5

Later Georgians

The death of his grandfather in 1760 brought the twenty-year-old George III to the throne and, for the first time in a long while, the Court was full of young people. Almost immediately upon his accession, George married Princess Charlotte of Mecklenburg Strelitz and soon their family was growing up around them. So, in spite of quite a large number of deaths among the older generations of royals, the prevalent climate was one of new life rather than death.

It is interesting to note that, a century earlier, of the fifteen children born to James II and his two wives, only five survived infancy. And then of course there was poor Queen Anne with her seventeen, none of whom survived childhood. By contrast, of the fifteen children of George and Charlotte, only two died in childhood and most lived to a ripe old age. Medicine and diet were improving all the time. Of course, it is well known that, over the population as a whole, infant mortality was rampant throughout the eighteenth and nineteenth centuries, but the royal family had the best medical attention available at the time and so tend to reflect an attainable ideal in this field.

The improvement in the health of the royal children may have been partly due to a new atmosphere at Court. George III was essentially a domestic man. This is not to say that etiquette at court was allowed to slip – Queen Charlotte saw to it that this did not occur – but he loved children, at any rate while they were small, and liked to live with them around him and to interest himself in their welfare. His children lived a more restricted life than most upper-class children of the time, but even they were affected by an embryo cult of childhood that was emerging in England at the time they were growing up. Their diet and clothes were more suitable than in former times and they took regular outdoor exercise even if it was only to take part in the daily parade on the terrace at Windsor.

The two deaths that did take place in this family of royal children were in 1782 and 1783 and hit the King and Queen very hard. On 20 August 1782 Prince Alfred, the baby of the family, died of tuberculosis at Windsor aged one year and eleven months. Mrs Delany, the well-known letter-writer, artist and embroideress, met the King and Queen a few weeks after his death and commented that 'they were not in spirits, especially the Queen, who seemed much affected, and that every word was an exertion, tho' always most gracious.'[1] Less than a year later they were to lose their next youngest son, Prince Octavius, also a consumptive, and his father's darling: 'There will be no Heaven for me if Octavius is not there,'[2] said the King, but Mrs Delany felt that 'their superiority of mind [would] support them under this tender [affliction], as they have recourse to that sublime consolation which can never fail them.'[3] Both princes were buried in Henry VII Chapel, but extremely quietly and privately with the barest minimum of ceremony. After this the family were blessed with twenty-seven years of freedom from death.

In the same year that Prince Octavius died, there arrived to comfort his parents Princess Amelia, the final child of this fertile couple. She, however, like her two brothers was tubercular and 'from earliest youth of a very tender and delicate constitution'.[4] It is strange that, when the rest of the family were so robust, the three youngest should all be tainted with this, at that time, incurable disease. All the same, Princess Amelia grew up to be a charming young woman of twenty-seven and her father's favourite child. Her death, in 1810 would be unimportant to this story if it were not for two things. Firstly, it was said to be her death and the strain of the long months of illness leading up to it that finally tipped her poor father, who had by that time been suffering from porphyria for more than twenty years, over the edge of insanity, and secondly, she was buried in St George's Chapel at Windsor which from then on became the regular resting place of the royal family in preference to Westminster Abbey. Presently the bodies of the princes Alfred and Octavius were moved there from the Abbey.

The King had visited his youngest and dearest child daily for many weeks as she grew weaker, and talked and prayed with her. One day towards the end, she put on his finger a ring she had had made containing a lock of her hair 'set round with a few sparks of diamonds'[5] (such *mementi mori* were becoming fashionable) and 'the agitated and anxious mind of the King sunk beneath the shock; nor was he afterwards found capable of transacting business'.[6] Her death, combined with a heavy cold laid him low and insanity ensued. This, it is now thought, was a kind of delirium caused by physical illness which had once before attacked him in 1788, and this time he was too old to shake it off. Soon the Regency was proclaimed and King George III was confined to his apartments at Windsor and never left them in the next ten years of blindness and increasing madness that remained to him.

Princess Amelia's will left everything to a Colonel Fitzroy with whom she had been secretly in love for years, but the Prince Regent disregarded this as being highly improper and distributed her jewels and effects among her sisters.

The reason for the change of burial place from Westminster to Windsor cannot be pinpointed, but it probably had to do with George III's essential domesticity. By 1810 Windsor had become home to him, though the Queen preferred Kew, and he looked upon himself as a country gentleman. He probably regarded St George's Chapel as his parish church and felt it natural to have his family buried there. Whether, if he had retained his faculties till the end of his own life, he would have thought it suitable for his granddaughter, as heiress apparent to the throne, or himself, as sovereign, to be buried there, and so set the pattern for the generations to come, will never be known.

During the preparations for the funeral, the Prince of Wales, typically for him, became very exercized as to whether collars and orders should be worn and if so by whom, and whether under or over the mourning cloak. This problem was finally solved by the Dean of Windsor who discovered that it was against the statutes of the Order of the Garter for it to be worn after sunset and so the matter was dropped.

In the descriptions of the funeral, which took place quite soon after the Princess's death on the evening of 13 November, several things are noticeable. Her brothers were all there, followed by their entire households and servants, but none of her sisters. It might have been expected that one of them would be chief mourner, but this function was performed by the Countess of Chesterfield and various other ladies of the Court were pall bearers. By this time it was clearly not thought proper for royal ladies to attend funerals at all and this was to be a long-lived tradition. Another change was that, instead of yards of cloth being issued for mourning clothes to courtiers and servants, on this occasion and thereafter, only scarves, hatbands and gloves were issued which must have seemed a poor substitute for a warm suit of clothes to the less affluent, and presumably they had to provide their own blacks. This may have been meanness on the part of the King who was well-known for his parsimony, but it must be remembered that England was, by 1810, sixteen years into the War with France and there may have been shortages, making it desirable for people to wear the black clothes that most of them would have already possessed. Many of the servants would have had to be helped with their clothes, but this was probably on a personal level within each household and not from the Great Wardrobe. Officers of the army and navy were to wear merely crape armbands with their uniforms as they do to this day.

And so, at an evening service with the Poor Knights of Windsor, now known as the Military Knights, tramping up the aisle, with a clatter of spurs and swords, at the head of the procession, as they have done at almost every service to this day, Princess Amelia was laid to rest in the vault that already held King Henry VIII and Charles I and was soon to hold so many more of her family.

The first really dynastically important death of George III's reign did not come until he had been on the throne for fifty-seven years. It seems incredible that, with fifteen children, King George and Queen Charlotte had only one legitimate grandchild, but such was the case. Several of their sons, desiring a simple, domestic life, had either married or set themselves up with ladies with whom they might have enjoyed a lifetime of married bliss but for the Royal Marriage Act which George had forced through Parliament in 1772 which rendered their marriages null and void. The act prevented any member of the royal family from marrying without the assent of the monarch and parliament and is still on the statute book to this day. Effectively this meant that they must marry only into other royal houses according to King George's rigid code of royal conduct. Two of the sons even had children (the Duke of Clarence had ten by his cosy actress, Mrs Jordan) but they, of course, did not count for the succession. Even the Prince of Wales had contracted a secret marriage with Maria Fitzherbert, but she bore the double bar of being not only a commoner but a Roman Catholic. The marriage was never recognized and in 1795 he married his cousin, Caroline of Brunswick. This marriage was a disaster and almost from the start they lived apart, but it did result in the birth of a daughter, Princess Charlotte, heir apparent to the throne. Charlotte, at twenty was a young woman

> about the middle size, inclining rather to embonpoint, but not so much as to impair the symmetry of her form. Her complexion was beautifully fair, her arms delicately rounded, and her head finely placed. There was a mingled sweetness and dignity in her look; a full, intelligent eye; and when she was engaged in conversation, she had much liveliness in the expression of her countenance. The resemblance to her illustrious father was striking.[7]

Between the lines of the *New Monthly Magazine*'s respectful euphemisms may be seen a big girl, rather too like her father for beauty. This likeness to the Prince Regent was always stressed as her mother was strongly suspected of dallying with other men. Something of a tomboy, Charlotte had an easy, friendly manner which made her popular with her inferiors. Unexpectedly, considering her parentage, she appears to have been religious and to have gone about the country giving signed bibles to worthy peasants.

In 1816, after one or two false starts, she married Prince Leopold of Saxe Coburg, a thin and somewhat humourless young man but adored by Charlotte and soon afterwards the hopes of the nation were raised by the news that the Princess was pregnant. She and her husband were living at Claremont, near Esher, where the young couple enjoyed the quiet country life. It was here, rather than in London with its superior medical facilities, that the birth was to take place.

Sir Richard Croft was appointed 'physician accoucheur' to the Princess and a Mrs Griffiths as nurse, and these two were constantly in attendance during the pregnancy. One medical man who was not appointed but was nevertheless in the house all the time was Dr Christian Stockmar, who had come from Germany with Prince Leopold more as secretary and friend than in any medical capacity. This young doctor was horrified at the frequent bleeding of the Princess throughout her pregnancy and also at the bland, protein deficient diet that they imposed on her. This was not the way that he had been taught to treat young mothers-to-be in Germany, but, for his own sake, he kept right out of the affair, deciding that no one would listen to him and yet if things should go wrong, which God forbid, all would be blamed on the 'foreign doctor'. But he befriended Charlotte and encouraged her to continue her walks and drives in the park at Claremont, trusting to her apparently strong constitution to see her through. She called him 'Stocky' and laughed and joked with him through the summer months. There were, all the same, some disquieting symptoms and a persistent pain in her right side for which she wore a permanent blister. In September Lady Holland wrote: 'Princess Charlotte is going on with her grossesse but there are some strange, awkward symptoms.'[8] She was immense and the doctors thought it might be twins and wondered if she would have the strength to go through with it. And then they had their dates wrong, announcing that the birth was expected on 19 October, the Prince Regent and the Queen making their plans accordingly so as to be at hand to gather, with the bishops and Privy Councillors at the scene of this important birth. By the time the Princess, at last, went into labour, almost three weeks late, they had dispersed, the Queen to Bath and the Regent to a shooting party in Suffolk.

It was an agonizingly slow labour, fifty-one hours in all, beginning on the evening of 3 November. Servants were sent flying about the country for the Archbishop of Canterbury, the Bishop of London, the Chancellor of the Exchequer and several other cabinet ministers who assembled at Claremont, and Sir Richard Croft summoned medical support. He sent to London for his brother-in-law, Dr Matthew Baillie and also a Dr Sims, an expert in caesarian sections and forceps deliveries, but in the event they decided between them, 'that it would be prudent to wait for the progress of natural energy, instead of the application of art to hasten the delivery.'⁹ In this century, a caesarian would undoubtedly have been performed, but in the days before anaesthetics and aseptic surgery, this was avoided unless all else failed.

Frequent bulletins were issued, assuring the public that 'The labour of Her Royal Highness the Princess Charlotte is going on very slowly, but we trust favourably,' and a little later, 'The labour . . . has within the last three or four hours considerably advanced, and will, it is hoped, within a few hours be happily completed.'¹⁰

'The Prince Leopold was incessant in his attendance, and no countenance could more deeply express the anxiety he felt.'¹¹ Indeed, of the two, it was the Princess who was the more cheerful. The slow hours must have seemed like a lifetime to them both, but Leopold hardly left his wife, often lying beside her on the bed while she toyed with his hair, and only leaving her 'when delicacy dictated'. Charlotte's strength was slowly ebbing. Some hours before the birth, the doctors suspected that something was very wrong, but they still did nothing to help her, and she was almost exhausted when, at 9 o'clock on the Wednesday evening, 5 November, she at last gave birth to a fine, large, but stillborn son. The doctors rushed it into the next room and worked frantically to revive it, rubbing its poor little body with salt and mustard and plunging it in hot water, but to no avail. It had probably been dead for some hours.

Charlotte appears to have behaved wonderfully well at this juncture, using all her remaining strength to comfort her husband on the loss of their baby. That she seemed very little affected herself was probably due to exhaustion – she had no strength left for emotion. Altogether,

Her Royal Highness was quite tranquil afterwards, bore the intelligence of the child being still-born with great resignation, submitting herself to the will of God, and seemed inclined to fall into a gentle sleep. So 'favourably . . . was she going on' that not only the great Officers of State [took] their departure, but even Prince Leopold and the medical gentlemen had retired to take some rest after the fatigue of long attendance and watching.¹²

Charlotte was given a little chicken broth, toast, barley water and a 'camphor julep' to sustain her, Mrs Griffiths slipped away for a few minutes to change her dress; 'How smart you are Griffiths,' murmured the Princess as she fell asleep. 'Why did you not put on the silk gown, my favourite?'¹³ Prince Leopold went off to write to the Regent, and Stockmar, before retiring to his own room, gave him a strong sedative. The household settled down for what they hoped was to be their first good night for some time.

Mrs Griffiths was dozing by the fire when, about midnight, she became aware that the Princess was restless. She had difficulty in swallowing a little gruel, brought it up again and complained of a ringing in her ears. Mrs Griffiths found that her pulse was racing and sent for the doctors. Baillie and Sims had actually gone to bed, but Croft hurried in and found his patient cold as a stone and flinging herself from side to side as she complained of a terrible pain in her abdomen. Terrified, he sent for his two colleagues and Stockmar, and then started plying the Princess with hot wine and brandy. When Stockmar entered, Dr Baillie tried to rally Charlotte, saying, 'Here comes an old friend of yours.' She eagerly clutched at his hand, murmuring, 'They have made me tipsy,'[14] and he surreptitiously felt her pulse which was now strong, now weak but all the time racing.

In the light of the post-mortem and from Stockmar's account, it appears that Charlotte was suffering from uterine inertia, that is that the womb was not contracting properly, and a concealed haemorrhage resulted in a clot reaching the heart. This being the case, Croft, with his hot wine, hot blankets and hot water bottles, was applying quite the wrong treatment; cold water, if necessary poured right over the patient, might have stopped the haemorrhage and might even have stimulated the uterus into contracting. However, it is today recognized that Princess Charlotte was suffering from porphyria, like her grandfather, and could never have borne a live child.

Stockmar now left the room to fetch Prince Leopold. He had tried before but found him too dopey to take in the danger. Now, as he went out, he heard the unmistakable sound of the death rattle in Charlotte's throat followed by a loud and urgent cry of 'Stocky! Stocky!'.[15] He hurried back and was just in time to see her roll over on to her face, draw up her knees in a last violent struggle and die. It was 2.30 on the morning of 6 November.

Leopold, when Stockmar finally succeeded in rousing him, seemed quite unable to take in that his wife was dead. He fell on his knees by the bed, calling to her and covering her hands and those beautiful arms with kisses. Then for days he sat seemingly unable to understand anything that was said to him. He would have nothing of Charlotte's touched, even insisting that her cloak and bonnet should be left where she had hung them over a screen in the 'sitting-parlour' on coming in from a walk on the day that her confinement began, and that her watch should remain on the mantelpiece where her own hands had placed it. Do we see here the seeds of that excessive mourning later indulged in by his niece, Queen Victoria? This was, perhaps, a Coburg characteristic. But Leopold may have derived some comfort from thinking of the misfortunes of others. At any rate, in the first days after Charlotte's death, he ordered £50 to be distributed among the workmen engaged upon improvements at Claremont whose labours were now suspended.

Meanwhile, messengers galloped hither and yon through a thick November fog, bearing the tragic news. The Privy Councillors had hardly reached their homes before they were overtaken by the 'melancholy intelligence'; the Prince Regent, upon hearing that his daughter was in labour, had set off from Suffolk to return to London. He met two messengers on his way with bulletins on the slow progress of the labour, but the third missed him in the fog and the dark and it was not until he reached Carlton House that he had any knowledge of the disaster. Then, most uncharacteristically for him, his first thought was for his much despised son-in-law. Striking his brow, he exclaimed, 'What is to be done for the poor man, Great Heavens!'[16]

The Queen and Princess Elizabeth, whose visit to Bath was proving a rapturous success, were just putting on their jewellery before going to receive the loyal address of the mayor and corporation, when the first dispatch about the stillbirth arrived. Five hours later, while they were dining at the Guildhall, the news of the death of the Princess was brought to them and 'the Dinner was broken up "with the most admired disorder"',[17] and 'All Bath wore a Face of Mourning'. Indeed, in those grim November days, it seemed that all England 'wore a Face of Mourning'.[18] Shops, theatres and even courts of law were closed and, from town to town, 'the dumb peals of tolling bells, spoke the general depression.'[19] Beacons and bonfires had been built the length of the country to announce the royal birth and Congreve Rockets were to have been let off at Dover Castle. Now all were sadly demolished. 'On the public at large, the effect was little less overwhelming than if one of its members had been suddenly ravished from every family. No event within [their] memory ever burst upon the country more unexpectedly.'[20] The House of Hanover was not, in general, popular, but Charlotte herself had been; she had been expected to sit on the throne, and who knew what they would get in her place?

The Regent actually carried his concern for Leopold so far as to offer him a bed at Carlton House, but this he refused, preferring to remain at Claremont where he could visit the 'beloved remains' every evening, 'and pour forth his sorrows over them.'[21] He guarded the body jealously and tried to protect it from the doctors who had failed Charlotte and now claimed her body for a post-mortem, which proved inconclusive, and embalming, which they performed not only upon her body, but upon that of the infant too. Such was the royal ritual and it could not be avoided. The Princess's body was then wrapped in several waxed 'cere cloths', enclosed in rich blue velvet tied with white satin ribbons. The procedure was exactly as it had

Mourning dress on the death of Princess Charlotte.

been for centuries.

Although the report of the post-mortem made no mention of neglect or malpractice on the part of the doctors in attendance, and although both Prince Leopold and the Prince Regent sent Croft supportive letters, gossip was soon rife

[113]

and fashionable young mothers who had booked him for their confinements began to back out. Some stuck by him, but when, three months later, he found himself faced with a similar case, his nerve cracked and he shot himself.

Four weeks' Court mourning was ordered, which does not seem much for one in such a high position, with the details of what should be worn exactly as they had been for some fifty or sixty years. The *Lady's Magazine* and *Ackerman's Repository* showed all their fashions for November and December in black and gave advice as to what to wear: 'Norwich crapes and bombazines are the most favourite materials for gowns', 'spencers of black cloth and rep silk', 'Evening turbans formed of black satin, sypress gauze, and chenille trimming, are in high estimation for dinner parties . . . surmounted by a plume of cypress feathers uncurled', 'Ear pendants of jet . . . of prodigious length . . . brooches of jet, in the form of crescents reversed, are most prevalent'.[22] Scarves, hatbands and gloves were distributed as before, including the whole choir and officials of St George's Chapel, Windsor, the organist having written to the Lord Chamberlain's Office to claim them. Possibly they had been left out last time.

The funeral was arranged for the evening of 20 November and was to be once more at St George's Chapel. Mr Banting of the undertakers France and Banting, arrived at Claremont some days before bringing the coffins in by the back door. The last task of Mrs Griffiths was to help to lay the Princess in her coffin. Mr Banting and his forty assistants had quite an impressive procession of their own when they brought the crimson-covered state coffins and urns from London. These enclosed the lead inner coffins and mahogany outer ones and were highly ornamented in silver gilt, for the Princess, and silver for the baby.

On the evening of 18 November these coffins were carried down the long steps of Claremont and placed in separate hearses, each drawn by eight black horses with nodding plumes. These took the road for Windsor, followed by a number of mourning coaches with drawn blinds, in the first of which sat Prince Leopold.

> As [the melancholy cavalcade] passed through the different villages, the bells tolled their funeral knell, the inhabitants gazed in solemn, breathless silence, and many were the tears which old, young, rich and poor shed, as they saw the melancholy array passing along.[23]

Arriving at Windsor at 2 o'clock the following morning, the cortège, now escorted by a detachment of the Royal Horse Guards, made for Lower Lodge where Princess Charlotte's coffin was taken in and placed where it was to lie in state until the following evening. As she lay there under a canopy and surrounded by candles and escutcheons, Leopold slipped silently in to take his last farewells of his wife.

Meanwhile the baby's coffin and urn were driven straight to St George's, where they were received by eight Yeomen of the Guard, carried into the Chapel attended only by the Dean, and lowered, in absolute silence and without any form of service, into the vault. A stillborn child, having no soul, did not warrant the prayers of the church.

The next day all was 'solemn bustle' in Windsor. The shops were all shut out of respect for the Princess and this gave their proprietors the chance to queue with other respectable citizens for the chance of a place in the Chapel. Those who did get in, later found they had made a mistake as they were

restrained to the north aisle, and a detachment of Guards, drawn up three deep, interposed between them and the space over which the procession was to pass. In point of fact, they might just as well have been miles off, for what they were allowed to see; and this was the case with ninety-nine out of every hundred who flocked from all parts to witness this solemn ceremony. Nothing, indeed, could exceed the want of the attention paid, by the managers of the Funeral, to that national but anxious curiosity which the public exhibited on this sad occasion. This was most impolitic and ill-judged . . .[24]

declared the author of one memoir of Princess Charlotte. Writers of the time may have excelled themselves as to flowery and eulogistic prose when applied to the deceased, but they could still be acid when they chose. Those spectators who fared best were those who managed to find a place in a window or even a roof-top along the processional route.

Much the same scenes of chaos were going on outside Lower Lodge where so many people were jostling to get in to the lying-in-state that the 'constables' were forced to send for a detachment of the Blues to help them keep order. The detachment did this in an exemplary manner by 'blending its sympathies with the sterner duties of military discipline.'[25]

'The quickened tolling of the bells, at half-past eight [p.m.] announced the removal of the Royal remains from the Lower Lodge to St George's Chapel.'[26] And the procession, when at last it came, was a very splendid sight, with the orange glare of thousands of flares casting their eerie light up on to the Castle ramparts and the muffled drums of the full band of the Royal Horse Guards setting a solemn, measured pace. All the royal servants were there in full state liveries with crape hatbands and black gloves and all bearing flambeaux. Then came the hearse with its plumed black horses each led by a liveried groom. After this came 'His

Majesty's Body carriage' bearing the chief mourner, Prince Leopold, and his supporters, the Dukes of Clarence and York, Princess Charlotte's two senior uncles. Following them came a number of closed empty carriages representing the Regent and other members of the royal family. This was a nineteenth-century custom, just coming into fashion, whereby people who either did not wish to attend the funeral or were, for one reason or another, debarred by protocol from attending, could pay the deceased the compliment of sending their carriages to swell the ranks of the procession. The Prince Regent, even though he was the father of the dead Princess, as surrogate king would not be there.

Outside the Chapel, the servants, grooms and bands filed off and the procession reformed with all the heralds, Poor Knights, courtiers, ministers of the crown and clergy which such an important state funeral demanded. And as they moved slowly up the aisle and into the choir, still by the light of flambeaux borne by soldiers, '"I know that my Redeemer liveth..." was played in the most tender manner, and sung in a style of pathetic solemnity, highly creditable to the gentlemen of the choir.'[27]

Less than two weeks had passed since the Princess's death and in that time St George's had been transformed. An 'elegant and extensive porch' festooned in black had been erected over the south door and the cortège moved through it and up into the choir on black baize, and here the stalls of the Knights of the Garter had been hung with black 'in rich draperies'. The cushions, seats, chairs for the chief mourner and supporters, and the altar were all black. In this suffocating atmosphere, like a black cave, poor Leopold, 'who moved in the mournful procession with an effort of firmness which only more painfully indicated the struggles of his heart',[29] was placed in a seat at the head of the 'corpse', with its coronet and cushion, and with the gaping mouth of the vault at his feet. It would have taken a strong man indeed to maintain that firmness as the beautiful words of the burial service unfolded and Dr Blake's lovely anthem from Psalm 16 vv. 9–11 was sung: 'Therefore my heart is glad, and my glory rejoiceth: my flesh also shall rest in hope.' Then, as the Dean intoned, 'Man that is born of a woman ...' the coffin was gradually lowered 'by imperceptible machinery into the vault below',[29] the effect of which was 'most awful', and Princess Charlotte joined her little infant whose coffin was then laid upon the top of hers. The Deputy King of Arms proclaimed her style and titles and, as the company slowly retired, 'the Dead March in Saul was exquisitely played by Mr Sexton, organist to the Chapel.'[30] And, as he left the Chapel, 'Prince Leopold was greatly agitated ... his pallied and agonised countenance, and unsteady step, excited the deepest sympathy in all the spectators. Immediately after the afflicting ceremony, His Serene Highness

Memorial to Princess Charlotte, by J and M Wyatt, in St George's Chapel, Windsor.

returned to Claremont with his faithful attendants,'[31] there to await his next opportunity to influence the history of Great Britain.

It is the greatest pity that during two centuries which are, in general, so rich in tombs and monuments to the dead, there is barely one commemorating a member of the royal family. Every church in England displays an abundance of seventeenth and eighteenth-century tombs and wall monuments – prone ladies and gentlemen of the Stuart period with their children and servants about them, splendid neo-classical draped figures, urns and obelisks, and dramatic baroque skeletons and weeping mourners. At the very beginning of the seventeenth century we have Queen Elizabeth's splendid tomb, followed by the little 'Rosebud' and her sister in Westminster Abbey and from then on the royal family lie in their vaults below the Henry VII Chapel commemorated by nothing more than a plain stone in the paving of the floor bearing their names and dates. Not until Princess Charlotte was the tradition of tombs and monuments temporarily revived with her delightful monument in St George's by James and Matthew Wyatt: a sort of apotheosis in white marble in which the Princess and her infant are supported heavenwards by angels leaving her draped corpse and two veiled mourners below. It combines neo-classical serenity with baroque shock tactics in a manner peculiar to the Romantic period. But the effort was not sustained and it was left to the Victorians, with their mausoleums and neo-medieval effigies to rectify the omission.

Less than a year after the country put off its blacks after Princess Charlotte's death, they were back in them for her grandmother and namesake, Queen Charlotte. The old Queen was, in 1818, seventy-five years old and, though she continued to play her part, holding drawing-rooms and receiving important visitors, all the more assiduously because of the King's long absence from them, her health was clearly failing. For some time she had been suffering from some heart complaint; she suffered acute spasms and shortness of breath, was often a livid blue colour and held herself hunched over to one side. Her always homely face had become downright ugly.

In July the Queen presided at the double wedding of her sons, the Duke of Clarence to Princess Adelaide of Saxe Meiningen and the Duke of Kent to the Dowager Princess of Leiningen, two of the four sons who, although now elderly, had obeyed the call to provide a legitimate heir to the throne, following the death of Princess Charlotte. But by the end of August the regular bulletins that appeared in the press were saying: 'Her Majesty was not so well yesterday as she was on Tuesday, and was not able to take her usual airing in her garden chaise', and 'The Queen has not had a good night'.[32] Clearly her condition was giving cause for alarm. In September, she was rather better and comparatively free from pain, but the *Lady's Magazine* 'wished that [they] could say that she [was] out of danger'. Indeed they 'regretted to say that in [their] next [bulletin, they] expected to announce tidings of a more melancholy nature.'[33] It is doubtful if a modern women's magazine would presume to 'kill off' a member of the royal family so prematurely.

In fact, Queen Charlotte lived another two months, but, as the summer turned to autumn, her condition gradually worsened and she developed dropsy in her right leg. The Queen was at Kew which was one of her favourite residences, and two of her daughters, Princess Augusta and the Duchess of Gloucester, were constantly with her, while the Regent and the Duke of York were always on call and visited her regularly. The youngest, Princess Sophia, herself delicate, lived permanently at Windsor and kept an eye on the poor old King who only intermittently knew who she was. She sent regular reports on his state of health to her mother who was afraid of his insanity and only rarely visited him. The Duchess of Gloucester gives us a glimpse into the Queen's bedchamber as the two sisters watched over her. She relates that she and Princess Augusta 'witnessed sufferings I can never describe, and, I trust, we shall never forget the Example she gave us of fortitude, and mildness, and every virtue, always trying to keep from us her anguish, and putting on a cheerful face when we came into her room, and receiving any little attention with pleasure.'[34] On 17 November 1818, with the two Princes and two Princesses at her bedside and her hand in that of the Prince Regent, her eldest son, Queen Charlotte died, and the husband to whom she had been married for fifty-seven years was beyond any awareness of it. The Duchess of Gloucester, describing her last moments, says: 'We had the consolation of seeing her expire without a pang, and a sweet smile on her face. My two brothers, Augusta and myself *nearly* received her last breath.'[35] And her epitaph from the same pen, states that,

> Her's was a long life of *trials*. Religion, and her *trust in God*, supported her under all her *various Misfortunes* and *so Virtuous a life* in this World *must* be *happy* in a *far better*; but we know that the *great link* of the *Chain* that brought us all together, and the World a *bright Example* ... we must feel the want of, and loss of, more and more every hour.[36]

How nice for any old lady to be so much loved by her middle-aged children.

Quickly the news was carried to London and the tolling of the great bell of St Paul's, taken up by all the other churches in the capital, told the people what they had for days been waiting to hear. All places of entertainment closed and in a

Queen Charlotte in mourning dress, possibly for one of her children, by I Cruikshank.

matter of hours people of all classes began to appear in black, or at least with some shred of black about their persons. It was fifty-seven years since a plain little princess had come over from Germany, calmly playing God Save the King over and over on the harpsichord through a shipboard storm that decimated her attendants, and no one could remember a time when Queen Charlotte had not been around.

Before the Earl Marshal had time to issue the usual proclamation on Court mourning, the *Lady's Magazine* printed their views on the subject:

> We trust that no affected display of grief will extend the period of public mourning to any thing like the term observed in the last reign, which was *twelve months*! The times are now materially altered; so much so as to make that period much too long. Considerable distress has always been occasioned by a general mourning. The present, however short, will be felt with more than its usual poignancy by the labouring class of manufacturers ...[37]

However, it was felt that almost everyone had had time during the Queen's long illness to supply themselves with some articles of mourning which, out of respect for Her Majesty, they would wish to wear for a short time. We have come a long way from the sumptuary laws forbidding all but the aristocracy from wearing mourning. In fact, two years previously, the Regent, no lover of blacks, had arbitrarily halved the period of mourning for all members of the royal family except those for whom it was already very short, and had further announced that after the first six weeks it would be worn only at Court. In this case the period was to be six months and the Earl Marshal directed all to put themselves into deepest mourning until after the funeral. But already, in December, *Ackermann's Repository* was shocked to find that 'Several trimmings, composed of black crape and intermixed with scarlet are ... in preparation for some very dashing *elegantes*. This mixture of black and scarlet has of late years been tolerated even in the deepest mourning; in our opinion it is far from appropriate ...' However, they believed it would, on this occasion, be confined to 'those ladies whom the French style *merveilleuses*'.[38]

In her will Queen Charlotte left her beloved Frogmore to her eldest unmarried daugher, Princess Augusta, and Lower Lodge at Windsor to Princess Sophia who, however, did not take it up. Her possessions, including many of her jewels, were left to her four youngest daughters but, incredibly, her executors decided that, with a few exceptions, all should be sold at public auction and this was done at thirty-three sales at Christie's during 1819. Her daughters found it a 'sad pill to swallow'.[39] Among the things the Princesses were allowed to keep was a quantity of unworn lace, and this they offered to Mrs Beckerdorff who, with her daughter, had devotedly looked after the Queen in her declining years. In those days lace could be as valuable as jewellery and Mrs Beckerdorff, probably fearing trouble if she took it, declined the bequest.

The Queen lay in state in the King's Dining Room at Kew on 1 December and a select public filed through to pay their last respects. In the black-draped rooms, they saw the Queen's coffin under its canopy, with the pall turned back at the foot to expose the coffin to the public view, set among a forest of candles and escutcheons, the tin gilt crown on its cushion and three veiled ladies who kept vigil throughout the day and the night that followed. Then they passed through two more rooms and out by the steps to the garden.

The following day Queen Charlotte's body was taken in procession to Windsor. Moving at two miles an hour, it was already dark by the time it reached the Home Park and, at Frogmore, was joined by the royal mourners. It was by now established practice that most of the outdoor procession consisted of servants, undertakers' men and empty carriages, with knight marshal's men and soldiers, in this case a detachment of Lancers, escorting it, the grander people joining either at the church door or at the approach to it. The full mounted cortège now wound through the trees with their guttering flambeaux illuminating with a rich glow the scarlet uniforms of the escorting troops, approached the Castle by the Long Walk and arrived at St George's Chapel nearly an hour early, 'some inconvenience resulting from this unusual excess of punctuality, several persons whose business it was to form part of the Chapel procession having arrived too late to gain admittance'.[40]

Once more St George's had taken on the appearance of a dark cavern, draped and upholstered in black, the procession entering by the 'elegant' tented porch over the south door where it was met by the Dean, the Archbishops of Canterbury and York and the choir with their lighted tapers. In those days there was no wide flight of steps up to the west door and so the south door was the one always used for ceremonial occasions.

The Chapel procession this time was a longer one than for Princess Charlotte, including along with the Poor Knights of Windsor, a fuller complement of heralds, politicians and great officers and courtiers of the King, the late Queen and the Prince Regent, all the Knights of the Garter, several bishops, endless physicians and apothecaries, and the curates and rectors of Kew and Windsor. The royal body on its 'car' specially constructed by Congreve of Congreve rocket fame, was followed, after the chief mourner and royal dukes, by all the late Queen's ladies, women and maids-of-honour. Ten Gentlemen Pensioners, with axes reversed and ten Yeomen of the Guard with 'partisans' reversed, closed the procession.

This time the Prince Regent was chief mourner to his mother and weighed down, not only by grief, which threatened to overcome him, and by his trained mourning cloak, but also by the large assortment of orders which he wore. The Prince had a passion for orders and, in spite of the ruling last time that they should not be worn, he was loaded with them. The *Lady's Magazine* tells us that

> The Royal Chief Mourner was magnificently attired in a large mourning cloak, decorated with a brilliant embossed star; above this appeared first the splendid Collar of the Order of the Garter, the Collar of the Bath, the Collar of the Golden Fleece and the Collar of the Royal Hanoverian Guelphic Order. His Royal Highness appeared much dejected and at one time sobbed aloud.[41]

The Dukes of York and Sussex followed their brother but the other four brothers were all abroad. And the *Lady's Magazine* noticed, somewhat tartly,

> the limited attendance and homage paid by the peerage on this occasion, as well as by other persons who occupy a distinguished rank in the state: neither was there, we believe, any female of rank who honoured the ceremony with her presence. The funerals of sovereigns are part of their State and should be attended with the same marks of exterior respect as any scene over which they may be called, when living, to preside. The choir was by no means filled...[42]

Queen Charlotte herself had been the strict arbiter of Court etiquette and with her removed, the aristocracy, whose manners had slipped along with their morals, neglected their undoubted duty.

It sometimes happens that death, having visited a family once, appears to remain with that family so that several other deaths occur in quite a short space of time. And so it happened that between 1817 and 1821 the royal family lost six of its members. At the end of the year 1819, while the public were anxiously scanning the bulletins on the health of George III, his fourth son, Edward, Duke of Kent, set off for Sidmouth to spend the winter with his wife and baby daughter, Princess Alexandrina Victoria, in a rented house on the balmy Devonshire riviera. His Royal Highness was fifty-two and a man of strong physique. After a life of soldiering and later of London life, always accompanied by his devoted mistress, Julie de St Laurent, the Duke had answered the call to supply the nation with an heir, following the death of Princess Charlotte, and, the previous year, had married Victoire, the widowed Princess of Leiningen and sister of Prince Leopold. In May 1819 the Princess, who was to become queen of a quarter of the world, was born and the Duke's domestic cup was full. He was, however, in serious financial straits and it was in a bid to economize, as well as for the health of his wife and baby, that he decided to winter in Devonshire.

On 13 January the Duke and his equerry went for a long walk along the beautiful coastline. It rained for much of the day and he returned in the evening to Woolbrook Cottage, the Regency villa he had rented by the sea, wet through. It was suggested to him that he ought to change, but he brushed the suggestion aside and sat down to play with his baby daughter. He had always enjoyed excellent health and, even when it was clear that he had caught a cold, he thought nothing of it. The cold quickly turned to pneumonia 'and though His Royal Highness lost 120 ozs of blood from the arms, and by cupping, he departed this life . . . at 10 o'clock on Sunday forenoon [23 January]'.[43] His wife had spent five nights at his bedside without even changing her clothes.

When news of the calamity reached Windsor the next day, the Duke's sisters were prostrated with grief. 'Think, my dearest Lady Harcourt,' wrote Princess Augusta to a close friend, 'that yesterday five weeks he was here on his way to Sidmouth, so happy with his excellent good little wife and his lovely child; and within so short a time was perfectly *well – ill* and *no more!*'[44]

The Duke's death left the Duchess, still a comparative stranger in this country, without even the means to settle up at Sidmouth and return to London until her brother, Prince Leopold, came to the rescue and carried her and little Drina and Princess Feodora, her daughter by her first marriage, back to Kensington Palace, their London home.

For some days the Duke's body lay in state at Woolbrook Cottage. The Devonshire people filed slowly through the darkened rooms and out again into the bright January sun. And as he lay there, news reached Sidmouth of the death of his father, King George III. Then he was put into one of the biggest coffins ever made, at any rate in Sidmouth, weighing 'upwards of a ton', and began his last journey back to Windsor.

There is a local legend in Devon that the cortège was held up at the Hare and Hounds on the road to Honiton by the enraged tradesmen of Sidmouth who refused to let it pass until their debts were settled. It was forced to return to Sidmouth and the Yeomanry were turned out to get it away under cover of darkness.

As the long cortège of closed carriages wound its way across the south of England, accompanied at each stage by 'an immense concourse of spectators from the surrounding countryside',[45] bells tolled in the towns and villages through which it passed and people stood in the streets to watch the sombre procession; the hearse with its nodding plumes, the mutes and the trays of feathers. It was a mounted procession and escorted by detachments of troops who were picked up or dropped off at the various garrison towns along the way. Four nights were passed on the road – at Bridport, Blandford, Salisbury and Basingstoke and at each place the coffin was placed in the church under a military escort.

At last they reached Windsor and a second lying-in-state at Cumberland Lodge in the Great Park until the funeral on the night of 12 February. The Duke was buried with full military honours, the pall and canopy bearers being all full generals, the Duke's own rank, and the chief mourner was his brother, the Duke of York, Commander-in-Chief of the Army. But the service, in the blackened Chapel, was more than usually gloomy. The liturgy was the same as ever and His Royal Highness's style and titles proclaimed, but, as a mark of respect to the late King who lay unburied in the Castle, there was no music. The procession moved in silence up the aisle, in silence the coffin was lowered into the vault, and in silence the royal Dukes retired to the Castle.

Edward of Kent was sincerely mourned by those who knew him personally as a friend or benefactor, but in spite of the traditional eulogies in the press the country at large knew him, if at all, as a soldier whose harshness had caused more than one mutiny or as a whining beggar to the government. Like other men, he had his virtues and his faults. He was also sincerely mourned by his widow who, in the eighteen months she had known him, had come to love him for himself, who was denied by protocol the consolation of attending his funeral and who was now left, on slender means, to bring up the daughter who would fulfil a gypsy's prophecy and become a great Queen.

As we have already seen, George III had been hopelessly ill and confined to his spartan rooms overlooking the North Terrace at Windsor Castle since 1810. At the death of Queen Charlotte, responsibility for his care was transferred to the Duke of York. The Duke was very glad of the extra £6,000 a year which went with the job, but he took his duties seriously and was up and down to Windsor all the time in the last few weeks before the King's death. Except for blindness, increasing deafness and mental illness, King George was in good health, and even, in flashes, recovered his intellect, made perfectly sensible conversation and continued to play beautifully from memory upon the piano and harpsichord. He was a goldmine to the medical profession, who came forward in droves with ever more eccentric cures, and the King showed that he was aware of this. The present Prince of Wales tells a story of how Dr Willis, who, with his son, had been in charge of the King

George III in old age: an engraving by Wilson Lowry after a drawing by M Wyatt.

since his earlier loss of reason in 1788, 'tried to make excuses for the ghastly treatment he was giving the King by saying: "Sir, our Saviour himself went about healing the sick." "Yes, yes," replied the King, "but He had not £700 a year for it." '[46] When he died it was calculated that £35,000 a year had been paid out in medical expenses since 1812. Parliament had consistently refused to pay, so all this came out of the King's private income.

But mostly he lived in a world of his own, conversing with friends long dead, addressing Parliament and unnerving his attendants by indecently exposing himself. This was, at least in part, senility, for the King was now eighty-one.

In the middle of November 1819 his doctors reported that 'without any apparent illness, His Majesty appears fast declining'. It was the first indication of any change for years but the official bulletins continued into January 1820 with 'His Majesty's disorder has undergone no sensible alteration. His Majesty's bodily health has partaken of some of the infirmities of age, but has been generally good during the last month.'[47] Indeed it was not until 27 January that he was confined to bed and then the end came quickly. On 29 January the Duke of York, who was with his father when he died, wrote to his brother, now George IV:

Dearest brother, It is my melancholy duty to inform you that it has pleased Providence to take to Himself our Beloved King and Father; the only immediate consolation under such a calamity is the almost conviction that his last moments were free from bodily suffering and mental distress. He expired at 38 minutes past 8 o'clock P.M.[48]

For some reason King George III was not embalmed. As soon as the post-mortem had taken place, the body was merely wrapped in a waxed linen 'cere cloth' and then sealed up in its leaden coffin.

Though George III had lived in seclusion for over nine years, quite removed from the public gaze, he lived on in the affectionate memory of his subjects, who now mourned him nationwide. The King is apt to be remembered, and blamed by history, for the loss of the American colonies, not least by the Americans, many of whom feel that they might have had a royal family to this day were it not for George III. But in 1820 the American colonies were not in the forefront of the minds of his people. Britain had fought a long war against Napoleon Bonaparte which had ended only five years previously; the King had stood with his people against possible invasion and they responded to him as a later generation of Britons was to respond to King George VI in the dark days of 1940. And there is another way in which George III may be compared with his great-great-great grandson. They both led blameless marital and domestic lives. This gained them both the admiration and affection of their subjects and George III, at any rate, was compared favourably with his sons. He was thought of by many as 'the father of his people' and his death was gloomily hailed as the passing of an era. While Queen Charlotte lived, there had been an air of decorum about the Court; now that they were both gone, who knew what to expect in the next reign?

'The King is dead; long live the King.' Immediately upon the death of the old King, his son, the Regent, became King George IV. He should have been proclaimed the following day, but 30 January was at that time still kept as a day of mourning for Charles I, the anniversary of whose death it was. It was, therefore, considered quite inappropriate to proclaim a new king on that day and the ceremony was postponed until 31 January, by which time the new King himself was gravely ill and, though far from popular, giving everyone a fright. Thomas Creevey MP gives us some idea of the general feeling:

> Now – the young King (in reign not years) has been as near death as any man but poor Kent ever was before – 150 ozs of blood let have saved his *precious* life. I never prayed so heartily for a Prince before. If he had gone, all the troubles of these villains [the Tory ministers] went with him, and they had Fred I, their own man for his life – i.e. a shady Tory professional King, who would have done a job or two for Lauderdale, smiled on Lady Jersey, been civil at Holland House, and shot Tom Coke's [later Earl of Leicester] legs and birds without ever deviating right hand or left, or giving them [the Ministers], politically, the least annoyance. This King they will have too, for the present man can't long survive. He [Fred] won't live long either; that Prince of Blackguards, Brother William [Clarence] is as bad a life, so we come in the course of nature to be *assassinated* by King Ernest I or Regent Ernest [Duke of Cumberland, the worst of the brothers, who was suspected of having murdered his valet].[49]

This was not to say that George IV was popular himself. He was not. People greatly disapproved of his mistresses, his treatment of his wife, of whom more later, and, perhaps most of all, his extravagance but, to Creevey and many others the alternatives were worse.

In keeping with the general feeling of family loss at the death of the King, there was a really public lying-in state. In other reigns it had always been 'the nobility and gentry' that had been admitted to pay their last respects to their sovereign. This time everyone who could appear in respectable mourning might enter and on the first of the two days before the funeral, thirty thousand did so.

The funeral ceremony in St George's Chapel, Windsor, of Princess Charlotte of Wales.
Aquatint by T Sutherland after C Wilde and J Stephanoff.

The Funeral Procession of Queen Caroline of Brunswick. A contemporary aquatint. At the death of Queen Caroline in 1821, Court Mourning was ordered but not General Mourning and some members of the public clearly thought it unnecessary to wear black for a disgraced queen.

Passing through St George's Hall, the crowd entered the King's Guard Chamber ... [and then] the throng moved at once into the King's Presence Chamber ... this spacious chamber was entirely hung with black cloth.

In the Presence Chamber were stationed a line of Yeomen of the Guard in full mourning. The next room, the King's audience chamber, was that in which the body lay in state. This chamber was hung with purple cloth from the ceiling to the floor, and lighted with a number of silver lamps and candelabra ... At the upper end, under the throne on which his late Majesty so often sat in regal state, was placed upon trestles the royal coffin.

The canopy of the throne was on this occasion considerably enlarged, so as to nearly extend over the whole surface of the coffin. The foot of the coffin was the only part exposed; the pall, which was of the richest black velvet, was there thrown aside, and the silver ornaments, richly gilt, lay open to view.[50]

The approach to the coffin was lined with Gentlemen Pensioners on each side, on each side of the coffin stood the late King's pages, in full mourning and at the foot, two heralds, their tabards trimmed with crape, and at the head sat a Lord of the Bedchamber. These attendants were all changed every two hours. 'This chamber was lighted in the most tasteful and appropriate manner, by a happy arrangement of the lamps,' and by three large silver candlesticks 'with very large wax lights'[51] on each side of the coffin.

Between 11 o'clock and four on the first day, the long silent line of mourners shuffled past their dead monarch, their eyes wide at the solemn majesty of all that they saw, and then they passed through the King's drawing-room and state bedroom and so out into the winter afternoon. And after the doors were shut to the public, 'the Eton youths were admitted. The Masters, Fellows and Scholars were all in deep mourning, with crape round their hats,'[52] mourning which, except for the hats, Etonians wear to this day.

On the second day, after the doors were shut, at 7 p.m., the chief mourner, the Duke of York, entered 'the Chamber of Mourning' and took his seat at the head of the coffin, and there he remained until a quarter to nine, when the coffin was removed and carried on the 'funeral car' first used at the funeral of Queen Charlotte, through the various rooms to take its place in the procession which had by now formed up.

It is interesting that, though the lying-in-state had been a more democratic affair in that a more lowly public was admitted than previously, the funeral procession was the opposite. Whereas in earlier times, monarchs were attended to their funerals by all their servants – Children of the Woodyard, Yeomen of the

Funeral procession of George III at Windsor Castle, showing the Duke of York as Chief Mourner.

Scalding House, Grooms and Clerks of the Pastry and Larder, and so on and on – this procession, though as long, was made up of courtiers, from the great officers down to gentlemen ushers and daily waiters to His Majesty, Pages of Honour, most of the aristocracy and their eldest sons, all the heralds, legal luminaries, Privy Councillors, royal physicians, the two archbishops, several other bishops and royal chaplains. The only servants included were the late King's pages and grooms of the Privy Chamber. There were no foreign ambassadors this time and, instead of poor men, there were the Poor Knights of Windsor. Before the coffin, under its pall of purple velvet 'adorned with ten Escutcheons' bearing the Imperial Arms, were carried, on purple velvet cushions, the Royal Crown of Hanover and Imperial Crown of the United Kingdom. It must not be forgotten that George III was also King of Hanover.

The Chapel was decorated in a style of splendour unexampled on any previous occasion. There was a raised platform, which extended through the South aisle, up the nave to the choir; it was covered with black cloth. Upon each side were ranged soldiers of the Foot-guards, every second man holding a wax light;

behind these were stationed the Eton Scholars, to the number of 500 at least, all of whom were admitted by special order of his present Majesty. In the north aisle, seats, elevated above each other, were arranged for the accommodation of those persons who had received tickets of admission . . .[53]

Clearly a lesson had been learnt at Princess Charlotte's funeral and the same mistakes were not made again.

As the procession entered and the body was received by the Dean, the organ played 'I am the resurrection and the life, saith the Lord', and when all were seated, with the Duke of York at the head of the coffin and his brothers ranged around him, which was not until 10 o'clock, 'the Anthem "Hear my Prayer" was sung by Masters Marshall and Dening in a superior style; and the celebrated Funeral Anthem by Handel, upon the death of Queen Caroline was sung . . .'[54] Garter King of Arms proclaimed the late King's style and titles, the coffin was lowered into the vault and the ceremony ended about 11 o'clock with a 'Solemn Voluntary' as the mourners filed out.

In the *Gentleman's Magazine* it was recorded that 'In the Metropolis, business of every description was entirely suspended. Minute Guns were fired in the Park, at the Tower, and on the banks of the Thames . . . Divine Service was celebrated in the Churches, while the deep funeral tone of the different bells proclaimed the obsequies of the Father of his People.'[55]

And, some days later, as the guard was being marched along the North Terrace at Windsor Castle under the windows of the late King, the ensign caught, out of the corner of his eye, a glimpse of the familiar white-bearded figure standing in the window. Without thinking, he gave the command, 'Eyes right' and the ghostly figure raised its hand in acknowledgment of the salute. It was not until later that the young officer and his guardsmen realized that the King had been buried for some days.

6

The end of the Hanoverians

It has never been denied that George IV was one of our most talented kings and may be compared for his culture and artistic ability to Charles I, and for his leadership of fashion to Charles II. We owe him much, for his building and embellishment of royal residences but in his day he was one of the most unpopular monarchs that ever sat upon the throne, at any rate in recent centuries. By his morals and extravagance he brought the monarchy into disrepute; he was hated by the common people for his treatment of his wife and daughter; and his bulky figure, gorgeously attired, was a gift to the lampoonist. The standard of behaviour that he set was followed by the aristocracy and this did not endear them to respectable society.

George IV was an idle and neglectful king except where it involved the planning and execution of ceremonial extravaganzas with himself as the central figure. His coronation in 1821 was an amazing spectacle for which he designed for himself completely new robes based on those worn by Napoleon when he crowned himself emperor. Yet a mere four weeks later, he allowed another ceremony to take place which for ramshackle lack of taste and decorum it would be hard to find an equal. This time it was not he who was the central figure – indeed he was not even there – but the body of his late, much hated wife. The two events, so close in time, point up the contradictions in the King's character and of all the indecorous royal events of that raffish period, the obsequies of Caroline of Brunswick must rank as one of the most extraordinary.

From her first arrival in this country in 1795 as the unseen bride of the Prince of Wales, Caroline was a source of controversy. Detested from the outset by her husband for her coarse, unbridled behaviour and uncorseted and none too fragrant person, she was none the less warm-hearted and unexpectedly practical and charitable which won her the love of the common people and the fierce loyalty of some influential members of London society, especially in the City. A six-year spell of roaming on the continent in doubtful company ended when she heard that her husband had succeeded to the throne, and she hurried back to England to take her place as his Queen. There followed a most humiliating experience when she was tried before the House of Lords on a charge of High Treason in that she had been unfaithful to the King. Though the case passed the House of Lords, it was then dropped as it was obvious that it would not pass the Commons. George IV was determined not to allow her her rightful place as Queen, and she was refused admittance to the coronation, being turned away from the very doors of Westminster Abbey.

Three weeks later, on 7 August 1821 at Brandenburg House, Hammersmith which had been her home since her return to England the previous year, Queen Caroline died. She suffered a painful illness – probably cancer – involving 'obstruction of the bowels', which was the subject of hourly and horrifyingly explicit bulletins. And her husband's only comment on hearing she was dead was 'Is she, by God!'.

We have a blow-by-blow account of the proceedings following her death in the last of four volumes of her biography published in 1822 by one of her staunchest supporters, J.H. Adolphus. Mr Adolphus had always been outraged at the treatment meted out to the Queen; now he exploded in a tirade against the shabby and indecent arrangements made for hustling her remains out of the country in the shortest possible time. His account is extremely partisan, but it makes amazing reading. For this reason it seems worth describing at some length.

Immediately on Caroline's death an unseemly quarrel broke out, and was publicly enacted, between the Queen's executors and the representatives of government and the Lord Chamberlain's Office. The King's orders were explicit. Caroline was not to be allowed to be buried at Windsor with her daughter Princess Charlotte, as had been her first wish. However, the Queen had foreseen this and had therefore chosen to be buried with her own family in Brunswick. Undue haste was complained of by her friends and household. The King was in Ireland, on a post-coronation progress and 'every day previous to the funeral was a day lost to the festivities of Dublin ... and the moment the body was embarked was to be considered the completion of her obsequies, and the late Queen would then be as though she had never existed'.[1] The Lord Chamberlain's Office hastily drew up a plan of campaign: the Queen's remains were to be privately removed from Brandenburg House on the Tuesday morning, one week after her death; this was considered scarcely decent in those leisurely days. The inclusion of troops in the procession was also objected to by her friends on the grounds that it was against the

Queen's wishes. Acrimonious notes flew to and fro between the Queen's household and the Lord Chamberlain, Lord Liverpool. Her faithful ladies, Lady Hood and Lady Anne Hamilton, grew more and more frantic in their correspondence: 'they would find it impossible to complete the requisite dresses by Tuesday', 'Why is Her Majesty's funeral thus indecently hurried?', and 'Why is there to be a guard of honour appointed to attend her funeral, which honour was never given her during her life? If this course [was] persisted in, [they] foresaw much mischief, even bloodshed'. But all to no avail. Lord Liverpool and the others fell back on 'His Majesty's express commands', and continued their preparations.

Brandenburg House was hung with crape throughout, a coffin was produced and a somewhat makeshift lying-in-state was arranged, attended by many hundreds of the curious amid scenes of confusion. Gradually the household and servants were fitted out in mourning and by the morning of Tuesday, 14 August all of London had managed to dress themselves in deepest black, and to have turned out into the streets in teeming rain.

At six o'clock a squadron of the Oxford Blues took up their station outside Brandenburg House and the mourning coaches in which the Queen's household and servants as well as officials of the establishment were to travel took their places, the passengers embarked and the head of the procession moved off. Then came what threatened to become a stand-up fight between the Queen's executor and doctor, Dr Lushington, and Mr Bailey, 'who had been appointed conductor of Her Majesty's funeral' over the 'forcing into the procession [of] a great body of soldiers' against her express wish. Dr Lushington 'command[ed] that the body be not removed till the arrangements suitable to the rank and dignity of the deceased [were] made'. Mr Bailey had his orders and passed these on to the undertakers. 'Touch the body at your peril,' declared Dr Lushington. 'You do not mean to use violence, and prevent, by force the removal of the body, I trust,' returned Mr Bailey. Dr Lushington did not intend to use force and admitted defeat. And so the coffin was loaded on to 'a rather poor hearse' with eight plumed black horses amid scenes of 'the most violent and impassioned grief'. Accompanied by a large number of carriages, Clarenceaux King of Arms in his state dress bearing on a cushion an imitation of an imperial crown, and all of the population of Hammersmith who were not crowding the windows, roofs and treetops, the hearse set off through the rain on its eighty-mile journey to Harwich.

'The great majority of female spectators were in tears, and many wept aloud as they took their last view of the hearse.' Mr Adolphus' loyalty to the Queen may have led him to overstate the 'overwhelming grief' expressed by the people of London and all along the route to Harwich. It is hard to see how people with little

[134]

Queen Caroline's funeral procession, headed by the children of Latimer School, Hammersmith.

or no first-hand knowledge of her could 'sob aloud' in large numbers all along the way and even 'faint with the emotion of the melancholy scene'. Part of their devotion to her was probably no more than the reverse of the unpopularity of George IV. Added to this, Londoners had not yet quite got over the excitement of the coronation only a month before, so that their feelings were easily whipped up into a state of mass hysteria.

As it passed through Hammersmith the procession was joined, unexpectedly and very affectingly, by the children of Latimer's Charity School who walked before it strewing flowers in its way.

So far so good – the crowd was well behaved and, except for an altercation as to whether the horsemen in the procession should pay toll on joining the turnpike, the cortège, over a mile long, moved slowly but steadily through the downpour along the road to Kensington. No one seemed to know the route which was to be taken, but rumour was rife and presently information was gleaned that at Kensington the procession was to turn left up Church Street to Bayswater, Edgware Road and a northerly route through Islington and the Mile End Road towards Romford. This meant completely missing out the City, where the

Queen's support was strongest, and the crowd were having none of it. Swift and effective action was taken. Carriages were commandeered and overturned to form a barrier across the bottom of Church Street, the cobblestones were taken up, trenches dug across the road and even the water pipes opened. This strategy succeeded; the cortège was halted and stood there in the rain while soldiers were sent tearing off to the Lord Chamberlain and to the chief magistrate of Bow Street for orders and support.

At last, at 11.30, authority yielded to necessity and 'gave orders for the procession to move on in a direct line, which was complied with amidst the stunning huzzas of the multitude', and the cavalcade moved on along Knightsbridge. At the first gate into Hyde Park there was another fracas. With cries of, 'She shall not go through the Park; let us die first', 'Every man into the breach', and 'I'll chop your hands off if you do not let go', the battle for the gates raged. More troops turned out but failed to move the mob and the procession moved on once more towards Hyde Park Corner.

Meanwhile a vast crowd, 'a moving cloud of umbrellas', rolled to and fro across the park at the whim of rumour and expectation. At Hyde Park Corner there was a brisk skirmish and the mob almost, but not quite, succeeded in forcing the procession along Piccadilly. At the Cumberland Gate a portion of the park wall and railing was torn down to provide ammunition, the Riot Act was read, shots were fired, two men were killed and others 'cut by sabres'. This had a temporarily sobering effect and the procession was able to take the Edgware Road and resume its appointed route. All went well as far as the top of Tottenham Court Road, but here 'a sudden and insurmountable obstacle presented itself'. The people had anticipated the arrival of the procession and had successfully blocked up the route. 'Every waggon, cart, coach and vehicle of whatever description, was seized, or rather spontaneously seemed to go and form itself into parts of a dense deep mass, extending the whole width of the road, and almost 100 yards in depth. Through such a compact body it was impossible to force any passage except by artillery.' The authorities admitted defeat and turned down Tottenham Court Road heading for the Strand and the City.

The Lord Mayor, hastily summoned from Guildhall, met the procession at Temple Bar and 'placing himself at its head' preceded it through the City.

On its way through the City it was also joined by a number of official and semi-official bodies of men, merchants and artisans: carpenters, brass-founders, morocco leather dressers, coopers etc. They marched in ranks, with banners and emblems of their profession. With the staunchly marching crowd keeping pace with them and a band playing somewhere among the ranks, the whole thing must have looked more like a modern-day 'demo' than a royal funeral. And added to this carnival effect was the hawking of pincushions with the Queen's head painted on the top.

In his account of their passage through the City, Adolphus mentions an interesting point. Here 'a very delicate mark of respect was shown ... towards the remains of our lamented Queen. The populace in the streets and the inhabitants at their windows, invariably stood uncovered while the hearse passed.' At a later date this fact would have gone unremarked, but from the illustration of the hearse passing through Hammersmith, it appears that it may not have been the usual custom at that time for men to remove their hats at the passing of a funeral.

At the City boundary at Whitechapel the Lord Mayor and the City contingents fell out and a party of mariners took their place at Mile End. It was by now 5 o'clock and the weary travellers had been nearly ten hours on the road in almost unceasing rain and still had some miles to Chelmsford which was scheduled as an overnight stop. The statutory four miles an hour was speeded up to an undignified degree but at eight o'clock they had only reached Romford and here it was decided that the exhausted suite should pass the night at the White Hart Inn and catch up with the procession before it left Chelmsford in the morning. The wretched troopers, horsemen and undertakers were forced to go on, 'winding slowly along, led on by the gleam of a hundred flambeaux; the arms of the soldiery glittering in the moonbeams', and it was four o'clock in the morning before the coffin was at last lifted out of the hearse and deposited on trestles in Chelmsford Church where it rested until mid morning.

And so this by now ramshackle cavalcade trundled on its way through the Essex countryside. In every town or village the populace turned out 'attired in deepest mourning' and many struggled to touch the hearse as it passed. In one place a deputation of inhabitants met the procession, 'each individual bearing a black wand, covered at the top with crape' which preceded it through the town. At another a body of local farmers on horseback escorted it on its way, and at yet another Mr Adolphus 'had neither time nor inclination to give much notice to the general demeanour of the populace, as [his] attention was rivetted most strongly to the grave and steady deportment of a body of gentlemen, who were marching "with solemn step and slow" to meet the funeral'. They entered Colchester with this escort, now increased to three hundred and fifty persons, linked arm in arm four or five abreast, headed by 'a clergyman of the Church of England in full canonicals', the bugles of the local garrison playing the Dead March in Saul, the bells of the different churches tolling.

The King's orders were to proceed straight on to Harwich with no more than a brief halt at the Three Cups Inn. This, however, was felt to be 'a serious inconvenience to the friends of Her late Majesty attending her remains' and they begged Mr Bailey to allow them to spend the night there. An undignified and public altercation took place and it seemed that 'silent submission was the only reply to commands enforced by military force', but in the end authority gave way and 'a night's repose was granted to the fatigued and harassed party'. 'Though the Royal remains had stood in the street during the time of refreshment, it was thought too indecent that they should be there kept during the night' and so St Peter's Church was hurriedly hung with black for the reception of the coffin. Here another unseemly wrangle took place about the affixing of a name plate on the coffin which had been omitted before leaving Hammersmith. The undertaker produced the official one from his pocket and was about to fix it on when the executors produced a rival plate inscribed according to her will 'Deposited, Caroline of Brunswick, the injured Queen of England'. This they succeeded in screwing on, but when they returned in the morning it had been removed by order of the Prime Minister, and the executors were told that they must wait until the coffin had left the country and then 'in Germany they might do ... what they thought proper'.

At dawn on the Thursday morning the cortège set out on the last leg of its journey and the sea was soon in sight. It was covered with vessels of all sizes, all with flags at half mast and crowded with spectators in 'decent black'.

It jogged along in fits and starts, frequently at the indecent pace of seven miles an hour and then stopping for a time in order not to cover more than the four miles allowed for the hour. At half-past eleven there wound down into the town of Harwich a procession 'which no-one would suspect of being the funeral of a queen ... A small advance guard of cavalry preceded, the undertaker on a lame horse headed; ten undertakers on horseback in pairs – a miserable spectacle, both as to cattle, dress and persons, some with shoes, some with gaiters, others in boots, some in spurs, others not – followed their leader.' A number of muddy coaches came next, then some more cavalry followed by Her Majesty's own carriage containing Clarencieux King of Arms, 'the cushion and the crown, a tawdry bauble decorated with white beads strung around in a manner that would have disgraced a country fair. Then followed the hearse ... no plumes on the horses, a few paltry feathers on the hearse. No plateaus of plumes carried, as is the case at almost all respectable funerals.' A few more carriages, some containing local notables, an empty gig and another detachment of dragoons 'closed the "*decent*", "*orderly*" and "*becoming*" funeral of the Queen of England – the wife ... of the most *potent* monarch, George the Fourth!!'[2]

At this point the Queen's friends and attendants had no idea of the procedure planned for the embarkation of the coffin, nor what was to become of them. In fact on arrival at Harwich the hearse was rushed to the end of the jetty, and the coffin, without even a pall to cover it, was already swinging out over the water from a crane, before any of them had time to climb down from their carriages. Mr Adolphus had never seen even a pauper's coffin so unattended; not even young William Austin, the Queen's residuary legatee and thought by many to be her son, was able to catch up with the bearer party. And this, 'as far as regarded England, was . . . the funeral of Her Majesty'. The lonely coffin was loaded on to the frigate Glasgow, the representatives of king and government departed, and the loyal executors and ladies-in-waiting, without any clear idea as to how they were to get to Brunswick or back, embarked on another of His Majesty's ships. Then the little flotilla passed out through the fleet of small boats crowded with mourners, and headed for the open sea. Caroline of Brunswick was on her way home.

In 1827 it was the turn of the King's eldest brother, Frederick, Duke of York, to die of dropsy, aged sixty-three. His wife had died in 1820 at their country house, Oatlands, near Weybridge, and had been buried in Weybridge churchyard, much to the delight of the parish and the local undertaker who was called in rather than the fashionable Banting of London. The parish clerk and sexton each received new black velvet-trimmed gowns for the occasion from the Office of Robes, and the Duke's pew and the two behind it were draped and trimmed up with black cloth. Things did not go entirely smoothly, though, as on the night after all the draping had been done, someone broke into the church and stole much of the black cloth, so that it had to be redone at considerable extra expense. A large amount of lavender water was also supplied and sprinkled liberally all around the open grave in the churchyard, 'to take of the unpleasant smells'.[3] This was an afternoon funeral, according to ordinary provincial custom.

However, there seems to have been no question of the Duke joining his wife at Weybridge. He died, for some obscure reason, in Rutland House, Arlington Street, rather than in his own house down the road in St James's Palace. He was the King's favourite brother and some days before his death, George visited him as he sat in the special adjustable chair in which he died.

His death was followed by a lying-in-state at St James's Palace for which tickets were issued to a select public to be admitted up to 11 a.m. Thereafter, for the two days it lasted, 20,000 people each day filed through the state rooms and past the coffin. Frederick had been Commander-in-Chief of the Army, though he had been disgraced by allowing his mistress, Mary Anne Clarke, to sell commissions, and his obsequies were distinctly military from the 'tentlike draping of the chamber of death' at St James's to the number of regiments and distinguished officers who took part in the funeral.

This time the King did take an interest in the proceedings. Greville, who had been the Duke's racing manager for some years, tells us that 'the King ordered that the funeral should be public and magnificent; all the details of the ceremonial were arranged by himself'.[4] He went down to Windsor in piercing January cold and selected a place in the vault close to their father. He, of course, did not attend the funeral in St George's Chapel, but was 'most grievously affected' and heard every minute gun 'as a nail driven into his heart and was [afterwards] very angry when he heard how miserably the ceremony had been performed'.[5] Greville says that 'nothing could be managed worse than it was, and except the appearance of the soldiers in the chapel, which was extremely fine, the spectacle was by no means imposing, the cold was intense, and it is only marvellous that more persons did not suffer from it'.[6] Lord Eldon followed George Canning's example and stood first on his cocked hat and then in a niche of carved wood where he was able to stand on wood',[7] there being no matting of any sort on the floor. However, much good it did Canning, for he contracted rheumatic fever, the Bishop of Lincoln died, the Dukes of Sussex, Wellington and Montrose caught bad colds, the Prime Minister, Lord Liverpool, had a stroke from which he never recovered, and 'it was alleged that the soldiers who made up the guard of honour expired at the rate of half a dozen a day'.[8]

But possibly the best comment, not only on the death of the Duke of York, but on the whole tone of those days, is by Prince Pückler Muskau, a minor German princeling, at that time on a visit to England. Writing to his mistress the day after the Duke's death, the Prince says,

The poor Duke of York is at length dead, after a long illness, and lay in state yesterday with great magnificance. I saw him in October, and found him, even then, the shadow of the robust stately man whom I had formerly so often seen at Lady L[ansdowne]'s, and at his own house, where six bottles of claret after dinner scarcely made a perceptible change in his countenance. I remember that in one such evening, – it was indeed already after midnight – he took some guests, among whom were the Austrian Ambassador, Count Meerveldt, Count Beroldingen, and myself, into his beautiful armoury. We tried to swing several Turkish sabres, but none of us had a very firm grasp; whence it happened that the Duke and Count Meerveldt both scratched themselves with a sort of straight Indian sword, so as to draw blood. Count Meerveldt then wished to try if it cut as well as a real Damascus, and undertook to cut through one of the wax candles which stood on the table. The experiment answered so ill, that both the candles, candlesticks and all, fell to the ground and were extinguished. While we were groping about in the dark, and trying to find the door, the Duke's aide-de-camp, Colonel C, stammered out in great agitation, 'By God, Sir, I remember the sword is poisoned!' You may conceive the agreeable feelings of the wounded at this intelligence. Happily on further examination it appeared that claret and not poison was at the bottom of the Colonel's exclamation.

The Duke seems to be much regretted, and the whole country wears deep mourning for him, crape on the hat, and black gloves, 'ce qui fait le desespoir' of all shopkeepers. People put their servants into black liveries, and write on paper with a broad black edge. Meantime the Christmas pantomimes go on as merrily as ever. It has a strange effect to see Harlequin and Columbine skipping about on the stage in all conceivable frivolities and antics, while the coal-black audience, dressed as for a funeral procession, clap and shout with delight . . .[9]

'So, poor Prinny is really dead – on a Saturday too, as was foretold'[10] wrote Creevey on 26 June 1830. For the whole of his reign, George IV had been suffering from arteriosclerosis, which, considering his enormous weight, might have carried him off at any time during the last eight years. Added to this he had dropsy, from which his limbs were monstrously swollen and another 'most painful and distressing complaint' which required the constant attendance of a surgeon and which Lord Grey told Madame de Lieven, the wife of the ex-Russian Ambassador, he could not describe to her but 'which was in itself mortal'.

In April he became seriously ill, but went on, often 'as clear, as communicative, as agreeable, nay as *facetious* in his conversation as he had ever been',[11] until the middle of June. He conducted business in his rather careless fashion and talked of his death as of some remote possibility until one day he suddenly announced to Sir Robert Peel that he would be dead by Saturday, and he was. In those last few days at Windsor the King was visited by his remaining brothers and sisters and received communion in his room, seeming to take comfort from prayers and from dipping into the bible that lay at his bedside, which was something new for George who had never been a religious man. At this time he was known to suffer a great deal of pain which caused him to groan so loudly that it could be heard by the sentries in the quadrangle below, who were moved to a greater distance in consequence.

On the night of 25 June, his old friend and physician, Sir Wathen Waller, was with him as he dozed rather restlessly and with much coughing in his chair, leaning on the table in front of him, as was his wont. At one time he took some medicine and sipped a little clove tea before dozing once more. Suddenly he felt faint and asked for the window to be opened, then a few moments later he clutched Sir Wathen's hand, which he was holding, looked him straight in the face, 'with an eager eye' and exclaimed, 'My dear boy! This is death!'[12] Then, leaning back in his chair, he closed his eyes and 'with a very few short breathings',[13] expired.

> Death came at last, and with a little pin
> Bored through his castle wall, and farewell – King.[14]

The post-mortem found that the King's heart was very much enlarged, that the valves of the heart had become 'ossified' and surrounded with fat, but that the immediate cause of death was a haemorrhage in the stomach caused by coughing.

Within the castle, when morning brought the spread of the news, there was real mourning, for George's immediate servants, many of whom had been with him for more than a quarter of a century, 'had been attached to him by the warmest ties of affectionate duty'.[15] All these, including the outdoor servants and their families, and all the household, were admitted that day to view the body as it lay on a couch with a sheet turned down to expose the face which 'appeared rather sunk, and the abdomen much raised'.[16] Then, that evening, it was wrapped in cere cloth only, not embalmed, and soldered up in its leaden coffin.

The King's will was opened that first day, but it was never proved. Large quantities of his effects were sold at public auction, including his outsize clothes, presumably to pay some of his innumerable debts, and Mrs Fitzherbert, whom he had married secretly more than forty years before, was assured the continuance of her allowance of £10,000 a year on condition that she renounced all claims to his estate and personal effects. A great many of his valuables did disappear, however, probably at the hands of his mistress, Lady Conyngham who, with her husband and daughter, carried away waggonloads of booty from Windsor, or so it was rumoured at the time. The King had asked the Duke of Wellington to be an executor of his will and had, at the same time, asked him to see that he was buried in his nightclothes and with any ornaments he might be wearing at the time. The Duke saw that this was done and when, on that first day, he saw the body, curiosity got the better of him and, seeing a narrow black ribbon at the neck of his nightshirt, tweaked it out and discovered it to be a miniature of Mrs Fitzherbert set in diamonds. When this was discreetly relayed to that lady, she remained silent but was seen to weep.

The formal lying-in-state took place on the two days preceding the funeral which was fixed for Thursday, 15 July at 8 p.m. Once again, it was for the nobility and gentry but, 'an intimation was given to some of the residents of Windsor, and

The Coffin of George IV on view to the public in the showrooms of Messrs Banting &
France, Upholsterers to His Majesty, James Street, Haymarket.

the tradesmen of the late King, that they and their families might have a private
view, from 9 till 11 o'clock ...'[17] on the Monday morning. Londoners had already
had a chance to view the empty coffin the day before as it stood in the showrooms
of Messrs Banting and France, the royal undertakers, or 'upholsterers', as they were
euphemistically called. Those who came to this Monday preview were in for a
surprise. This time there were no black draperies, no 'appropriate glooms'. The
King's coffin stood on a low 'car', partially covered with a gorgeous purple velvet
pall in the brilliantly lit crimson and gold splendour of the King's quite newly
decorated small drawing-room. And beside it, on each side, stood two of his
favourite pages.

Huish tells us that the real lying-in-state on the Wednesday and Thursday was
very ill-prepared. The splendour and solemnity of the occasion was quite marred,
at least for the early comers, by the banging of hammers, the bantering shouts of
workmen and the sight of sweeps and bricklayers in their ordinary working clothes

pressing through the crowd or leaping the barriers. And the crowds themselves were no better, screaming and bandying 'rude and indecent jokes' around, so that the 'whole scene [had] more the appearance of a crowd hastening to a raree-show, than to a chamber of death'.[18] Once inside the 'chamber of mortality and woe', however, the spirits of the crowd were subdued by the solemn grandeur before them as they passed through the Great Drawing-Room, 'the murmur of breathing, or the rustle of the sable suit' being the only sounds heard as they shuffled in a continuous stream over the black baize floor. But the scene was altogether less black than at previous lying-in-states. George himself had decreed that, among others, the Yeomen of the Guard were not to be issued with 'black dresses', and the King's pages were to wear their usual 'Full dress, Drawing-room coats' (scarlet) with black accessories. Thus the effect was one of brilliance with 'the richness of the purple canopy – the superbness of the coffin and its costly covering – the pall – the splendid masses of bright and flaming hues from the golden drapery of the royal standard – the crowns and heralds uniforms – imparted a death-like and spectral paleness to the heads of the household mourners which had an intensely interesting effect'. Truly, 'The pomp of death is more terrible than death itself'.[19]

In the early hours of the day of the funeral, 'a party of artillery, with twelve nine-pounders, arrived from Woolwich and bivouacked under the trees of the Long Walk'.[20] At 4 a.m. they started firing and continued at five-minute intervals until the funeral began at 9 p.m. Thereafter they fired minute guns while the service lasted.

As the procession wound its way down from the state apartments, it was immediately noticeable that there were some newcomers in the ranks. The Poor Knights of Windsor had now been renamed, by George IV, the Military Knights to distinguish them from the Naval Knights of Windsor, six of whom now fell in behind the Military Knights, wearing splendid long purple cloth mantles with silver tissue badges bearing St George's Cross upon gilt anchors with gold cordon cables. There were, at that time, eleven of these old naval lieutenants living in the building below the Castle which is now the Choir School. But these old sea dogs were a troublesome, rumbustious lot; they imported women from the town to attend to their comforts, refused to attend chapel twice a day, for which it is hard to blame them as they had to climb the hundred steps and several of them had wooden legs. These they would take off when they got drunk in the town and use to belabour each other with. After much trouble, they were disbanded in Queen Victoria's reign.

The most important innovation at George IV's funeral was the decision of his brother, the new King William IV, to perform the role of chief mourner dressed in a cloak of purple velvet, rather than black, and with no less than five orders round his neck. With a few exceptions, it had never been the custom in England for sovereigns to attend funerals. And, from his behaviour, it seems that it would have been better if this one had not. Coming up the aisle, he was observed glancing eagerly from side to side and 'talking incessantly and loudly to all about him, so that the most frivolous things were heard'.[21] The congregation by that time had been assembled some two hours and had grown restive and loudly conversational. But for their sombre dress, they might have been gathered together 'upon some joyous festival',[22] and the soldiers on duty in the Chapel joined in the general hubbub of conversation and 'commonplace jokes'. And outside it was the same; some of the spectators even climbed upon some railings to gain a better view of the platform along which the coffin and the mourners were to pass on their way from the Castle to the Chapel. Never a word of praise or regret for the late King was heard.

Once the procession arrived and the service began, most people settled down and it was considered very fine, though to some a thing of 'too much tinsel magnificence':[23] a tawdry show which would have horrified the late King. The *Times* reporter, however, noticed that, during the singing of one of the hymns, a piece of carving which hung over one of the stalls in the choir fell on top of Sir Astly Cooper, striking him on the forehead and drawing blood. Sir Astly clasped a handkerchief to his head and resolutely remained in his place.

The King continued to chat throughout the service, and some of the mourners in the choir looked quite ludicrous:

Sussex and Cumberland looked awfully fierce in their black cloaks ... The Duke of Buckingham squatting down in a stall exhausted (for he had held a corner of the pall) looked exactly like a giant tortoise, then the vulgar, insolent air of Lord Ellenborough in a coat covered with gold – the greasy importance of Verulam carrying a banner, and old Cathcart with another which he could hardly support – the horrid nervous grimaces of the Duke of Norfolk and the awkward gestures of Lord Conyngham were all in their different ways most ludicrous ... Mount Charles was much affected and I think no one else.[24]

The new King did not even wait to see his brother's remains lowered into the vault below, whence they were trundled into George III's vault under the Wolsey Hall, now known as the Albert Memorial Chapel. As soon as the funeral rites were ended and while the anthem was being sung, he stumped out, with a nod to the

Earl Marshal; but who can blame him, for the service had already lasted two hours and there must have been many among the elderly gentlemen gathered there who envied him.

It is, however, only fair to say that Lord Ellenborough gives a very different account of the funeral: 'All the people were very decent in their dress and their conduct was perfect,' and, though the King 'nodded occasionely as he recognised people . . . when his countenance was still he looked very grave,' and altogether, 'It was very well arranged.'[25]

At the end of the day, 'All Windsor drunk!' declared Joseph Jekyll. 'Suppers and champagne for parties who remained there, and everything but grief or respect'.[26] It was to be many a long day before this country was to earn its present reputation for the superb organization of its state occasions.

Of course there was a flurry of official eulogies on the death of George IV both from great public figures and from some of the press. But by no means all the press considered it necessary to praise him, and among these was *The Times* which devoted two issues to outright vilification and character assassination in a manner unthinkable today. They attacked his extravagance, his morals, his behaviour to his wife and even his taste, and in doing so they felt secure in finding favour with their readers. George IV left much to posterity, especially to the royal collections, which are enjoyed and appreciated today, but in his own day his admirers were heavily outnumbered by his detractors. He was a highly unpopular king, yet no one can deny that he was, in the words of the French Foreign Minister, Prince Talleyrand, 'Un roi grand seigneur'.

The reign of William IV was not a long one, and the seven years saw only one royal death, that of William Frederick, Duke of Gloucester, first cousin and brother-in-law of Kings George and William, as he was married to their sister Mary. He died on St Andrew's Day in 1834 at his home, Bagshot Park, and was buried on 11 December in the Gloucester vault at St George's. Though an unimportant royal occasion, the funeral was not without its complications as the house at Bagshot had to be fitted up for a private lying-in-state followed by a more formal one at Cumberland Lodge, Windsor Great Park, on the day of the funeral. Thus there were two processions, with sixteen horses to be stabled meanwhile at Cumberland Lodge and countless others in the immediate neighbourhood. The whole thing was rendered almost impossible by Mr Banting the undertaker being subpoenaed to appear at a trial at the Court of Exchequer. The Lord Chamberlain was obliged to send to the Court demanding his presence, as 'his services could *not* be dispensed with'.[27] Luckily for him he was released and made £1039 3s. 8d. on the contract.

A range of porcelain commemorating royal deaths from Princess Charlotte (1) to Edward VII. The highly flattering portrait on the large jug commemorates the death of George IV.

Though not long, indeed it seems no more than an interregnum between those of George IV and Queen Victoria, and though not glamorous, the reign of William IV is not without importance. The 'Sailor King' was a solid, bluff, hail-fellow-well-met man who took every man as he found him in a straight and unaffected way. When he first came to the throne he shocked the Court by walking up and down St James's Street and greeting perfect strangers with a hearty handshake, and a nation which had come to abhor the monarchy responded to him and gave him their affection. Though not clever, he had some common sense, could see when he was beaten, as with the Reform Bill of 1832 which he opposed, and gave in with a tolerably good grace. Thus he played his part in steering Britain through the rocks and shoals which were the political scene of the 1830s, and with the help of his quiet and supportive wife, Queen Adelaide, and the idyllic domestic life which followed his less respectable earlier life with the actress Dorothy Jordan, the throne which he passed on to his niece, Queen Victoria, was a much securer one than that which he inherited only seven years before, and well rooted in the affections of his people.

In 1830 King William moved himself and Queen Adelaide out of Bushy Park which had been his home for most of his married life, and thereafter they moved between Buckingham Palace, Windsor Castle and even, on occasions, the Pavilion at Brighton. But Windsor was his favourite residence and it was there that he fell ill in May 1837. For years he had suffered from asthma and, at seventy-two, he was worn out with it; his heart was affected and by the middle of the month he was subject to alarming fits of fainting. He knew that his end was near, but was determined not to die before his niece, Princess Victoria, reached her majority at eighteen on 24 May. This would remove all question of a Regency by her mother, the Duchess of Kent, who, with her advisers, was loathed by the King, and he could not rest in peace with the thought of them as powers in the land. Fortunately this hurdle was cleared and from then on, though he continued to receive ministers and sign papers, the King's health declined steadily. The Queen went alone to Ascot and then dismissed the house party in the middle of the race meeting. This brought the gravity of his illness home to the public who were being officially kept in the dark. It was not until a few days before his death that bulletins were issued, and then they were displayed in St James's Palace to which the nobility and gentry were admitted. And the order for him to be prayed for in churches was not sent out until Friday, 16 June and then by post so that many churches had not received it by the Sunday.

The next hurdle to be cleared by the King was Waterloo Day, 18 June. 'Doctor, I know that I am going,' he said, a few days before it, 'but I should like to see another anniversary of the battle of Waterloo. Try if you cannot tinker me up to last out that day.'[28] He did last it out and lay clasping a tricolour captured at Waterloo and insisting that the annual Waterloo Dinner at the Castle should go ahead as usual.

Queen Adelaide was with him constantly, reading prayers to him and passages from the Prayer Book which appeared to give him great comfort. It was reported in the press that for more than a week she never took off her clothes, always recognized by them as the mark of extreme devotion. In her exhaustion, she, on one occasion, burst into tears. 'Bear up! Bear up!'[29] exclaimed the King bracingly.

On Sunday the Archbishop of Canterbury came to give him Communion and on the Monday he returned to read the prayers for the dying and then members of the royal family and some of his ten children by his mistress Dorothy Jordan came to say goodbye as he sat propped up in his leather chair, gasping for breath. At twelve minutes past two on the morning of Tuesday, 20 June, King William's life was gently snuffed out and Lord Conyngham, now Lord Chamberlain, and the Archbishop set out for Kensington to break the news to an eighteen-year-old girl that she was Queen.

'Poor man, he was always very kind to me and he *meant* it well, I know,' confided the young Queen Victoria to her journal that day. 'I am grateful for it and shall ever remember his kindness with gratitude. He was odd, very odd, and singular, but his intentions were often ill-interpreted.'[30] Not a bad epitaph for King William IV, but whereas the death of George IV had been greeted with general indifference, this time the news was received everywhere like the loss of a member of the family.

That very day a post-mortem was carried out which showed that the valves of the heart were ossified, the lungs full of blood and the liver and spleen much enlarged. He was then embalmed, unlike his brother and father, and sealed up in the leaden coffin before the day was out.

The true grief of Queen Adelaide, now the Queen Dowager, comes down to us clearly and poignantly in the note she sent to Queen Victoria on the day of the King's death, ending with the words: 'Excuse my writing more at present, my heart is overwhelmed and my head aches very much. Accept the assurance of my most affectionate devotion, and allow me to consider myself as your Majesty's most affectionate Friend, Aunt and Subject.'[31] She asked if she might remain at the Castle until after the funeral, and the new Queen begged her 'to consult nothing so much as [her] comfort and convenience'. When the time came she quietly moved back into Bushy Park and the obscurity she sought, taking with her nothing but the silver cup from which she had fed William during his last illness and a family group portrait of his illegitimate children grouped round a bust of their father. This she hung in her own room at Bushy.

Not everyone, however, was as forbearing as Queen Adelaide. It was not long before Lord Conyngham struck again, this time in his role as Lord Chamberlain. There had in Stuart times been a custom, mentioned earlier, whereby one or two courtiers nearest to the deceased royal person had some claim on the furniture in his employer's private apartments. This custom had long since fallen into abeyance until Lord Conyngham chose to revive it to his own benefit, claiming three writing tables, a bookstand, a tortoiseshell and Buhl clock and sundry ornaments and figures from the room in which King William died.

Meanwhile the arrangements for the lying-in-state and funeral were going ahead. Letters were sent to all the theatres ordering them to close on the evening of the day of the death and the day of the funeral. The Royal Academy was not ordered to close, but did so by order of the President. The funeral was fixed for the evening of 8 July and for the two days before the King lay in state in the Waterloo Chamber. To this the public were admitted. Then, in the evening, guardsmen stationed themselves all along the route down from the state apartments to St George's Chapel and flambeaux were distributed to them by Banting's men and 'moons' to others who lined the staircase where the mourners were to assemble for

[149]

the procession. The Duke of Sussex, who was becoming something of a professional, was once again chief mourner in his huge black cloak and several of the King's illegitimate 'Fitzclarence' sons had places in the procession.

So all was well – the planning was there, but once more the funeral turned out to be a travesty of what it could have been and not at all worthy of a king universally mourned, at least by his ordinary subjects if not by the cynical aristocrats who attended the funeral. Charles Greville was there and was very much shocked by what he saw.

> It is a wretched mockery after all, and if I were a king, the first thing I would do should be to provide for being committed to the earth with more decency and less pomp. A host of persons of all ranks and stations were congregated, who 'loitered through the lofty halls', chattering and laughing, and with nothing of woe about them but the garb. I saw two men in an animated conversation, and one laughing heartily at the very foot of the coffin as it was lying in state. The chamber of death in which the body lay, all hung with black and adorned with scutcheons and every sort of funereal finery, was like a scene in a play, and as we passed through it and looked at the scaffolding and rough work behind, it was just like going behind the scenes of a theatre. A soldier's funeral, which I met in the morning – the plain coffin slowly borne along by his comrades, with the cap and helmet and sword of the dead placed upon it – was more impressive, more decent, more affecting than all this pomp with pasteboard crowns, and heralds scampering about, while idleness and indifference were gazing or gossiping round about the royal remains. I would rather be quietly consigned to the grave by a few who cared for me ... than be the object of all this parade and extravagance.[32]

Doubtless this is as biased a view of King William's funeral as Lord Dover's was of George IV's or Adolphus's of Queen Caroline's; there were probably others who found all three perfectly respectable, yet they have a ring of the whole disreputable tone of the period which is inescapable.

Strictly, of course, with the accession of Queen Victoria, we pass out of the Hanoverian age. This is because Hanover came under Salic law and no woman could sit upon its throne. Therefore the bad old Duke of Cumberland, as the next surviving son of George III, acceded to that throne and it was separated for ever from that of Great Britain. However, for purposes of convenience the remaining members of that generation are included in this chapter.

In the 1840s and 1850s, once more the emphasis at Court was on youth. The

The funeral procession of Princess Sophia of Gloucester showing the flares which lighted the proceedings and the bearskin caps of the officers draped in crape.

young Queen soon married the young Prince Albert of Saxe Coburg and their numerous children came thick and fast. But, after the departure of the Duke of Cumberland to Hanover, there were still five of the Queen's old uncles and aunts alive in this country, as well as Queen Dowager Adelaide and the Queen's mother, the Duchess of Kent, and one by one they died, plunging the Court into mourning. This had, however, become quite brief by then, generally three weeks, though for Princess Sophia Matilda of Gloucester, the Queen's first cousin who died in 1844, it was cut to a mere ten days. Her funeral is worth mentioning as the first occasion on which the railway played a part in royal funeral arrangements. The body of the Princess, who had died at Rangers Lodge, Blackheath, was transported by rail from Paddington to Windsor.

Princess Augusta, the eldest survivor, died in 1840, followed by her brother the Duke of Sussex, of whom more later, in 1843 and by Princess Sophia in 1848. Queen Adelaide died in 1849, the Duke of Cambridge in 1850 and last survivor of that vast family, Mary, Duchess of Gloucester, in 1857 at the age of eighty-one.

Although the period of Court mourning at that time was not long, a much more staid atmosphere had come in with the new reign, and the undertakers, who by now had taken full charge of the proceedings following a death, were playing their role to its full potential. No funeral was complete without as many mutes as possible carrying trays of black plumes or draped wands, long weepers trailing from their hats. No mourner would be seen without his trailing weeper and mourning scarf crossing his breast. The black plumes nodding on the horses' heads had assumed enormous proportions and, at royal funerals, even the guardsmen had their bearskins swathed in black crape which presented a ludicrous appearance. Courtaulds, the inventors and producers of weatherproof crape, were making a handsome fortune. It was the undertakers who carried the responsibility of seeing that everyone coming to the funeral had black scarves and gloves delivered to them before the event and of distributing the mementoes which had been so popular since the previous century. These were usually rings or brooches with the name and dates of the deceased and often contained a lock of hair. Messrs Banting were still known as Upholsterers to the Queen, in deference to everybody's delicate sensibilities, but by now they were taking almost all the responsibility for royal obsequies off the shoulders of the various departments of the royal household.

By 1843 the old Duke of Sussex was seventy. The sixth son of George III and Queen Charlotte, Augustus had lived most of his adult life under a cloud. He had married twice, though neither of his marriages had been recognized under the Royal Marriages Act of 1772, and had a son and a daughter. He lived quietly at Kensington Palace and gave himself up to amassing a vast library of mostly religious books and to charitable works. He may be seen in the background in paintings of such events as Queen Victoria's Accession Council and her marriage, identifiable by the little black velvet cap without which he was never seen.

Among his charitable works, the Duke was on the governing body of the new public cemetery at Kensal Green, a scheme which had his enthusiasm to the extent of his declaring his intention of being buried there himself. It may also have had something to do with the fact that his second wife, Cecilia, known as the Duchess of Inverness after one of the Duke's titles, could join him there. It would have been impossible for her to be buried in a royal vault at Windsor. The Lord

The body of Augustus, Duke of Sussex, lying in state at Kensington Palace. The walls and floor of the room are completely covered with black cloth. The Duke of Cambridge sits at the head of his brother's coffin. The ladies must surely have been in black.

Chamberlain's Office were dubious about allowing this; however, the Freemasons represented that they ought to have 'an opportunity of displaying their regret at the funeral by a manifestation of their respect to the memory of their departed Grand Master'.[33] Somebody murmured the number twenty-five thousand and the Queen, appalled at the thought of such an invasion at Windsor, quickly gave her consent.

The Duke's other wish, expressed at the time of the Anatomy Bill of 1832, was to donate his body to one of the London hospitals for dissection. This was really too much for the royal family to swallow and his wish was not carried out but it was agreed that the findings of the post-mortem should be published if they might be of any 'beneficial interest'. As he did not die of anything interesting, the matter was finally dropped.

The Duke had always suffered from asthma and with old age this overcame him and affected his heart, and in April 1843 he died. A lying-in-state was arranged at Kensington Palace where the now deserted rooms where the Queen had grown up were draped and tented in black, hung with hatchments and escutcheons, and lit by candles in silver sconces. As the public filed through, fifty at a time and out into the garden by way of some wooden steps, they noticed that the coffin was flanked by two heralds in their brilliant tabards and attended by members of the Duke's household servants, including his German *jäger* and his Burmese page. 'All the arrangements,' declared the *Illustrated London News*, 'were in excellent taste',[34] and the *Pictorial Times* exclaimed at 'the gorgeousness of grief'.[35]

The funeral was arranged for midday, on Thursday, 4 May and for several days before there was a brisk trade in tickets for windows on the long processional route, rooftops and for seats in the official stands with their reassuring message that they had been 'approved by the Surveyor of Woods and Forests'. By six o'clock in the morning, London was thronged with 'persons anxious to obtain a sight of the solemn and imposing ceremony',[36] for the most part 'suitably attired' and with the 'respectable classes' in deep mourning. The shops of Kensington were all closed for the day, everywhere mourning flags and banners were displayed and the bells of the City churches tolled mournfully. The cortège was over a mile long when it got under way at 8 o'clock and moved slowly out into Kensington High Street, Church Street and the Uxbridge Road, and 'When the procession reached the Paddington Canal-bridge the sight was very striking. The sides of the canal were densely crowded as far as the eye could reach and the surface of the canal itself . . . was completely covered with barges, occupied by throngs of spectators . . .'[37] Prince Albert, as chief mourner, had his own procession from Buckingham Palace and entered the cemetery, where, according to the *Illustrated London News* the twenty-five thousand Freemasons were assembled, by a temporary bridge of planks over the canal and watergate.

After the service in the modern chapel, for which six hundred tickets had been issued, the body was temporarily deposited in the vault underneath while a handsome grave was built outside. It is in fact a heavy red granite stone resembling nothing so much as a double duvet, under which now repose the remains of His Royal Highness and his second wife who, in due course, joined him there. Much prettier is the light classical sarcophagus on a high plinth above the grave of his sister, Princess Sophia, who, for some reason unknown, chose to be buried close to

Queen Adelaide in mourning for King William IV. Note the 'weeper' cuffs.

her brother at Kensal Green. Theirs are among the very few royal graves to be seen and Sophia's sarcophagus comes right at the end of an era rich in monuments of classical allusion. In the 1840s, religious thinking of the Church of England turned away from the old pagan classical sculptured forms so beloved of the eighteenth century, and insisted that only explicitly Christian forms of ornamentation were acceptable in their graveyards. From then on we see crosses, recumbent figures and angels, as opposed to putti, in abundance, but sarcophagae, obelisks, pyramids, broken columns, torches, and other classical or Egyptian objects are only seen in Non-conformist cemeteries where such imagery remained permissible. Christian symbolism in England had gone out with the Reformation; now the Ecclesiologists of the mid nineteenth century brought it back with a vengeance, both for monuments within the church and for graves outside.

In 1841, when she was forty-eight, Queen Adelaide was very ill. She thought she was dying and lying in bed she pondered on what was to happen to her remains, did not like what she knew of English royal funeral tradition and summoned all her strength to write, in her own hand, her last will and testament regarding her obsequies. In fact, the Queen did not die. She lived another eight years, but when she finally came to die in 1849, Queen Victoria, touched by the little document and the insight it gave into the character of this little known, gentle and supportive Queen Consort, took the unusual step of having this private document published in the *London Gazette*:

I die in all humility, knowing well that we are all alike before the Throne of God, and I request therefore that my mortal remains be conveyed to the grave without any pomp or state. They are to be moved to St George's Chapel, Windsor, where I request to have as private and quiet a funeral as possible.

I particularly desire not to be laid out in state, and the funeral to take place by daylight; no procession; the coffin to be carried by sailors to the Chapel.

All those of my friends and relations, to a limited number, who wish to attend may do so. My nephew, Prince Edward of Saxe Weimar, Lords Howe and Denbigh, the Hon. Wm. Ashley, Mr Wood, Mr Andrew Barnard and Sir D. Davies, with my dressers and those of my ladies who may wish to attend.

I die in peace, and wish to be carried to the tomb in peace, and free from the vanities and pomp of this world.

I request not to be dissected, nor embalmed; and desire to give as little trouble as possible.

November 1841.   (Signed) Adelaide R.[38]

Dear Queen Adelaide – diffident and self-effacing to the last.

Adelaide died in a rented house, Bentley Priory, near Stanmore in Hertford-shire, and her wishes were carried out to the letter. Her body was brought very discreetly, by night, from Stanmore to Slough where it was met by the carriages of the Queen and other members of the royal family and escorted to Windsor. The service in St George's Chapel was small and intimate; no tickets were issued and such close relations, including some royal ladies, household and servants as assembled, filled only the choir. It was a nice thought on the part of the widow of the 'Sailor King' to ask to be carried to the grave by sailors and they carried her proudly – the first time that the Navy had taken any major part in a royal funeral.

Queen Victoria and Prince Albert mourned Queen Adelaide as 'the kindest and dearest of friends' and the English people, who had only got to know her after her husband's death, agreed with them. Her dignified simplicity and her unassuming strength were recognized and there was universal sorrow at her death.

Mourning was set at seven weeks in all; five weeks first mourning (black bombazine, plain muslin, crape hoods, shamoy shoes and gloves, crape fans), one week of second mourning (black silk, fringed or plain linen, white gloves, necklaces and earrings, but no diamonds, black or white shoes, fans and tippets), and one week of third mourning (black silk or velvet, coloured ribbons, fans and tippets). It was worn gladly by a wide section of society, well beyond the confines of the Court.

Of course, by far the grandest funeral almost of the whole nineteenth century was that of the Duke of Wellington in 1852. Though not royal, and therefore not strictly within the scope of this book, some mention should be made of this momentous event. The Duke died at Walmer Castle on 14 September 1852 and his funeral took almost three months to plan and arrange. Royal funerals were becoming increasingly private family affairs, but this was to be a public military spectacle on a really grand scale. The procession from The Royal Hospital, Chelsea, to St Paul's was the longest, in an age of long funeral processions, that anyone could remember, and the immense triumphal funeral car which carried the coffin was only moved with difficulty by sixteen horses.

At the time of Queen Victoria's accession, there had been considerable bad blood between the Queen and her mother, the Duchess of Kent. Victoria blamed her for her difficult teenage years, for the rows with William IV and for her attempts, with her comptroller, Sir John Conroy, to gain control of the throne. Consequently, once on the throne, she made certain that she was completely free of them both; for some time she hardly saw her mother and pushed her into the background, humiliating her deeply. However, in 1840 the Queen married the

Duchess's nephew, Prince Albert of Saxe Coburg and, with his tact and loving care for them both, he soon healed the breach and their relationship became increasingly affectionate. The Duchess was an excellent grandmother – loving and interested to the last in the doings and saying of her grandchildren – and she and her daughter were in almost daily touch. Indeed, it would be almost true to say that, by the 1850s, her mother was Queen Victoria's 'best friend'.

By now the Duchess was installed at Frogmore and, when the family were at Windsor, one or more of her grandchildren would come down to visit her every day and the Queen and Prince Albert looked in whenever their engagements permitted. This was an idyllic old age, but ill health in the shape of cancer was claiming the Duchess and, on the evening of 15 March 1861 the Queen and the Prince Consort were suddenly summoned from London to her bedside. When they arrived she was already unconscious and they saw that she was dying. All through the night with eighteen-year-old Princess Alice, they sat with her, or knelt round the bed, the Queen holding her hand, and she has left a very vivid description of the scene:

> As the night wore on ... I heard each hour strike, the cocks crow, the dogs barking in the distance. Every sound seemed to strike into one's innermost soul ... All still. Nothing to be heard but the heavy breathing and the striking of every quarter of the old repeater, a large watch in a tortoiseshell case which had belonged to my poor father, the sound of which brought back all the recollections of my childhood, for I always used to hear it at night, but had not heard it now for twenty-three years.[39]

Surely anyone who has sat up with a dying relative will recognize the scene.

At nine o'clock in the morning the Duchess of Kent's life flickered gently out and the Queen was utterly devastated by grief. Prince Albert was all loving tenderness and comfort, and also, with some firmness, tried to instruct her in how to cope with bereavement. (Could it be that he knew that an even worse grief was about to engulf her and wished to help her while he could?) But she was inconsolable.

Everyone feels that they could have done more for their mother, if only they had known ... but there was a possible added ingredient to Victoria's grief. Though long forgotten on both sides, and though the Queen never admitted any blame for the breach of so long ago, it is probable that now it all came crowding back with remorse for her part in the old quarrel.

The Duchess died on a Saturday; the funeral was fixed for the Tuesday week and was to be very private and at 11 o'clock in the morning. The old tradition of night-time funerals, which had endured for over two hundred years, was dead. Court mourning was ordered from 21 March and covered all appearances by anyone at Court during the period named. Therefore, when the Queen returned miserably to her duties that summer, and the season for Drawing Rooms, at which debutantes were presented to the Queen, came round, they were known as 'black drawing rooms'. Agnes Strickland, who was at that time a middle-aged woman, attended one and described the scene to her mother:

You will be glad to hear that I got through the black drawing room yesterday quite well. I wore a black velvet train, black silk underdress, and a black velvet tiara, lappets and plumes. I fear that head-dress must have given me the look of Bellona. However, as everybody wore the same style of headgear, it did not much signify; but I found it very hot and heavy. The young ladies who were presented, were all costumed in lily-white with garlands and bouquets of flowers of the same spotless hue. It was really a fine sight to see these grand black dresses and sable plumes, blazing with diamonds, intermingled with the white dresses of the young ladies.[40]

At a slightly later date (1888), Marie Mallet, a Woman of the Bedchamber to Queen Victoria, wrote: 'I find I shall have to wear black feathers at the Drawing Room and black lappets so that I shall present a hearse like appearance.'[41]

There was no outdoor procession at this funeral; before dawn on the day of the funeral, the coffin was conveyed from Frogmore to Windsor and deposited in the nave of St George's Chapel. A special train brought the hundred or so mourners down from London and

When all were placed in the Choir, softly began Croft's solemn Anthem, 'I am the Resurrection and the Life, saith the Lord', and at the plaintive music of this dirge, which sounded like a wail through the building, the procession moved slowly forward. The cortège [with the Prince Consort as chief mourner supported by the Prince of Wales and the Duchess's son, the Prince of Leiningen] occupied the full length of the nave and part of the choir, with the bier in the centre, covered by the outstretched pall, creeping by an unseen motion noiselessly and stiffly on.[42]

This ghostly motion was achieved by the bearer party moving along underneath the stiffened pall which stuck out over their heads and shoulders and hung down to below their waists. The anthem was an old favourite of the Duchess's, Luther's great hymn:

> Great God! What do I see and hear?
> The end of things created:
> The Judge of mankind doth appear,
>   On clouds of glory seated.
> The trumpet sounds! The graves restore
> The dead which they contained before:
>   Prepare my soul to meet Him.

For a while the Duchess's remains were lodged in the royal vault, but in the August of that year they were transferred to a granite sarcophagus in the pretty mausoleum, by A.J. Humbert, set into a bank in the gardens of Frogmore. The Duchess had planned this last resting place herself and it was already nearing completion when she died. Here the Queen often visited her in the years to come.

The Duchess's will, of which the already dangerously overworked Prince Albert was the sole executor, left a confusion of mementoes to a large number of people. The bulk of her estate passed to Queen Victoria but she left £3,000, which the Queen made up to £5,000, to be divided between her servants, according to their length of service and position in the household. This was a generous gesture which, in those pensionless days, must have helped the more elderly of her staff to a comfortable retirement.

Gradually during the months that followed, with their regular pattern of events and visits to Osborne and Balmoral, the Queen began to come to terms with her mother's death, and she had almost recovered when, at the end of the year, she was hit by a fresh blow, so much worse, so terrible that she was never fully to recover in the forty years of life that were to remain to her. And the cult of widowhood was to cast a dark shadow over the rest of the century.

Queen Victoria's Funeral Procession passing Buckingham Palace. Watercolour by J Walter West, 1902. This picture shows how colourful the Queen's funeral was in comparison to earlier ones, notably that of the Prince Consort.

The body of the Duke of Windsor lying in state in St George's Chapel, Windsor, guarded by four officers of the Foot Guards.

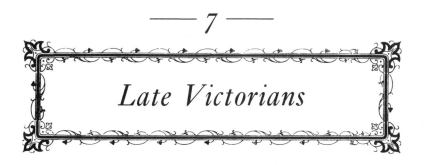

7

Late Victorians

Preoccupied as she was with her own grief for her mother, Queen Victoria quite failed to notice that the Prince Consort was thinner and more weary as day succeeded day. She did think he was overworking and often urged him to cut down on his multifarious activities, but half-heartedly and at the same time continuing to load him with drafts to be written for her, papers to be read, advice to be given, all on top of the endless meetings and events he insisted on attending. Surely the modern concept of royal duties must stem from Albert. Some of the sons of George III were connected with various charities and took a serious interest in them but Albert, starting out as a serious, educated and immensely energetic young man in a difficult position in a foreign country, had succeeded by 1861 in making himself almost indispensable to the smooth running of his adopted country. By his tact and sound advice to the Queen, he had raised the throne to a position of stability and international respect, and by sheer hard work and the force of his personality had done the same for British education, industry and the arts. He was a pioneer in the fields of model housing for the poor and hygiene, and in pursuit of all these aims, chaired innumerable committees and then forced through their findings. And with all this he had a charm and a lightness of touch with which he is not often credited.

Many fathers fail to appreciate their sons, especially when they fail to live up to the very high ideals of manhood and of royalty which Prince Albert set. Poor Bertie, the Prince of Wales, at nineteen could do very little right in the eyes of his parents. In the autumn of 1861 there was a society scandal when he was at an army camp at the Curragh, outside Dublin, and a young woman was smuggled into his room in the mess. She then followed him to Windsor and the story got about. In the previous generation such a scrape would have passed quite unnoticed, but times had changed, and Albert, the chaste husband of an adoring wife, felt it necessary, on a cold November day, to go in person to Cambridge and remonstrate with his wayward son. In search of privacy, they walked the lanes around Grantchester, got drenched with rain and Albert became throughly chilled on the evening train journey back to Windsor. That was the start of the Prince's last illness and the reason for a period of dislike for her son on the part of Queen Victoria which took some time to pass off.

Prince Albert was now said to have influenza, but still did not give up work, going up to London for meetings and drafting dispatches for the Queen. For some months he had been working frantically as though he feared he would not long be able to continue and must see through as many tasks as he could. As his illness progressed, he felt worse and worse, but continued to get up and dressed and attended meals although his appetite had quite gone. He took his nephew, Ernest Leiningen, out shooting and, although stiff and aching, shot as well as ever. On 24 November he was able to walk with the Queen to the Duchess of Kent's mausoleum at Frogmore and on 29 November reviewed the Eton College Volunteers, but commented, although dressed in a fur-lined coat, that he felt 'as though cold water was being poured down his back'.[1]

By 4 December any attempt to eat nauseated him and he could do little more than lie on a sofa, still fully dressed. It must have been obvious to all that he was seriously ill, but the doctors kept on telling the Queen that it was nothing more than overwork and worry, and the Queen believed what she wanted to believe. She was not even seriously alarmed when on 6 December they diagnosed typhoid fever. She had had that herself in her girlhood and wrote briskly to her Uncle King Leopold of the Belgians: 'Our beloved invalid goes on well – but it *must* be tedious, and I need not tell you *what* a trial it is to me. Every day, however, is bringing us nearer the end of this tiresome illness, which is much what I had at Ramsgate, only that I was much worse, and not at first well attended to.'[2] Albert was not well attended to either, but was allowed to wander about in the night from room to room in an unheated castle, in only a silk dressing-gown. He had been ill many times before, but up until 1858 he had always had the devoted care and expert nursing of his valet Kurt. Kurt was now dead and no one took firm charge of the patient, plied him with drinks or wiped the cold sweat from his brow. And Victoria, who had a low opinion of the stamina of men, looked in on him frequently but did nothing for him. She was still much taken up with the effect of the illness on her: 'I cannot describe the *anxiety* I have gone through! I feel today a good deal shaken, for for four nights I got only two or three hours' sleep.'[3] Albert's restless prowling continued. He could not remain long in one place and, as he became weaker, had his sofa pushed from his bedroom to his dressing-room, to the Blue Room, nearer to the window, nearer to a favourite picture, and round and round again.

The real heroine of the piece was eighteen-year-old Princess Alice who sat with her father, read to him, fed him with beef tea and talked to him when he wanted to talk. One day he asked Alice if she had written to her sister Vicky, Crown Princess of Prussia. 'Yes,' she replied, 'I told her that you were very ill.' 'You did wrong,' he said, 'You should have told her I was dying.'[4]

Albert had by now taken up permanent residence in the Blue Room, in which both George IV and William IV had died, almost as though he had gone there to die. But at least it was bright and cheerful. 'When I returned from breakfast,' wrote the Queen later,

> I found him lying on the bed in the Blue Room and much pleased. The sun was shining brightly, the room was fine, large and cheerful, and he said: 'It is so fine!' For the first time since his illness he asked for some music, and said, 'I should like to hear a fine chorale played at a distance.' We had a piano brought into the next room, and Alice played, 'Ein feste Burg ist unser Gott', and another, and he listened, looking upwards with such a sweet expression, and with tears in his eyes.[5]

She was beginning now to be seriously worried, however, for she adds that she had been to church, it being Sunday. The Reverend Charles Kingsley, remembered today as the author of *The Water Babies*, had preached, 'but I heard nothing.'

By now it was impossible to keep the Prince's illness from the public, and bulletins were issued. The Prime Minister, Lord Palmerston, and other ministers of the government made constant enquiries. They all knew the Prince well and were seriously alarmed at the notion of running the country without him. Albert's far-sightedness, tact and knowledge of the international *dramatis personae* were so valuable to them.

The patient now became intermittently irritable and wandering in his mind, but at other times almost his old affectionate self, enjoying Scott read aloud to him, passing urgent messages to Palmerston, laying his head on the Queen's shoulder, stroking her face and calling her 'liebes Frauchen' and anxious to have the letters of his young sons Alfred (Affy) and Leopold, both of whom were abroad, read to him. But he was rapidly sinking.

The doctors, however, still kept up their myths of improvement. Early on the morning of 14 December they came to tell the Queen of such an improvement and, 'I went over at 7 ...,' she writes,

It was a bright morning, the sun just rising and shining brightly. The room had the sad look of night-watching, the candles burnt down in their sockets, the doctors looking anxious. I went in, and never can I forget how beautiful my darling looked, lying there with his face lit up by the rising sun, his eyes unusually bright, gazing as it were on unseen objects, and not taking notice of me.[6]

It was a glorious day and the Queen went out once or twice 'for a breath of air', cautioned not to go far. On the terrace she and Alice found 'the military band playing at a distance, and [she] burst into tears and came home again',[7] where she found that the doctors had shifted their position to 'very much frightened but don't and won't give up hope'. The pulse kept up, but the Prince's breathing alarmed them all. It was increasingly quick and shallow and there was 'a dusky hue about the face and hands which [they] knew was not good.'[8]

At one time Alice, momentarily alone with her father, felt that he was struggling to tell her something. She bent her head close to his lips but could make out nothing from the stray phrases she was able to hear. Was he commending her mother to her care, or giving instructions about his funeral? We shall never know.

During the afternoon, as the Queen sat at the bedside, Alice brought the younger children to see their father for the last time. She kissed him and he took her hand, but when the others approached, one by one, to kiss his hand, 'he was dozing, and did not perceive them.'[9]

So the long day passed into evening with the Prince dozing, yet sometimes recognizing his wife, kissing her and murmuring to her and sometimes even opening his eyes and asking for one member or other of his household. So that, as the evening advanced, the room became quite crowded with mournful figures and the Queen, who every now and then slipped out for a few moments to 'give way to her grief in an adjoining room', and then returned to kneel by his side and clasp his already cold hand. On the other side was Princess Alice; at the foot, the Prince of Wales and Princess Helena; and in other parts of the room were the three physicians. Prince Ernest Leiningen, Albert's nephew, his valet, Lohlein, the Dean of Windsor, General the Honourable Robert Bruce, knelt opposite the Queen with Sir Charles Phipps and General Grey, all of his household. There was a deep and solemn hush in the room, each one feeling their very breathing crushed by the weight of their grief as they waited through the long evening. 'The castle clock chimed the third quarter after ten', writes Martin:

Calm and peaceful grew the beloved form; the features settled into the beauty of

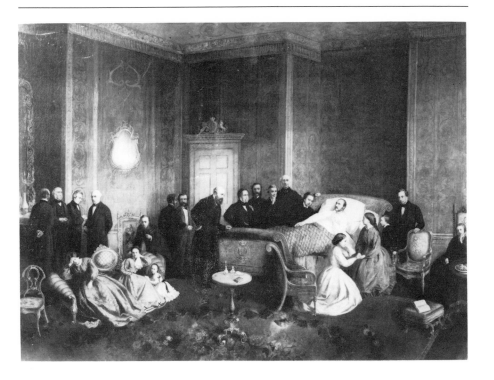

'The Last Moments of HRH The Prince Consort'. An oil painting by Oakley painted some time after the event.

a perfectly serene repose; two or three long, but gentle breaths were drawn; and that great soul had fled, to seek a nobler scope for its aspirations in the world within the veil, for which it had often yearned, where there is rest for the weary, and where 'the spirits of the just are made perfect'.[10]

The Prince was dead, and within an hour 'the solemn tones of the great bell of St Paul's – a bell of evil omen – told all citizens how irreparable has been the loss of their beloved Queen, how great the loss to the country.'[11] Nevertheless, communications at that time were not what they are today and, outside London, many churches were still praying for the Prince's speedy recovery the following day.

Contrary to popular belief, based on Lytton Strachey's biography of her, the

Queen did not shriek or sob or rend her garments. Some time after her husband's last breath had been drawn, she was helped from the room and sat in an anteroom perfectly calm, while her children and many members of her household came to offer their condolences. 'You will not desert me? You will all help me?'[12] was her pathetic plea. Disraeli relates:

> It seems that the departed Prince had lectured the Queen severely about giving way so completely on the death of her mother, and told her to remember that the blow was dealt by the hand of the Allwise. She remembers this now, and keeps saying 'Now you see I am calm; I am profiting by his advice, I am doing what he wished.'[13]

But she was completely crushed and unable to visualize life without Albert. To her uncle Leopold, King of the Belgians, she wrote,

> The poor fatherless baby of eight months is now the utterly broken-hearted and crushed widow of forty-two! the world is gone for me! If I *must live* on (and I will do nothing to make me worse than I am), it is henceforth for our poor fatherless children – for my unhappy country, which has lost *all* in losing him – and in *only* doing what I know and *feel* he would wish, for he *is* near me – his spirit will guide and inspire me! But oh! to be cut off in the prime of life – to see our pure, happy, quiet, domestic life, which *alone* enabled me to bear my *much* disliked position, CUT OFF at forty-two – when I *had* hoped with such instinctive certainty that God never *would* part us, and would let us grow old together (though *he* always talked of the shortness of life) – is *too awful*, too cruel![14]

Unable to bear the preparations for the funeral at Windsor, she soon fled with Alice ('Good Alice has been and is wonderful')[15] to Osborne where she was joined by dear Uncle Leopold, who, not well enough to attend the funeral, did his best to comfort her.

By 1861 post-mortems and embalming of members of the royal family had been abandoned (or if post-mortems were carried out, their findings became strictly confidential and have remained so to this day) so that it is difficult for modern medical opinion to comment on the causes of Prince Albert's death. Typhoid remains the official cause of death, but there is reason to doubt it. Daphne Bennett, in an appendix to her book, *King Without a Crown*, makes, with medical assistance, the following observations:

[166]

The diagnosis of typhoid does not fit all the facts. There is evidence that Albert had been in declining health for some time. There is general evidence from those who knew him that his health was being undermined (supposedly from overwork) and specific evidence that he appeared thin and may have had swelling of the abdomen (and possibly the ankles) before his last illness. This suggests that he may have been suffering from a chronic wasting disease before the final episode. The final acute phase does not sound like a characteristic attack of typhoid. There is no clear report of high fever; nor of the prostration which is usual; nor of delirium, which is common. Albert was moving about, although weak, almost to the end [indeed he was even able, when his bed was to be changed, to get out of bed unaided on the very evening of his death]. There is no evidence of the source of infection, nor was there an epidemic of typhoid at the time – it is necessary to exercise great caution before questioning the diagnosis of the physicians who were present. But diagnosis was less exact in 1861 than it is today, and the Royal physicians were under considerable pressure to give a precise cause of death. The surviving evidence gives grounds for thinking that they were mistaken in diagnosing typhoid, and for believing that Albert's final illness may have been a terminal episode following a more chronic but ultimately fatal disease such as cancer, or hepatic or renal failure.[16]

As can be imagined, eulogies flowed from newspapers and pulpits like a stream of treacle, though the clergy tended to pass quickly on from the Prince's perfections to the salutary Victorian lessons to be learned from his death, and even the *Observer* dwelt on this aspect of his death:

Prince Albert is dead! It was only yesterday that he was, as it were, full of 'lusty life', today he lies in 'cold obstruction'. Alas for the Queen! who has lost the partner of her life – the first and dearest object of her affections. Alas for pomp and vanity! that this erstwhile mighty prince should now be insensible to praise or blame, food for the worm.[17]

However, by the next day they had pulled themselves together and a much more sensible and balanced obituary appeared.

In the Prince, notwithstanding his German education, we have had as true an Englishman as the most patriotic native of these islands. He has had the sagacity to see and feel that the interests of his family and his dynasty had claims upon him superior to others, and at no period has our foreign policy been less subject to the imputation of subservience to foreign interests and relations than during the last twenty years.[18]

And in the same paper, Princess Alice received well earned recognition. Following a description of the deathbed, they go on to say:

Of the devotion and strength of mind shown by the Princess Alice all through these trying scenes, it is impossible to speak too highly. Her Royal Highness has, indeed, felt that it was her place to be a comfort and support to her mother in this affliction, and to her dutiful care we may perhaps owe it that the Queen has borne her loss with exemplary resignation, and a composure which under so sudden and so terrible a bereavement could not have been anticipated.[19]

Even *Punch* produced its eulogy, set in the fashionable mould of chivalry:

How should the Princes die?
　　With red spur deep in maddening charger's flank,
　　Leading the rush that cleaves the foeman's rank,
And shouting some time-famous battle cry?

Ending a pleasure day,
　　Joy's painted goblet fully drained, and out,
　　While wearied vassals coldly stand about,
And con new homage, which they long to pay?

So have the Princes died.
　　Nobler and happier for the fate that falls,
　　On him who mid yon aged castle walls,
Hears, as he goes, the plash of Thames's tide.

Gallant, high natured, brave,
　　O, had his lot been cast in warrior days,
　　No nobler knight had won the minstrel's praise
Than him for for whom the half-reared banners wave.

After six more verses in the same vein, they summed up, touchingly:

When with a kind relief,
   Those eyes rain tears, O might this thought employ!
   Him whom she loved we loved. We shared her joy,
And will not be denied to share her grief.[20]

Queen Victoria may have behaved with the composure that Albert had taught her, but she was unable to carry out his wishes all the way. He had said, at the time of the Duchess of Kent's funeral, that he would like a similarly simple, private family funeral and this, as far as possible for a much more public figure, was arranged. No tickets were issued and only close personal friends and relations and those who had worked closely and intimately with the Prince were invited. Looking at the century since the death of George II, it is possible to see that as the lives of the royal family became simpler and more family orientated, so a tradition of more private funerals was emerging.

Albert had also had a horror of black hangings, but here the Queen ignored his wishes and so many miles of black cloth were hung in Windsor Castle that all available stocks were used up and more had hastily to be dyed. He had also said that he did not wish so much as a single bust of himself to be made, and yet we all know how Victoria adorned towns and public buildings throughout the land with statues, culminating in the massive Albert Memorial in Kensington Gardens.

The deepest possible Court mourning was announced, everything of the most unshiny, and lavishly trimmed with crape, and the Earl Marshal proclaimed that 'it [was] expected that all persons do forthwith put themselves into decent mourning.'[21]

The funeral was quickly arranged in just over a week for Monday, 23 December at noon. This gave very little time for foreign relations like Albert's brother, the Duke of Saxe Coburg, and son-in-law, the Crown Prince of Prussia, to travel from Germany to the Isle of Wight to offer their condolences to the Queen at Osborne, and thence to Windsor. Other foreign royals such as the three Princes of Belgium, Princess Alice's suitor, Prince Louis of Hesse, the Princes of Saxe Weimar and Leiningen, and Queen Victoria's godson, Maharajah Duleep Singh, gathered in London and came down to Windsor by special train on the morning of 23 December. The night before, the body of Prince Albert lay in the Audience Chamber at the Castle and a select press were admitted, but there was no lying-in-state. The *Daily Telegraph*, in commending the strict privacy of the funeral, commented that 'no amount of backstairs influence . . . would have been successful in gaining admission.'[22] Apart from the Queen's and the Prince's households, British and foreign royals and representatives of absent members, all of whom were to form part of the procession, only a number of past courtiers and a very few notables such as the Duke of Buccleuch and the Archbishop of Canterbury were invited, together with a handful of private persons with some close connection with His Royal Highness. No Military Knights, no Yeomen of the Guard and no women were invited, though some of the Queen's ladies viewed the ceremony from the black-hung royal closet overlooking the altar. The only touch of state ceremonial was the escort of the Life Guards which, on that bleak and cheerless morning, accompanied the horse-drawn cortège from the Castle to the Chapel, and also the Guard of Honour of the Grenadier Guards drawn up outside the Chapel. To modern eyes, a highly ridiculous touch was the helmets and bearskins of the officers draped with crape.

A selection of respectable newspaper correspondents was invited to view the ceremony from the organ loft and the next day the *Daily Telegraph*'s man really spread himself. Beginning 'It is part of the state of princes to be buried almost by the side of their beds and to look from their palace windows into the mouths of their sepulchres . . .' and contrasting this with the enviable state of the common man who 'can be borne in peace and tranquillity to some placid cemetery where their children can come year after year and tend the little flower garden that has blossomed over their ashes . . .', he went on,

> but they of royal lineage . . . must be buried in purple and crimson . . . the splendid but ghastly toilet of the grave . . . Not for him the quiet country churchyard – the verdant 'God's acre' where the lambs browse and the wild flowers bloom – the Prince must pass but a few paces from the Chamber of Death to the House of Silence.

He welcomed, however, the relative privacy and lack of lying-in-state where people were often 'crushed to death' and there were accidents from blazing torches and horses' hoofs. This 'was from its commencement, a sumptuous and majestic ceremony . . . entirely devoid of unnecessary display.'[23]

During the long wait in the cold chapel the reporter gave his readers a vivid description of the scene around him:

> Now and then some official in deep mourning, with fluttering scarf and drooping hatband would hurry towards the choir or hold a whispered conference . . . Then the locomotive capacity of the bier would be tested and grave-looking undertakers' assistants put their shoulders to the cumbrous chariot and roll it backwards and forward a few steps. The silence was

The funeral procession of The Prince Consort arriving at St George's Chapel.

something awful . . . Then sounds, trifling in themselves, would come and break the monotony of immobility. The pace of the policeman outside crunching the gravel of the path . . . the sharp reaping noise of the brooms with which the vergers were sweeping the last vestiges of the workmen's litter from the carpeting . . . a subdued sound of whispering and rustling . . . one of the minor chapels had been converted . . . into an undertaker's workshop. And there were the busy bees of Death . . . – plump men in raven black, rosy girls in brand new sables – stitching and tacking and folding scarves, and tying bands and sewing on rosettes, until the very last moment . . . cheerful and nimble and business-like . . . ever ready to make Death elegant, and dress the grave up with millinery.

After a description of the black drapery everywhere, the commentary continues, 'The desks of the canons and vicars choral are laid with programmes of the ceremonial, which, in tiny patches somewhat relieve the mass of shadow.' And in contrast, 'Higher still hung, in a glittering file, blazing with heraldic devices and silver and gold, the banners of the [Garter] Knights.'

At about 11.15 the small congregation began to arrive in their stalls and all the while the bells of St George's and of the other churches of Windsor were ringing single and double knells and the artillery were firing minute guns in the Long Walk.

Then, as 12 o'clock struck, 'the deepest and most awful silence prevailed. A sort of shivering presentiment chilled every heart that the Hearse was at the door, and that It was coming . . .' The black hangings over the south door were gathered into festoons and 'the body of the Prince Consort was brought in to be buried in peace.' Silently the procession fell in and as it moved sadly on, all eyes were on the chief mourner,

> so close to the coffin of his father that he could touch it; that slight fair haired young man, with his blue Garter ribbon just peeping from beneath his close buttoned mourning garment [no long-trained cloak this time, for they were a thing of the past] was the Hope of England, the Heir of immeasurable power, the present inheritor of unutterable woe.
>
> The Prince of Wales bore up bravely, but he was obviously suffering profound anguish . . . his whole bearing marvellously expressive of dignified resignation, he disdained to hide his face with a handkerchief . . . not a sob escaped him; but his closely-drawn lips and from time to time a convulsive twitching of the shoulders showed how much he was enduring.

At his side was eleven year old Prince Arthur 'in a black dress of Highland fashion . . . and the poor little boy sobbed and wept as though his heart would break. It is good for little children to weep thus,'[24] commented the reporter. And he was not the only one in tears; Albert's German *jägers* in their green and gold uniforms, wept bitterly 'for their kind master'.

The service – the full choral burial service of the Church of England – was beautiful but simple. The *Daily Telegraph* could not resist a dig at the Roman Catholics when he described how 'the severe, majestic, magnificent simplicity supplied the place of fuming incense, of embroidered copes and jewelled mitres.'[25] 'I am the Resurrection and the Life' and 'I know that my Redeemer Liveth' were followed by the thirty-ninth Psalm to Beethoven's Funeral Music. Then, after a reading from I Corinthians XV, came three German chorales: 'I shall not in the grave remain, Since Thou Death's bonds hast severed' and Martin Luther's 'Great God, what do I see and hear' and 'Ein feste Burg is unser Gott' were

The coffin of The Prince Consort entering the Chapel, the bearers walking under the stiffened pall which was normally held out by the pall bearers.

interspersed between the prayers.

> The lowering of the coffin into the vault ... was performed with far greater celerity than on the occasion of the funeral of the Duchess of Kent, when fifteen to twenty minutes were occupied in its descent. In the present instance, either the machinery was in better gear or the conductors of the ceremony were mercifully desirous to spare the feelings of the Prince's children in the agony of a protracted disappearance of the receptacle of his remains.[26]

While this went on, Garter King of Arms, in ordinary black clothes rather than heraldic dress, read the Prince's style and titles and then the coffin was placed for safe-keeping in the tunnel to the royal vault from where it was later moved to the mausoleum which Queen Victoria had already ordered to be built in the gardens of Frogmore, close to that of her mother, and where she would one day join him. At the same time she commanded that the old Wolsey Chapel at the east end of St George's should be renamed the Albert Memorial Chapel and should house a handsome monument with a recumbent effigy by Triqueti.

Queen Victoria never really recovered from Albert's death; for years the Widow of Windsor shut herself away and earned the disapproval of her subjects, who, though she worked assiduously on her boxes and gradually returned to seeing statesmen and diplomats, accused her of neglecting her royal duties largely because they never saw her. She wore exclusively black till the day she died, setting a standard of mourning which was adopted by large numbers of her subjects. Young Marie Adeane, joining the household in 1887 as a maid-of-honour, found that

> The Court had never gone out of mourning since the death of the Prince Consort. The Ladies-in-Waiting always wore black but the Maids-of-Honour with regard to their youth, were permitted white, grey, mauve and purple, except when one of the numerous Court Mournings occurred, when all the Ladies wore unrelieved black with jet jewelry.[27]

Victoria encouraged a cult of widowhood and surrounded herself with widowed ladies. And, up to five years after the Prince's death, every letter, memorandum and dispatch that left any of the Queen's residences was still edged with black.

The Queen developed a passionate interest in funerals; every time she was represented at one, the representative was obliged to write the fullest of descriptions to Her Majesty. On one occasion her Private Secretary, Sir Henry Ponsonby, was required to write a memorandum requesting her Chargé d'Affaires in Dresden 'to take a less humorous view of royal funerals'.[28] She had never attended a funeral herself but after a time she became unable to resist the temptation and by the 1880s it seemed quite normal for the Queen and the other royal ladies to attend family funerals at Windsor. The family was a large and widening one, with the Princes and Princesses gradually marrying and the next generation coming along, so that though the Prince Consort's is often thought of as the definitive Victorian funeral, and indeed there was never another quite like it, there were quite a number of royal funerals in the forty remaining years of Victoria's reign and, going through them, a gradual change is noticeable, bringing them up to very much what we would expect to see at a royal funeral today.

Opposite: The interior of the Royal Mausoleum, Frogmore. Watercolour by H W Brewer.

For almost ten years all went well with the family, and then in 1871 the Prince and Princess of Wales lost their third son prematurely born and hastily christened Alexander John Charles Albert only just before his death at twenty-four hours. The Wales family had by now made their permanent home at Sandringham in Norfolk, and it was in Sandringham Church, with the Queen's permission and at the wish of the parents, that the infant Prince was buried some days later. The Princess of Wales, grieving bitterly and blaming herself for the premature birth, watched from her bedroom window as the Prince, holding by the hand seven-year-old Prince Albert Victor and six-year-old Prince George, who wore little grey kilts, crape scarves and black gloves, followed the tiny coffin through the grounds to the village church. There after a completely private service, at which the presence of the Dean of Windsor was the only thing which marked it as different from any other village funeral, it was interred in the churchyard and Princess, later Queen, Alexandra tended the tiny grave for the rest of her life.

During the 1870s the funerals of three exiled foreign royals took place in England. These are mentioned only as examples of the diplomatic problems they posed for Queen Victoria. In 1873 the exiled Emperor Napoleon III of France died at his rented house, Camden Place, Chislehurst. Britain was by then on good terms with the French Republic and, though Queen Victoria was fond of the family, and particularly of the Empress Eugénie, it would have been impolitic for the ex-Emperor's obsequies to be too officially recognized here. His lying-in-state in a *chapelle ardente* set up in the house was the focus of large numbers of the French community in this country, and some of the local population but no official from the Court or government attended it. There was a brisk trade in 'immortelles', small china wreaths bearing the name of the deceased which in France took the place of the variety of mementoes – mugs, pins, pincushions etc. – customarily sold in England at the death of an important personage. The funeral in the tiny St Mary's Roman Catholic chapel in the grounds of Camden Place was not attended by any of the British royal family and the Lord Chamberlain's Office was not involved, though the Lord Chamberlain himself, Lord Sidney, attended in his private capacity as neighbour and friend.

Six years later, Napoleon's son, the Prince Imperial, followed him to the vault in that little chapel in Kent. The young prince was an officer in the British Army and was killed in Africa in the Zulu wars. This time the funeral was semi-military and was granted much more recognition by the royal family, though still unofficially. Lord Sidney still attended privately and his department was not involved at all, but the pall bearers were members of the British royal family along with the Crown Prince of Sweden, acknowledging the Napoleonic French origins of the Swedish royal family. The coffin was borne by officers of the Royal Artillery, the Prince's regiment. Even the Queen, though she did not attend the service, travelled to Chislehurst and sat with the Empress Eugénie during the funeral of her son.

One more funeral of an exiled monarch took place in England during that period, that of the ex-King George of Hanover, but this time it was a different proposition as George was also the Duke of Cumberland, grandson of George III and first cousin of Queen Victoria. Thus he was a member of the British royal family and entitled to be buried in the family vault at Windsor. He had lost his throne in the Prussian takeover of Germany, died in Paris in 1878 and was refused the right of burial in Germany by the new German government. After a 'military state funeral' at a Protestant chapel in Paris, at which the chief mourners were his son, now known as HRH The Duke of Cumberland, and the Prince of Wales, the body was brought to England by a steamer of the Royal Navy and conveyed to Windsor Castle for burial in George III's vault in St George's Chapel. Overnight the coffin lay in the chapel and the Queen and Princess Beatrice laid flowers upon it. The service at which *The Times* approved an 'almost entire absence of pomp of state, but ... all the substance of quiet magnificence',[29] was, as to music and ceremonial, very much modelled on that of Prince Albert, though on a smaller scale, but there was one major difference – the presence of ladies. All the ladies of the royal family were in the Garter Stalls, with their ladies-in-waiting below them, and the Queen herself attended the ceremony, the first time she had ever done so, though she sat, accompanied by her youngest daughter, Princess Beatrice, half hidden in the Royal Closet. And at the end of the service, while the organ played the Dead March in Saul, instead of retiring, as the Royal Family always did at this point, the Queen and all the Princesses descended into the vault to take a last look at the coffin. The considerable expenses of the funeral were covered by a Parliamentary grant for the family of George III.

All this was seen, as it was probably meant to be seen, as an act of sympathy and support to the ousted Hanoverians and was not appreciated by the new Imperial Germans. Indeed, the Queen found herself in a cleft stick over the matter of the wording of the depositum plate for her cousin's coffin: 'ex-King of Hanover' offended the Hanoverians and 'King of Hanover' offended the Germans. In the end the Queen's feeling for her cousin won and the plate was worded 'King of Hanover and Duke of Cumberland'. Apart from Hanover, Queen Victoria was continually faced with such problems over Germany at this time. While her eldest daughter was Crown Princess of the new German Empire, two other daughters were married to the princes of states swallowed up by the Prussians and all were furiously loyal to their several causes.

[177]

In 1884 there died, at Cannes in the South of France, Queen Victoria's youngest son, Prince Leopold, Duke of Albany. This was a heavy blow to her, not that Leopold was her favourite son, but because, growing up delicate and studious and unable to pursue a more active career, he had come in his early twenties to assume in some very small part the role of his father. A number of people recognized a likeness to the Prince Consort in his brilliant public speaking and extensive committee work; both Gladstone and Disraeli leant upon him for advice and influence with the Queen and the Queen herself made him her personal assistant.

Prince Leopold had been born with haemophilia, the first of a number of Queen Victoria's descendants to suffer from this crippling and tragic disease. As a result, he had suffered several serious illnesses but the word haemophilia seems never to have been mentioned. Certainly its hereditary implications seem not to have been recognized in the royal family and in 1882 he married Princess Helen of Waldeck-Pyrmont. The marriage resulted in the birth of Princess Alice, later Countess Athlone, the last of Queen Victoria's grandchildren to die – in 1981 at the age of ninety-seven, and their son was on the way when Prince Leopold went off with his private secretary and a doctor to winter in the South of France.

On 27 March 1884, in excellent health and spirits, he dashed up the stairs two at a time at the Cercle Nautique, slipped and knocked his right knee. The slight injury was immediately taken seriously; the Duke was rushed back to his villa and to bed, and the leg immobilized with splints to minimize the danger of internal bleeding. However, though the doctor stayed at hand, no real danger was anticipated. The Prince read the papers and chatted gaily, ate a hearty tea and supper and then read some more before settling down for the night.

At 2.30 the next morning, his doctor, who was in the adjoining room, was woken by the sound of heavy breathing, rushed in to his patient and found him in a fit. Six minutes later he was dead of an 'effusion of blood on the brain, inducing an epileptic convulsion'.[30]

Queen Victoria was 'thoroughly prostrated with grief' when the news was broken to her, but at once sent Princess Beatrice over to Claremont to break the news to the young Duchess of Albany who was 'in a very delicate state of health'.[31] The Prince of Wales was at the races at Aintree when he was informed. He immediately left the course and the news was made public, the wildest of rumours going about 'that the Duke's death was caused by a shock upon receiving the news of the failure of his brother's horse, The Scot . . .'[32] The Empress Eugénie was able to return the Queen's kindness to her at the death of her son, five years earlier, by travelling at once to Windsor and doing what she could to comfort her.

A member of the royal family dying abroad is always a complicated matter even today. Apart from straightforward questions of transport, there are possible diplomatic problems and the customs of the host nation to be considered. At once two equerries were dispatched to Cannes to handle the affair at that end and after a French semi-military procession from the villa to Cannes station, with soldiers carrying rifles like shot guns under their arms, the body of the Prince was brought by special train via Paris to Cherbourg, where it was joined by the Prince of Wales. There it was met by HM Yacht Osborne, carried over to Portsmouth and thence to Windsor by train. At Windsor station the coffin was received by Queen Victoria herself who then drove with other royal ladies in the procession of closed carriages to St George's Chapel. There, after a short service in the Albert Memorial Chapel, it was left until the next day. The Prince of Wales and other men of the royal family, followed the coffin on foot. And here a new development can be seen which was soon to become standard practice in the obsequies of royal men and sovereigns: the coffin was borne, not by Mr Banting's men, but by soldiers of the Seaforth Highlanders, of which the Duke was Colonel-in-Chief, and instead of a hearse, the coffin was carried to the Castle on a gun carriage of the Royal Horse Artillery and draped with the Union Flag.

In spite of never having been a soldier, the Duke of Albany's position with the Seaforths was to make his funeral a military one but, whereas the many former royal military funerals had all been very much in the hands of the undertaker and his art – plumed horses, plumed hearse, stiffened pall hanging over the heads and shoulders of the undertaker's men, crape everywhere – this and subsequent royal military funerals, though no less grand, were to follow precisely the lines of an ordinary military funeral.

This, and the fact that so many royal funerals were now private, illustrates the gradually narrowing gulf between the royal family and ordinary aristocratic and upper-class society. By this time they stayed in other people's houses, Queen Victoria even stayed in hotels abroad, and they were beginning to marry commoners. Their funerals, therefore, followed the general trend.

Prince Leopold's funeral, on 5 April, was necessarily small as there was repair work in progress in the nave of the Chapel. Nevertheless, Queen Victoria was present, this time openly, sitting with Princess Beatrice in seats on the north side of the altar steps; the young widow was not well enough to attend.

Once again, the coffin, under its Union Jack, was borne by men of the Seaforth Highlanders and the chief mourner, the Prince of Wales, and his two supporters, the Crown Prince of Germany and the Grand Duke of Hesse, brother-in-law of the deceased, wore uniform with black armbands, as did many of the congregation. The draping of caps, helmets and tunics with crape was dropped, while the Queen and other ladies wore bonnets with elbow length veils. Simplification was in.

The service too was more modern with the congregation joining in the singing of the hymns 'O God our help in Ages Past', and 'Lead kindly Light', and as the coffin was lowered into the vault, a piper of the Seaforth Highlanders played the lament 'Lochaber no more' as the last of the minute guns sounded from the Long Walk.

Queen Victoria had first ordered that her son should be buried in Prince Albert's Mausoleum at Frogmore, but when she learned that Prince Leopold had, at some stage, expressly wished to be buried in the Royal Vault at St George's, she gave in and so he was buried in the vault which already held so many of his forebears.

As funerals became more private, so memorial services began to gain in importance. When the Duchess of Cambridge died in 1889, her funeral at Kew Church was very small and private, just for family, her own household and friends. The only thing that distinguished it from the funeral of any elderly local lady was the presence of the Lord Chamberlain, walking before the coffin as he had done at every royal funeral since his office was instituted and as he continues to do to this day, however private the funeral. But a few days previously, there had been a memorial service in the Chapel Royal at St James's Palace which was attended by diplomats, members of Parliament and officials of the various organizations with which the Duchess had connections, as well as several members of the royal family.

The next important death in the royal family was that of Prince Albert Victor, Duke of Clarence and eldest son of the Prince of Wales, in 1892. And because he was heir presumptive to the throne, his death had dynastic consequences. Neither Prince Eddy's character nor his intellect can be said to have been desirable in an heir to the throne. Scandal followed scandal throughout his youth and it was whispered that his 'wild oats' included not only tarts but male prostitutes and male brothels, and he seemed totally incapable of acting with discretion or of seeing the pain he was causing his family nor the damage to the royal image. Since the Prince Consort, princes were no longer expected to have mistresses publicly and of right. His father only just got away with it, but at least his affairs all involved the opposite sex. Everyone was convinced the cure for Eddy was marriage and there was much relief all round when, after an abortive engagement to the politically highly unsuitable Princess Hélène d'Orleans, daughter of the Bourbon pretender to the French throne, the Duke of Clarence became engaged to Princess May of Teck. May, at that time twenty-four, was the daughter of the impoverished and only semi-royal Duke of Teck (his parents were morganatially married) and the English Princess Mary-Adelaide of Cambridge. She had been born and brought up in

Funeral of Leopold, Duke of Albany, Queen Victoria's youngest son, 1884. This was the first occasion on which the Queen appeared openly at a funeral.

England and was a handsome young woman of strong personality and pride which had helped her through a difficult youth rather on the fringes of the royal family. It is hard to believe that she could have liked the idea of marriage with Eddy, but it would give position to her family and she would be able to help them financially. If anyone could have 'cured' Eddy it was probably May, but the thought of Clarence succeeding his father to the throne in 1910 leads one to wonder whether, by now, the British throne might not have gone the way of so many European thrones. At any rate, Princess May was saved the horror of marriage to Prince Eddy by his death from pneumonia at Sandringham on 14 January 1892, six weeks before the wedding was to have been solemnized.

First, the coffin, made on the estate, lay in Sandringham Church. Then, in the small hours of the morning of the funeral fixed for 20 January, the Sandringham tenantry turned out and followed as it was drawn on a gun-carriage of the Royal Horse Artillery to Wolferton station, where a guard of honour of the Norfolk Militia was drawn up, and thence by train to Windsor. Here it was the 10th

Hussars, with whom the Prince had served, who had the honour of providing the bearer party.

The funeral at St George's was a bigger one, in keeping with the Duke's position so close to the throne, but otherwise it followed very much the pattern set at the Duke of Albany's funeral. The Queen wanted to attend but was dissuaded in view of the time of year and attended a memorial service at Osborne at the same hour. Outside ladies were not invited to the funeral but the Princess of Wales and her daughters and several other royal ladies were present and the bereaved fiancée and her mother sat in the privacy of the Royal Closet. Among the men there was a larger than ever number of British and foreign royals due not only to the widening family connections, but to the ever improving travel facility. It was now easily possible for people to make their arrangements and travel from all parts of Germany, Scandinavia and even Russia within a week.

The service, conducted by the Bishop of Rochester, contained much new music including the anthem, 'Brother thou has gone before us' to music by Sullivan from 'The Martyr of Antioch,' and then the remains were removed to the Albert Memorial Chapel where they were later interred. Memorial services were held in the Chapel Royal, St James's, in St Paul's Cathedral and in many parts of the Empire.

The magazine, *The Gentlewoman*, regularly published a gossip column entitled 'Overheard by the Little Bird'. A few days after the funeral of Prince Eddy there appeared such a column from which the following is a selection:

At Sandringham – That the Royal Family are naturally hurt at the indelicacy of some of the papers in giving imaginary details of the late Duke's last moments.
In Several Places – That to talk of marrying Prince George to the sweet lady who is so broken-hearted is, at such a moment, positively indecent.
In a Boudoir – That on the only occasion that the dead Duke spoke to 'The Little Bird' she thought him the gentlest and kindest of nature's gentlemen.
In Clubland – Poor Prince Eddie was a capital shot ...
In Romany Circles – That two gypsies told the lamented Duke of Clarence that his marriage would mean his death.[33]

Prince Eddy's grief-stricken mother, the Princess of Wales, shut herself up at Sandringham for some months and would be found sitting all alone in her son's bedroom. Years later a visitor to Sandringham was shown over the house by Queen Alexandra.

She took me to the little room where my poor cousin Eddy had died nearly four years before. The room was never used, and everything had practically remained untouched since his death. His bed was in the same place, and on it were some faded flowers. My aunt looked at the bed with an expression of deep grief and whispered, 'Here he died!' She placed some fresh flowers on the pillow and in silence we left the room.[34]

This keeping of everything just as it was in the lifetime of the loved one, like Queen Victoria and the Prince Consort, was an acceptable Victorian way of demonstrating grief, though it seems morbid today, and who is to say that it did not help them to bear the grief. 'Motherdear', as she was always known in the family, adored her children, especially her sons, and the loss of one of them was a kind of death to her. But what of Princess May? She did the sensible thing and married Prince George, with whom she was much better off, and became Britain's much-loved Queen Mary, surviving into the reign of the present Queen.

In 1885 Princess Beatrice, youngest daughter, companion and confidential secretary of Queen Victoria, had married Prince Henry of Battenberg. The Queen could not bear the thought of losing Beatrice and only gave her consent to the marriage on condition that the young couple should make their home with her. It must often have been hard for Prince Henry, or Liko, as he was affectionately known in the family, but he was a cheerful soul and entered the perambulatory life of Windsor, Osborne, Balmoral and London with a good grace. Four children were born to them and it must have been a joy to the Queen's household to have a young family in their midst after the years of unrelieved gloom.

In 1895 trouble brewed up in Ashanti, West Africa. It was decided to send a volunteer force out from England and Prince Henry asked the Queen's permission to join it. With memories of the Prince Imperial dying in Zululand, Queen Victoria tried to refuse, especially as fever-ridden West Africa was well known as 'the white man's grave'. However, with his wife's support, Liko insisted, hoping thereby to prove his devotion to his adopted country, and at last the Queen gave in.

Alas, how right she had been in her fears. Scarcely had the expeditionary force started its march towards Kumasi than the Prince went down with malaria, was carried back to the coast and re-embarked for England. His campaign for all his noble intentions, had been a short and not very glorious one. All the same, no one was seriously alarmed for his health and, after much to-ing and fro-ing of telegrams, it was decided the Princess Beatrice should join him in Madeira for his convalescence. But it was not to be; a sudden turn for the worse and the Prince was dead as HMS Blonde steamed off the coast of Sierra Leone.

Poor Princess Beatrice was quite unprepared for the blow that was to befall her. She was stunned as she read the telegram, and murmuring only, 'The life has gone out of me,'[35] she fled to her room. The Queen too was shattered for 'dear bright Liko' had brightened her life too – 'A terrible blow has fallen on us all, especially on my poor darling Beatrice. Our dearly loved Liko has been taken from us ... What will become of my poor child?'[36] But, all the same, 'She will not hear of it being said that [he] ought not to have gone, and in a way she is right,'[37] confided the Queen to her Journal.

The problems of bringing a body all the way back from West African waters were very real; normally it would have been buried at sea but since it was a member of the royal family it was not to be thought of and so some improvization was called for. At last a large tank was fashioned from biscuit tins and 'the beloved remains' were brought back to Portsmouth pickled in naval rum. There the body was hastily transferred to a proper coffin and, on board the Royal Yacht Alberta, with Princess Beatrice and other members of the royal family in attendance, was brought over to Cowes. Here the Queen herself takes up the story:

> To describe this mournful day and all that took place at Portsmouth would be impossible. I will try and put down what I saw. Directly after luncheon, heard that the Alberta was in sight, and I hurried off as quickly as I could, driving down to Trinity Pier with Louise, Drino, Ena [the two elder Battenberg children] and Jane Churchill. The two younger children followed with the governess and nurse. The minute guns began their sad solemn salute, the bells in the ships tolling, and Alberta with the Royal Standard at half mast, slowly passed the Flying Squadron, gliding noiselessly up to the pier. In another minute my carriage drew up and I got out. Arthur [Duke of Connaught] was there to meet me, and I was rolled across the gangway, and then walked to where, on deck, between the funnels and the saloon, covered with the Union Jack and flowers, the beloved remains were resting, guarded by the two brothers and nephew, and sweet Beatrice entirely veiled in black standing at the head of the coffin.
>
> I can hardly write about it, the scene was so terribly affecting and pathetic, on a beautiful evening all lit up by a glorious setting sun. I was completely ovecome when I placed my wreath ...[38]

The next day, at a simple service in Whippingham Church, close to Osborne House where ten years before he and Beatrice had been married, poor Liko was buried in what was to be known as the Battenberg Memorial Chapel. The coffin was carried by men of the Scots Guards and the Queen herself walked in the procession. Some time later Beatrice's sister, Princess Louise, a very competent sculptress, made a beautiful monument to Prince Henry which may still be seen in Whippingham Church, and here Princess Beatrice joined him eventually.

It was not the first time that the four little Battenbergs were plunged into black. There had been several periods of family mourning during their lives, some of them for relations of the wider foreign family. Queen Victoria always insisted on the children going into black and that even the tiniest baby should be put into black ribbons for the full period.

The last royal death of the nineteenth century was that of Princess Mary Adelaide, Duchess of Teck, née Cambridge and mother of Princess May, Duchess of York. She was a large, expansive, generous lady whose purse unfortunately was far from matching her figure or her nature. 'Fat Mary' was a much loved figure of the London scene for she was tireless in her charity work to the end, her house, White Lodge at Richmond, perpetually overflowing with bundles of old clothes for distribution to the poor. Although a granddaughter of George III, Princess Mary Adelaide was a minor member of the royal family; nevertheless, when she died following a minor operation at the age of only sixty in the autumn of 1897, soon after the triumphant family reunion of Queen Victoria's Diamond Jubilee, she was mourned with tears throughout the country. Withered bunches of wild flowers arrived at White Lodge from as far afield as Scotland and Wales, as did a wreath simply inscribed 'From a Flower Girl of Plymouth'. Even the Queen, though she was often irritated by her fecklessness, was sad. She wrote in her Journal: 'It seems like a horrible dream. She was so warm-hearted and kind, and ever ready to help in doing good, so universally popular and courageous and full of spirit, so loyal, and such a charming companion, talking so well and such a good mimic.'[39] Evidently Queen Victoria was sometimes amused!

The Cambridge vault at Kew would have been the logical place for the Duchess to be buried but in spite of having been married there she had an aversion to that church. The Queen was asked if she might be buried in St George's Chapel: 'I answered, of course, in the affirmative, and am glad to think it will be so.'[40] And so, on the night of 2 November,

the cortège wended its way across the Park [on its way from Richmond to Windsor by horse-drawn hearse]. In front walked the guides carrying lanterns to show the road ... The wind soughed drearily amongst the trees, while the measured tramp of the horses' feet and the sound of the wheels alone broke the silence of the night. Now and then the moon struggled to pierce the heavy clouds – but soon all was darkness again, and the little band of mourners closed up their ranks as if the utter loneliness was too much for them to bear.[41]

The next day, while a simple but dignified burial service was taking place in St George's Chapel, memorial services were held at Westminster Abbey, at St Paul's Cathedral and at churches throughout the country. And the floral tributes at Windsor completely filled the Albert Memorial Chapel and drew large crowds for several days afterwards.

So the nineteenth century drew to a close and still the old Queen carried on. She was now eighty and surrounded by three generations of her family. Deafer and blinder and more rheumaticky but with her spirit undaunted, as the new century opened it was 'business as usual' at Windsor, or Osborne, or Balmoral – wherever the Queen happened to be. She now ruled over a quarter of the world; very few could remember a world before her reign began and no one could conceive of a world without her.

— 8 —

Queen Victoria

13th January (1901): – Had a fair night, but was a little wakeful. Got up earlier and had some milk. Lenchen came and read some papers. Out before one, in the garden chair, Lenchen and Beatrice going with me. Rested a little, had some food, and took a short drive with Lenchen and Beatrice. Rested when I came in, and at five-thirty went down to the drawing-room, where a short service was held by Mr Clement Smith [Vicar of Whippingham] who performed it so well, and it was a great comfort to me. Rested again afterwards, then did some singing, and dictated to Lenchen.[1]

Thus Queen Victoria passed a quiet Sunday at Osborne following a very sensible routine for an almost blind eighty-one-year-old lady who nevertheless had a job to do. And how deadeningly monotonous and boring it was for the younger members of her family and household, including the devoted daughters Beatrice and Helena (Lenchen, Princess Christian). But this was to be the old Queen's last entry in the journal she had kept for almost seventy years.

On the Monday the Queen was up as usual and received Lord Roberts, the Commander-in-Chief, with news of the war in South Africa. He was her last official visitor, but he found her as shrewd and on the spot as ever. On Tuesday she tried to go out as usual in her 'garden chair' and even sat in it under cover for some time, but the weather was too bad and the attempt was abandoned. On Wednesday 16 January it became known in the household that the Queen was unwell, but she had been unwell many times in the last few years and no one was alarmed. Soon, however, they became conscious that the Queen's condition was deteriorating; her mind, always so clear and sharp, was going, a heart and lung specialist was summoned from London, and on 18 January the Prince of Wales and other members of the family were informed. For the first time also the public were informed by means of a bulletin posted at Buckingham Palace and passed to the press: 'The Queen during the past years has had a great strain upon her powers, which has rather told upon Her Majesty's nervous system. It has, therefore, been thought advisable by Her Majesty's physicians that the Queen should be kept perfectly quiet in the house, and should abstain for the present from transacting business.'[1] Little did the public guess from the careful, guarded phrases, that she would never 'transact business' again and that a mere four days would see the advent of a new reign. It was quite unthinkable. In those days before radio or television, the Queen's life was very much more private than is today's Queen's, and her day-to-day state of health was not known. Whenever she was seen she looked as she had for years, a tiny figure, shrouded in black, if a little smaller and frailer. Besides she had *always* been Queen, and, illogically, it seemed she always would be.

Meanwhile the royal family were assembling at Osborne and, typically on such occasions, the Queen took a turn for the better, so much so that the Prince of Wales decided to return to London. The Duke of Connaught (the Queen's favourite son, Prince Arthur) was in Berlin when the news of his mother's illness reached him, and he was not altogether pleased when the Kaiser insisted upon coming to England too. The family all disliked their nephew, William, and so there was general gloom at the prospect of his arrival at Osborne. However, when he did arrive with the Prince of Wales on 21 January, they all thought he behaved very well, keeping in the background, only saying that he would like to see 'Grandmamma' if at all possible, but if not, he would quite understand.

By now the Queen was worse again and clearly dying. Bishop Randall Davidson of Winchester arrived, having come over on the late Saturday night boat along with a rowdy crowd of footballers, and he and the rector of Whippingham hovered around, held short comforting services for the family and household and held themselves in readiness to go to the Queen. It was typical of the Queen's tact that, while she was still able to speak, she had commanded Mr Smith to be summoned as well as the bishop, fearing that he, who had ministered to her spiritual needs at Osborne for so long, would be hurt if he was left out.

On Monday, 21 January, the Queen once more rallied. Bishop Davidson wrote that 'During the morning she brightened up and said to Sir James Reid [her doctor] "Am I better at all?" He said "Yes" and then she eagerly answered "Then may I have Turi?" [her little Pomeranian dog]. This was sent for, and she eagerly held him on the bed for about an hour.'[3]

Then the Prince of Wales went in to see her and she held up her arms and cried,

Reading the bulletins, outside the Mansion House, on Queen Victoria's last illness.

'Bertie', with a glad smile, but it was the last word she spoke. It was only a fleeting improvement and by evening she was once more slowly and peacefully sinking. Her doctors warned that she could die at any time in the night, but on Tuesday morning she was still there.

At last the public realized that this time it was serious. The newspapers were full of the Queen's illness and the whole Empire, indeed the whole world seemed to hold its breath and wait for news. Telegrams of good wishes and anxious enquiry flooded into Osborne and gave the household some welcome work to do.

As the day went on, the family gathered in the Queen's bedroom, which would have annoyed her had she been aware of it. She hated crowded deathbed scenes, perhaps remembering Albert's. But now she was beyond knowing or caring. There were occasional flickers of life but they were fewer and further apart. The bishop and the rector took it in turns to read prayers and hymns aloud but Davidson did not think she heard. At least not until he came to the last verse of her favourite hymn, 'Lead kindly Light' –

And in the morn those angel faces smile
Which we have loved long since and lost awhile.

Then he had the distinct impression that she was listening. For her the waiting would soon be over now.

As the sun set that winter's evening, the Kaiser, knowing only that he was her grandson, knelt beside her and supported her with his good right arm while Sir James Reid held her from the other side. For two and a half hours they knelt here without moving. Beatrice, Louise and Lenchen were at the end of the bed and the Prince of Wales and the others grouped around. It grew dark and soft lamps were lit, but no one moved. Afterwards the Duke of Argyll, husband of Princess Louise, told a member of the household that 'the last moments were like a great three-decker ship sinking. She kept on rallying and then sinking.'[4] And then, at last, she rallied no more and at 6.30, 'Her Majesty The Queen breathed Her last ... surrounded by Her Children and Grandchildren.'[5]

When the news was posted at the gates of Osborne House, there was a wild and most unseemly rush down the hill to Cowes by the assembled newspaper men shouting 'Queen dead! Queen dead!, as they dashed to the Post Office to wire their papers.

It has been said, notably by Jeffery Lant, that 'Nothing, absolutely nothing was ready.'[6] But this is not entirely true. Mr Lant founds his statement almost entirely on the account of Captain, later Sir Frederick, Ponsonby who was a young equerry in the household at the time and found himself heavily involved, and indeed responsible for large sections of the funeral ceremonial. To him, no doubt, it seemed that nothing, but nothing had been planned, but in fact the Queen had planned quite a lot herself and given detailed instructions as to the funeral service, the music, readings, etc., and the fact that it was to be a military funeral. This was perhaps curious for a woman, but, with the Boer War then raging, the Queen had lately been in military mood and at one with her troops fighting so far away. She also demanded that her pall should be white – no black for the joyful occasion of her reunion with 'beloved Albert'. Nor was there to be any lying-in-state in

London, much to the disappointment of Londoners who had hoped to be able to pay their last respects to her in St Paul's. As it was, London's part in the proceedings was to be reduced to the time it takes to march in slow time from Victoria to Paddington Station, the long way round by St James's. The Queen had passed these instructions to the Prince of Wales by memoranda in 1897 and 1898 so she at least was thinking ahead, even if no one else was.

Nevertheless, the ceremonial had not been planned at all, and, at the death of the sovereign, ceremonial takes over right away, nor who was to be invited, who to take part in the various processions and even who was to do the arranging. Today it seems extraordinary that not even a skeleton plan had been laid, when the monarch was already eighty-one, but at the time it appears to have been considered 'gruesome' to even discuss such an eventuality. There had not been a death of a monarch for sixty-four years and, though there was a frantic searching through old files, in a changed world the old rules simply did not seem to apply. For one thing this was a vastly more complicated affair than the simple Windsor funerals of George IV and his brother William. It embraced three quite separate places, the Isle of Wight, London and Windsor, and involved a sea voyage. For another thing, both as regards family and the Queen's now worldwide rule, this had to be an immeasurably more international event.

The Queen was laid out in her bedroom and the bishop, who knew exactly what should be done from his angle, held several 'calm and bright little services' for the family there. He described the scene where 'lay the little Queen with fresh flowers arranged on the bed, the small Imperial Crown lying by her side, her face . . . most calm and peaceful'. He found a Communion service quite difficult to organise as 'the room was not large and the furniture was plentiful,'[7] but he managed somehow and was very moved at the sight of the new King and the German Emperor kneeling side by side to receive the sacrament.

Soon the coffin and the leaden shell arrived, and the Kaiser, who was taking it all as an entirely personal bereavement, would have lifted his grandmother in himself, but this time her sons claimed the right for themselves. Bertie and Arthur lifted her tenderly in, dressed in a white gown and her wedding veil. (She had abolished shrouds and cere cloths for the royal family early in her reign.) They were astonished at how light she was.

Part of the dining room was now turned into a *chapelle ardente* hung round with hastily assembled crimson curtains, a huge Union Jack at one end and huge silver candlesticks set round the coffin which was draped with the Queen's state robes for want of a pall. On it the King set her little diamond crown and the insignia and ribbon of the Garter. Meanwhile, in London a bevy of ladies at the Royal School of

Needlework were stitching night and day on a white satin pall embroidered with a gold cross in the middle and the royal arms in the corners. Under the coffin was the Royal Standard and under that an Indian shawl. Clearly they were using everything they had to hand.

Straight away it was realized that they must have some soldiers to stand guard and add dignity to this little makeshift chapel. The nearest available were the 60th Rifles at Parkhurst Barracks on the island, and a detachment of these was instantly summoned. But when they arrived, it was realized that they had no idea of the necessary drill. They had never been taught how to reverse arms and the drill book was no help. However, a resourceful young officer worked out how it should be done and devised a drill for relieving the guard every hour, it having been found that the sickly smell of massed flowers made the men faint if longer vigils were attempted. Unfortunately for the 60th, no sooner had they perfected their drill than the Duke of Connaught decreed that to mount guard over the sovereign's body was the exclusive prerogative of the Queen's Company, Grenadier Guards, and they were hastily summoned from London. At first they knew no better than the 60th how to carry out this exercise and simply carried on the same drill, but soon an officer who knew what to do arrived, and Fritz Ponsonby had to admit that the changing of the sentries, all in slow time, with arms reversed, became a most impressive sight. For three days the chapel was open and was visited by servants, tenants and neighbouring gentry. Until the Queen's body left Osborne it was all a very intimate family affair, but then it was to move out on to the wider international stage. This reflects the two distinct roles of the Queen – the cosy grandmother and the Great White Queen of a quarter of the world. Meanwhile frantic preparations for the funeral were under way and these got off to a difficult start with the Lord Chamberlain and the Earl Marshal quarrelling as to who should have the overall direction of the ceremonial. The Lord Chamberlain argued that his department had much more experience of such things, having handled a number of royal funerals, but the Earl Marshal insisted, and rightly, that the funeral of the monarch was his right, as well as duty, and he was not going to be done out of it. The King detailed certain members of the Household to take charge of the arrangements in the various locations, and the brisk and efficient young equerry, Fritz Ponsonby, found himself in charge of Windsor though it was impressed upon him that the service at St George's was in the hands of the Dean and the Lord Chamberlain, and he was not to interfere there.

Fritz decided to go at once to Windsor and telegraphed the mayor, the head of the police and the officer commanding the troops to summon them to a meeting. Between them they arranged that, instead of going straight from the station to the

Castle, the procession should go down the High Street and Park Street and then turn into the Castle via the Long Walk which would allow a far larger number of people to see it as it passed. They were only able to block out a very vague plan as nothing was known as to how many and who were to walk in the procession, what troops would be involved, and what the timing would be. The next day, therefore, Fritz

> rushed off to London and went at once to the Earl Marshal's office where [he] found absolute chaos. The Heralds, who claimed the right to manage the funeral under the direction of the Earl Marshal, had little precedent to work on since there had been no Sovereign's funeral for sixty-four years and being accustomed to work out coats of arms and geneaological tables at their leisure, were swept off their feet with the urgent arrangements for the funeral. There appeared to be no system and everyone was engaged in working out the little bits of detail most suited to their capacity.

Ponsonby asked for the programme of the Windsor part of the ceremonial and was told that they had not yet started on it. '"We haven't finished Osborne and London yet", cried one of them. "But", I argued, "has it not occurred to you that the funeral starts from Osborne tomorrow?" I suddenly realised that the Windsor part would be a fiasco, and I should be blamed.'[8]

Ponsonby then demanded to see the Earl Marshal himself and here, to his surprise, he found in the Duke of Norfolk a thoroughly business-like man dealing with a flood of memoranda and telegrams from the Lord Chamberlain, the Master of the Horse and half a dozen other departments and offices. He was firing off a quick succession of crisp orders and imagining that they were being carried out as quickly. One of the troubles was that as fast as he tried to plan the various processions the Lord Chamberlain's Office kept supplying him with more and more kings and princes to be accommodated in the processions. It seemed that all Europe, indeed a good part of the world, was determined to send some representative, and the protocol thereof was rapidly becoming a nightmare. The Duke suggested that Ponsonby had better consult the Commander-in-Chief as to the deployment of troops. 'So off to the War Office I went, but when I got to the Commander-in-Chief's room I was told that Lord Roberts could see no one. I, however, wrote on my card, "Funeral arrangements – urgent". I was at once ushered in . . .'[9] Here he gained Lord Roberts' permission to give what orders he thought fit to the troops at Windsor. Back to the Earl Marshal's office and Fritz called for a shorthand writer and got down to dictating a skeleton programme as

[193]

best he could, keeping everyone in categories: English royal family, foreign countries, foreign suites etc., with each category bulging a bit more as further names came in. Nerves were fraying and the heralds complained that Fritz was rude to them, to which he tartly replied, while apologizing to the Earl Marshal, that had he not come to London and tried to hurry them, there would have been no arrangements of any sort for the Windsor part of the ceremonial. After having his skeleton programme printed and rushing it round to the War Office and the Admiralty, Ponsonby returned wearily to Osborne, arriving at 2 a.m. From then on he had to trust to luck, and the officers on the spot, as he was to be in close attendance on the coffin all the way from Osborne to St George's Chapel and could do nothing further about the arrangements. Today we take for granted that we can fix everything with a few telephone calls; in 1901 it had all to be done with telegrams, which is not at all the same thing.

The next day, after a short service in the house, a bearer party of sailors of the Royal Yachts bore the Queen out of her home for the last time and Fritz Ponsonby admitted that his colleague at that end had arranged everything beautifully, with everyone knowing exactly what they had to do and where they had to go. The coffin, now draped in its white and gold embroidered pall and surmounted by the crown, orb and sceptre, and the collar and insignia of the Garter, was placed on the gun carriage with eight horses of the Royal Horse Artillery and drawn slowly away towards Cowes. Following on foot were the King, the Kaiser, the rest of the royal family and the household, with two pipers walking immediately in front of the gun carriage playing from the house to the Queen's Gate. As soon as the gun carriage had reached the carriage drive, the massed bands formed up, then moved off, playing a funeral march. On either side of the coffin marched the bearer party of the Queen's Company, Grenadier Guards, and beyond them the equerries and ADCs including Fritz Ponsonby. At the back of the procession, eight abreast, walked the servants and tenants of Osborne estate.

On arrival at Trinity Pier, the bands ceased playing, though the drums continued a muffled roll, while the coffin was unloaded and carried on board the Royal Yacht Alberta. It then struck up again and played softly as the little ship moved slowly out into the Solent. Two ladies-in-waiting accompanied the coffin, the royal family and the rest of the household travelling in the Victoria and Albert, the Osborne and the Kaiser's yacht, Hohenzollern.

The short voyage across the Solent must have been something which nobody who witnessed it ever forgot. Thirty-eight ships of the Royal Navy were formed up in double formation at Spithead – battleships, cruisers and destroyers – and in addition there were five German ships, one Portuguese, one French cruiser and

Queen Victoria's coffin, on board the Royal Yacht Alberta, crossing the Solent. The ship in the foreground is a battleship of the Imperial Japanese Navy.

one Japanese battleship. All had their national flags at half mast and their decks lined with sailors and marines. As the Alberta passed slowly between the lines of towering ships with the coffin on her deck, the guard on each one presented arms and then rested on their arms reversed while bands played the Dead Marches of Chopin and Beethoven until the procession was well past. And all accompanied by the 'sullen roar' and the drifting smoke of the minute guns fired from every ship. Added to this already unforgettable scene, a glorious winter sunset flamed and lit up the little Alberta as she emerged from time to time from the acrid clouds of smoke.

The shore on both the Gosport and Southsea sides were crowded with black-clad people who stood silently as Alberta glided out of sight into Clarence Yard, the other yachts anchoring in the harbour.

The night was passed on board, but Fritz Ponsonby's sleep, and probably that of others, was disturbed by wondering how the ceremonial of the next day would go. Fritz had no contact with Windsor and his nerves had been further frayed that evening by being ordered by the King to take charge of the arrangements for the interment at Frogmore which was to take place on Monday.

> There was I at Portsmouth on board the Osborne with nothing to refer to, no precedent to go by, and no idea who would attend this last ceremony ... I was dead tired, having been all day on the go, with very little sleep the night before. I realised that the next day all the shops would close early to enable people to see the funeral and the day after was Sunday. Up to that moment Arthur Davidson had managed everything so well that he had set a very high standard and I felt that there was every possibility of the Windsor part being a fiasco. If, in addition to this, I mismanaged the final ceremony, what little chance I had of being taken on by King Edward would evaporate.[10]

Here we see the same uncertainty that troubled the courtiers of King James I – who was going to be taken on by the new King and who would be dropped? Far into the night Ponsonby worked on his programme on the premise that only those staying at the Castle were to be included. Telegrams flew to and from the Master of the Household and the printer at Windsor who was to produce the final programme. Fritz could only hope that he had got it right.

The following morning, Saturday, 2 February, two trains set off for London. The first contained the King and all the other members of the royal family and household, the train carrying the coffin and its attendants coming later.

At Victoria Station, officials and distinguished mourners began to assemble soon after nine, although the royal trains were not expected before eleven, 'and the railway station soon became a brilliant kaleidoscope of gold and scarlet.'[11] The King of Portugal, the Crown Prince of Siam, the Grand Duke Michael who represented the Tsar of Russia, the King of the Hellenes and numberless other princes, grand dukes, archdukes and other personages with their respective suites all in glittering uniforms, gradually gathered on the arrivals platform. When the first royal train arrived, King Edward, the Kaiser and other members of the royal family took up their positions in a pavilion near the spot where the car carrying the coffin was to draw up. The Queen and other royal ladies went to stand near the closed carriages which were to draw them in the procession. All was subdued bustle which, as the hour drew near, subsided into a tense silence.

At eleven minutes to eleven a pilot engine came briskly into the station, and all knew that the Royal train was not far behind. A few minutes later there was a hush, and all eyes were drawn to to the gun carriage which, drawn by a team of eight cream coloured ponies, wearing trappings of woe about their heads, slowly skirted the pavilion and took up its position by the arrival platform at the spot where it had been arranged that the saloon containing the Royal remains should be halted.[12]

Cream coloured ponies were a welcome change from the inevitable blacks that always pulled hearses, and the 'trappings of woe about their heads' did not include the usual nodding plumes. They appear to have been black or purple ribbons plaited into the manes, and the postilions were in the usual brightly coloured royal livery. Indeed, as far as all the men were concerned, mourning seems to have been reduced to a black armband for officers, nothing for other ranks. Gone were the weepers, the crape scarves, the cloaks and trains, and gone also was the dulling of paintwork and blacking of brass on carriages. There had, however, been less change for the ladies involved, both royal and otherwise. Black from head to foot, with a great deal of crape and bombazine was the order of the day, with elbow-length veils attached to 'Mary Stuart caps' to be worn indoors and out. Princess Marie Louise, one of Queen Victoria's granddaughters, recently returned after a disastrous German marriage, wrote that, 'Strange as it may seem, I was appealed to as knowing what was de rigeur on such sad occasions.' These caps, which must have been very like the 'Paris heads' of Queen Elizabeth's day, were, she says, 'most becoming' and, when all the Princesses were gathered together, the sight was 'really rather imposing'.[13]

But to return to Victoria Station, at two minutes to eleven, all hushed conversation ceased as the royal train was seen approaching. At this point a 'mounted signaller . . . galloped out of [the] station yard with the news of the arrival . . . rode to a point at which the waving of his flag could be seen by the next; and by each of the twelve mounted signallers in turn the order for the advance was conveyed along the line of the route to the head of the procession,'[14] which was already in St James's Street. The naval and military guards of honour came to the salute as the train glided silently into the platform and was met by the Earl Marshal, the Lord Chamberlain, the Lord Steward, the Master of the Horse and the Master of Ceremonies. The coach containing the coffin was, *The Times* tells us, one belonging to the Great Western Company, whereas the rest of the rolling stock belonged to the Brighton Company. This was at the request of the King, being one in which the Queen had particularly enjoyed travelling when she travelled on the

Great Western system.

As the train drew up, the bearer party of twelve non-commissioned officers of the Foot Guards and Household Cavalry marched across the platform and bore the coffin out to the waiting gun carriage preceded by four ADCs carrying the pall on which still lay the crown, regalia and Garter. At this funeral and hereafter, the real crown and regalia were used, not tin-gilt 'fairground stuff' as in Georgian days and before. The procession then formed up for the slow march to Paddington Station through streets hung with purple and densely crowded with black-clad people, all 'most reverent and silent'.[15]

Lists of names make tedious reading, but it is necessary to give some idea of the size and range of this procession. Headed by the bands of the Household Cavalry, the first part was made up of detachments of all the regiments and corps that could possibly be mustered in London – cavalry, infantry, militia, yeomanry, county volunteers, the Colonial Corps, the Indian Army, the Veterinary Corps, the Army Pay Corps, Army chaplains, Riflemen, Highlanders, Guardsmen, gunners, and behind them, the senior service, the Royal Navy and the Royal Marines. Then, after another band came foreign military attachés, the headquarters staff of the Army, Gold Sticks, White Staves, the Earl Marshal and great officers of the late Queen's household, and her ADCs. And at last came the gun carriage flanked by the bearer party and fourteen equerries. Close behind it came the Royal Standard borne by a non-commissioned officer of the Household Cavalry and then, on horseback, rode the King, with the Kaiser on his right and the Duke of Connaught on his left. And behind them came two more Kings, of the Hellenes and Portugal and no less than thirty-eight princes. Many of these were related to Queen Victoria but they included also the Crown Prince of Siam and a Prince of Egypt. Both of these must surely have been in the country already for some other purpose as, even with the improved transport it would have been impossible to get from Siam in ten days and difficult from Egypt. They were followed by the foreign suites and a deputation from the German army which included a small party from a regiment called 'Queen of Great Britain and Ireland'. Behind them came six carriages bringing the Queen and other royal ladies, the King of the Belgians, who was not well enough to ride, the ladies of the Queen's household and that of the late Queen. The procession closed with an escort of Household Cavalry.

Slowly this vast cortège paced through the streets of London – Buckingham

Opposite: King Edward VII and Kaiser Wilhelm II riding together in Queen Victoria's funeral procession.

[198]

Palace Road, The Mall, St James's Street, Piccadilly, up through the Park to Marble Arch, Edgware Road, Praed Street and so to Paddington Station, to the deadened beat of the muffled drums and the minute guns in Hyde Park and lit by a fitful sun which succeeded the freezing rain of early morning. And all the way the streets were lined with troops, many of whom had left their barracks in the north of England and Scotland the night before and gone straight on duty.

There exists to this day a film of the procession, one of the first great events to be so recorded, with all the figures strutting jerkily along. At one point it can clearly be seen that King Edward has noticed the 'photographer' at the side of the road for he stops dead and stops the Kaiser at his side and together they pose for the cameraman who would naturally have preferred them to go clopping by with jangling bits and tossing plumes.

Having arrived at Paddington, the coffin was once more placed in the train and the mourners and their attendants embarked on three 'specials' and were carried to Windsor where Fritz Ponsonby's wildest nightmares were exceeded. The coffin was placed on the gun carriage to which were harnessed eight beautifully schooled horses of the Royal Horse Artillery. Then, having received the King's command to start the procession, Fritz stepped well out into the road, held up his hand, the drums began to roll and the head of the procession set forth to the opening bars of the Dead March in Saul.

The horses of the gun-carriage had, however, been standing still in the cold for some time, and as the lieutenant in charge never gave the command 'Walk march', the two wheelers suddenly started off before the leaders, and finding an unusually heavy load, began to kick and plunge. Away flew the traces and the gun-carriage remained still. I had contemplated all sorts of things going wrong, but such a mishap never occurred to me.

Meanwhile the front of the procession, unconscious that anything was wrong, had marched slowly on and the band had already turned the corner when I sent a non-commissioned officer to stop them. I found then that the traces were broken and everyone was trying to get the horses clear while several officers were engaged in trying to devise some makeshift, but naturally the first thing was to inform the King of what exactly had happened. I did so, and on coming away, Prince Louis of Battenberg said, 'If it is impossible to mend the traces, you can always get the naval guard of honour to drag the gun-carriage.' I went back to the horses where I found that it was contemplated getting two horses only to drag the gun-carriage with the leaders' traces. The general impression, however, seemed to be that this was a most hazardous solution of

The horses of the Royal Horse Artillery kicking over and breaking the traces attaching them to the gun carriage bearing Queen Victoria's coffin. This resulted in the Naval Guard of Honour assuming the duty of drawing it through the streets of Windsor and the birth of a Royal tradition.

the difficulty as it seemed very doubtful whether the two horses would be able to drag the gun-carriage up the steep hill into the castle with traces that were only makeshifts, and which might easily snap. Another solution was suggested, and that was that the gun-carriage should go up by the shortest way to St George's, but this was dismissed as it would have meant disappointing a crowd of several thousands.

[201]

So I determined to adopt Prince Louis's suggestion and accordingly went a second time to the King and said, 'Have I Your Majesty's permission to take out the horses and let the men of the naval guard of honour drag the gun-carriage?' The King said, 'Certainly'.[16]

And so a new royal tradition was born. In spite of a storm of protest from the Artillery which provoked the King into saying wearily, 'Right or wrong, let him [Ponsonby] manage everything; we shall never get on if there are two people giving contradictory orders,'[17] and so it was arranged. After spurning the steel cable brought by the station master, which proved to be the communication cord of the train, all he could lay his hands on, the sailors fastened together the remaining traces and at last the procession got under way. The effect was so striking that the King would have had them draw the gun-carriage on the final stage to Frogmore, and Ponsonby had difficulty persuading him that this would give unnecessary offence to the Artillery.

The procession through Windsor, smaller than the London one, had very much the appearance of a more ancient royal funeral cortège. In place of troops were all the heralds, Pursuivants and Kings-of-Arms in their tabards, interspersed with high officers of state and household before the gun-carriage and, after the cloud of foreign royals who followed the King, a large number of representatives of foreign states: ambassadors, ministers and envoys extraordinary of such places as Uruguay and Turkey, Bolivia and Bulgaria. This procession was entirely on foot and, to bring up the rear were the Gentlemen at Arms and the Yeomen of the Guard.

Fritz Ponsonby was in a fever of anxiety as to how it would go, especially on the very steep hills up to the Castle and down to St George's Chapel, but the sailors managed magnificently and created a great impression among the spectators along the route to whom this was a complete surprise. Minute guns were fired in the Long Walk and, as at the funeral of George III, the boys of Eton lined the route to the Castle.

Meanwhile, the ushers in the Chapel were having trouble; as more and more people crowded into the nave it became obvious that the Earl Marshal's representative there had forgotten to allocate seats in the choir and was still in the process of picking out the more important and moving them up there when the procession arrived at the west door and was greeted by the Archbishops of Canterbury and York as well as the Dean of Windsor with his canons and choir. The Queen and other royal ladies had gone by carriage by the direct route to St George's where they were conducted via the Wolsey Chapel to the Royal Closet and the pew adjoining. There they joined the royal children, headed by Prince Edward of York.

The service was rich in music and liturgy and beautifully sung by the choir, though, contrary to established practice by this time, there were no hymns for the congregation to join in. There were several old favourites but, among the newer music was Gounod's setting of The Lord's Prayer.

At the end of the service, instead of being lowered into the vault below the choir, the coffin was carried into the Albert Memorial Chapel where it was to rest until the interment at Frogmore on the Monday. All the foreign sovereigns, princes and representatives repaired to the Castle where they were revived with a buffet luncheon.

So far so good, but Fritz Ponsonby could not yet relax. He had Monday's ceremonial to arrange and he was quite determined that nothing should go wrong this time. A ghostly rehearsal was held by lantern light at Frogmore at 11 o'clock that night. A suitably weighted box had been provided and this was drawn on the gun-carriage to the steps of the mausoleum where two bearer parties, one from the Life Guards and one from the Foot Guards, were waiting motionless on the steps. The two bearer parties had been provided because of the great weight of the coffin. This is strange since one had managed it on the Saturday with the length of St George's as well as the steps to be negotiated, and having two parties involved a very complicated drill of changing from one bearer party to the other half way up the steps. It was lucky that they had the rehearsal as, when the sham coffin was carried into the mausoleum, it was realized that they would have to place the coffin on the tomb 'head to toe' with Prince Albert's effigy and that therefore it had somehow to be turned round during the change over on the steps. After several practices all went smoothly and Fritz thanked his lucky stars that he had been saved from another fiasco.

At 6 o'clock on the morning of Sunday and Monday rehearsals of the procession from St George's to Frogmore were held and every possible problem which might upset the horses was thought of and ironed out. The Artillery were taking no chances this time. The rest of Sunday was spent by Fritz working out who was to be admitted to the private grounds at Frogmore and sending tickets to this strictly limited list. The procession itself and attendance in the mausoleum was a family-only affair.

That night it looked as if everything had been thought of and tied up, but in the morning Fritz found that he had been over sanguine. Anyone who has ever arranged a wedding or large family gathering of any kind knows that, by some awful mischance, an important member of the family is always forgotten. Queen

Victoria's funeral was no exception. After breakfast, Fritz was sent for by the King and he found him with an enraged Duke of Fife, his son-in-law, who had somehow been completely omitted from the ceremonial for that day. The King reprimanded Fritz very severely, much to the satisfaction of Fife, but when, after the Duke had stalked huffily away, Fritz reminded him that the lists had been on his own table all Sunday and that neither he nor anyone else had noticed the omission, Edward softened, admitted to his anger being largely for Fife's benefit and congratulated Fritz on all his arrangements so far.

This last part of the funeral went without any hitch. The coffin was brought out of the chapel at 3 o'clock in the afternoon and drawn, on its gun-carriage, out of the castle and down the Long Walk to Frogmore, followed by all the old Queen's family, British and foreign, including ladies, their suites and the royal servants, the horses behaving perfectly this time. Again there was an eighty-one gun salute in the Long Walk and pipers played from the Frogmore gates to the mausoleum. There was a beautiful short service in the mausoleum and then Queen Victoria was placed in the sarcophagus at Albert's side and was left alone with her husband in the place that had been waiting for her for nearly forty years.

There was, however, a curious incident at this last part of the obsequies of Queen Victoria. Fortunately the royal family were unaware of it, but Fritz Ponsonby tells the story:

An officer in khaki came to see me [the day before] and applied for tickets for the Mausoleum. I told him that no one but the Royal Family would go to the Mausoleum, but I would give him tickets for the private grounds. He was a dignified gentlemanly-looking man with several medals. I never gave him another thought, but it appeared that . . . he stepped out of the crowd and joined the German suite in the procession. They very naturally thought he was connected with the arrangements and took no notice of him . . . Suddenly [in the Mausoleum] a voice whispered in my ear, 'Who is the old bird with a beard?' I looked round and saw the khaki officer, who was pointing to the King of the Belgians. I said 'Hush', took him by the arm, led him to the door and forcibly ejected him. . . When I got outside I espied my khaki friend and told him what I

Opposite: The last stage of Queen Victoria's funeral: the family procession from St George's Chapel to the Royal Mausoleum, Frogmore is seen crossing the Quadrangle, the coffin escorted by the bearer party from the Queen's Company, 1st Battalion, Grenadier Guards.

thought of his conduct ... I added that I wanted his name and regiment as I should report him to the Commander-in-Chief. He gave me his name and regiment, saluted and walked away ... [On returning to the Castle] I entered the Quadrangle [and] saw the Royal Family and foreign Sovereigns and Princes talking together at the Sovereign's Entrance, and in the midst of them was my khaki friend. He had apparently come up in a carriage with the German suite ...

Once more he was ejected, to the relief of the royal family and this time Fritz delivered him into the hands of a policeman who took him away. It turned out that 'the poor man had been invalided home from South Africa ... and was mentally deficient'.[18]

With the end of the lengthy funeral proceedings, everyone at last realized that the book was closed on the long reign of Queen Victoria. A new book was opened and imperceptibly the Edwardian age was ushered in. New brooms swept through Buckingham Palace with its rigidly nineteenth-century ways and the Marlborough House set were in. Many of the old household found themselves out of a job, but Fritz Ponsonby, who had obviously impressed the King at the time of the funeral, found himself in the new household with the twin positions of Assistant Private Secretary and Equerry to King Edward VII.

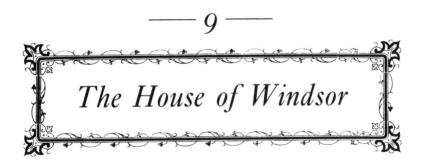

9

The House of Windsor

The reign of King Edward VII opened with a buoyant surge of something almost like youth in the air. It could not quite have been youth as the new King was not far off sixty and no longer in the best of health but he was a welcome change at a time when, after the first shock of the old Queen's death, people felt ready for it. The ponderous old ways, the dusty widows and the heavy respectability were swept out and the age of *fun* was ushered in. Slightly rakish fun it was, to be sure, but none the less welcome for that. This King was no remote figure on a distant throne, but a thoroughly approachable genial man who strode about racecourses, spas and pheasant coverts and loved a good party. British society threw itself with gusto into the Edwardian era and followed the example of their King in eating and drinking and womanizing too much.

But there were members of the royal family who were even older than the King and death continued to take its toll. In the August after the death of Queen Victoria, the Empress Frederick of Germany, the King's elder sister, Vicky, died. She was buried in Germany but a memorial service was held for her in the Chapel Royal, St James's Palace, where she had been married in 1858. Normally there would have been a considerable period of Court mourning for her, but as the Court was already in mourning until the following January for Queen Victoria, this passed unnoticed.

In March 1904, Field Marshal His Royal Highness the Duke of Cambridge died. George Cambridge was exactly the same age as his first cousin Queen Victoria; a fierce old man, he had been Commander-in-Chief of the Army for thirty-nine years until, in his old age, his refusal to countenance any changes or reforms in the Army led to his resignation. He was married to the actress Louisa Fairbrother, to whom he was devoted, but the marriage was never recognized by the Queen and so their three sons, with the surname of Fitzgeorge, were considered illegitimate although legally they had been born in wedlock. In King Edward's reign, one of them became ADC to the King. Louisa died in 1890, to the Duke's lasting grief, and was buried at Kensal Green and this determined the Duke to be buried there with her. When he died, his wishes were respected but first there was a grand military funeral service at Westminster Abbey at which 'Onward Christian Soldiers' was rousingly sung. His niece, May, now Princess of Wales, found it all so moving that she 'cried floods all the time'.[1]

The procession, employing large numbers of troops, was most impressive. There were five Field Marshals and eight full generals amongst the pall bearers. The route was lined with soldiers all the way to Kensal Green where sixty-six years before the Duke's Uncle Sussex had been buried. The King and other male members of the royal family, both British and foreign, followed in a procession of twenty-one carriages. Having arrived at the cemetery, the coffin was stowed away beside Louisa's, in a little mausoleum which looks like nothing so much as a child's 'Wendy house' with the coffins on benches along the walls and just room for two of the sons underneath.

As King Edward's reign drew on, it became obvious that this was no playboy King. He was deeply devoted to his country and worked hard throughout his reign to further Britain's aims in Europe and in the world at large. This, with his natural diplomacy and wide knowledge of Europe and its leaders, he was uniquely cut out to do. The King was related to many of the rulers of Europe; indeed he has been called the Uncle of Europe. It is possible to argue that never before nor since has Britain had so much influence on European politics and the Entente Cordiale with France of 1904 is often attributed to his diplomacy. It was not King Edward but his great uncle King George IV who was called 'The First Gentleman of Europe' but Edward had, in his day, as much claim to the title and for more solid reasons. It will be seen that his funeral reflects this claim.

In his later years, the King formed the habit of spending some weeks at Biarritz. His health and vitality were waning and he suffered from chronic chest trouble. The winters were becoming increasingly trying to him and he found that a sojourn at Biarritz, where the climate suited him, set him up for the rigours of the summer season. Unfortunately, in early March 1910 he elected to stop in Paris, went to the theatre and caught a chill which turned to bronchitis. However, six weeks of the bracing Atlantic air, of walks with his terrier, Caesar, and picnics with his charming and discreet mistress, Alice Keppel, did their work and on 27 April he returned to a wintry London looking more fresh and vigorous than he had for some time and plunged straight back into the backlog of work that was waiting for him.

In spite of the long journey he had undergone, he felt strong enough to go straight out, on the evening of his arrival home, to hear Tetrazzini in 'Rigoletto' at Covent Garden. Queen Alexandra was holidaying in Corfu and, at the weekend he went down alone to Sandringham to supervise some work in the grounds. The weather was wet and windy and the King once more caught a chill so that he returned to London on 2 May with all the good of Biarritz undone.

The King refused to stop work, however, seeing ministers and even dining out with his friend Miss Agnes Keyser (Sister Agnes of King Edward VII Hospital for Officers fame).But he was clearly very unwell, often unable to speak or get his breath for coughing, and his household saw fit to send a telegram to the Queen in Corfu. At the King's insistence, they stressed that there was no cause for alarm, but the Queen read between the lines and decided to return at once. By the time she arrived, on the evening of 5 May, her husband was too unwell to meet her at the station, a fact so unusual that the Prince of Wales was able to persuade him that a bulletin should be issued saying that His Majesty was suffering from bronchitis and that 'his condition causes some anxiety'.[2]

The Queen could see at once that he was seriously ill but the next day he insisted on getting up and dressing in the frock coat he always wore to receive people. When his old friend and adviser, the banker Sir Ernest Cassel, arrived, he insisted on rising to greet him and made a great effort at conversation but he so obviously found talking, and even breathing, difficult that Sir Ernest cut his visit short. He admitted to feeling 'very seedy', indeed 'wretchedly ill' but his smile for his old friend was as warm as ever. The fact that he could only manage half a cigar was considered by his household as a very bad sign.

In the afternoon the King was persuaded that he would be more comfortable in bed and soon afterwards the crowd outside the Palace saw the Archbishop of Canterbury (Randall Davidson, previously Bishop of Winchester) arrive. A last glint of interest came when it was announced to the King that his filly, Witch of the Air, had won an exciting race at Kempton Park. 'I'm very glad,'[3] he murmured, and, suitably, they were the last recorded words of this great man of the turf. But, as the day turned to evening, it was obvious that he was dying. He knew it himself and faced it cheerfully and the Queen, with her now famous 'gesture of heroic magnanimity',[4] summoned Mrs Keppel to his bedside. Edward's heart was affected and he frequently lapsed into unconsciousness. Bulletins now spoke of his condition as critical and through the evening the crowd at the gates grew and grew as the news spread. Slowly the beat of the old heart grew fainter and fainter. The Archbishop said the Commendatory Prayer 'and a few moments afterwards [11.45 p.m.] he simply ceased to breathe. I have seldom or never seen a quieter passing of the river.'[5]

Archbishop Davidson had been the first person to greet King Edward as sovereign at Osborne in 1901, now he was the first to greet King George V when, after a few minutes, the family came out of the old King's bedroom.

'Gentlemen, the King is dead,' announced, in gravest tones, a member of the household to the waiting crowd who pressed against the railings, and the news was received in stunned silence. It was unbelievable! It was only ten days since the King had arrived looking tanned and fit from Biarritz. It could not be true! But then almost at once came the official bulletin, fixed to the railing for all to read, and signed by four eminent doctors:

> Buckingham Palace May 6th, 1910, 11.50 p.m. His Majesty the King breathed his last at 11.45 tonight in the presence of Her Majesty Queen Alexandra, the Prince and Princess of Wales, the Princess Royal (Duchess of Fife), the Princess Victoria and Princess Louise (Duchess of Argyll). Signed F.H. Laking MD, James Reid MD, Douglas Powell MD, Bertrand Dawson MD.[6]

Meanwhile the new King, who was to be proclaimed King George V the next day, was sending a telegram to the Lord Mayor of London: 'I am deeply grieved to inform you that my beloved father, the King, passed away peacefully at 11.45 tonight.'[7] So it was official, and London society could get out their blacks once more for another whole year of mourning – just at the start of the London season too. Many a pretty young debutante must have wailed and torn her hair at the news, and not wholly out of grief for the King. There they all were, stuck in London, and there would be no balls and parties for them that summer. The glamorous Edwardian age had died with the genial monarch who was its inspiration, and nothing would ever be quite the same again. His festive personality had sent ripples circling out to embrace all classes of his subjects and all now mourned him deeply. Kenneth Rose relates that 'One hostess of the late monarch threaded black ribbons through her daughter's underclothes; another tied a large black bow of crepe round a tree which he had planted five years before and a grocer in Jermyn Street saluted the passing of a dedicated trencherman by filling his window with black Bradenham hams'.[8]

King Edward's body remained in his bedroom at Buckingham Palace for over a week and here came a number of his old friends, invited by Queen Alexandra to say goodbye to their 'dear King'. The Queen 'in a simple black dress' received them in the King's room 'moving gently about his room as if he were a child asleep'.[9] In fact he looked as though he was asleep,

The rush to buy mourning on the sudden death of Edward VII.

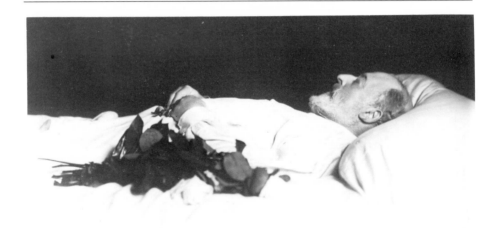

The body of King Edward VII the day after his death. Queen Alexandra allowed photographs to be taken and commissioned an artist to make a drawing which was released to the Press.

Opposite: King Edward VII lying in the throne room at Buckingham Palace before the public lying-in-state at Westminster Hall.

lying on the bed in which he always slept. His head was inclined gently to one side. No appearance of pain or death. There was even a glow on his face and the usual happy smile of the dead who die peacefully. The Queen talked to me for half an hour . . . with only a slight diminution of her natural gaiety, but with a tenderness which betrayed all the love in her soul . . .[10]

Once or twice, in a favourite gesture, she gripped Lord Esher's arm and he 'kissed both her hands when [he] left her, and came back across the room to kiss them again and to express all the devotion to her service which I owe her for all the happy days of the last ten years.' He left in tears.

Fritz Ponsonby had not been in waiting when the King died, but he hurried back and he too was taken in to see the King,

lying apparently asleep. I was very much awed and hardly liked to speak except in a whisper, but the Queen spoke quite naturally and said how peaceful he

looked and that it was a comfort to think he had suffered no pain. She said she felt as if she had been turned into stone, unable to cry, unable to grasp the meaning of it all, and incapable of doing anything.

She dreaded, she said, 'this terrible State Funeral and all the dreadful arrangements that had to be made.'[11]

On 10 May Queen Alexandra had a Letter to the Nation published in all the morning papers.

> From the depths of my poor broken heart I wish to express to the whole Nation, and our kind People we love so well, my deep-felt thanks for all their touching sympathy in my overwhelming sorrow and unspeakable anguish. Not alone have I lost everything in him, my beloved husband, but the Nation too has suffered an irreparable loss by their best friend, father, and Sovereign thus suddenly called away.

It has the feeling of having been written by the Queen herself with a scarcely perceptible unEnglishness of expression and it undoubtedly expressed her feelings at the time. She went on to invoke God's help for them all in bearing their loss, thanked all who had sent 'touching letters and tokens of sympathy', and ended by confiding her 'dear son' into their care and begged them to 'show him the same loyalty and devotion [they] showed his dear father.'[12]

At last the King's body was sealed up in an oak coffin and the first of the lyings-in-state in the purple-hung Throne Room of Buckingham Palace took place. This was entirely in accordance with time-honoured practice, but now a quite new tradition was instituted. Never before had St Stephen's Hall at Westminster been used for the lying-in-state of a dead sovereign. At the death of Edward VII it was decided to carry him to Westminster in order to give all his subjects the opportunity of paying their last respects to their King. This was something planned by King Edward himself. He had been so shocked by the unpreparedness of his mother's funeral that he gave orders that all should be planned in advance of his own death in consultation with himself. In the event, however, King George was much annoyed by the repeated incompetence of the Earl Marshal, the same Duke of Norfolk, and the College of Arms.

So on Tuesday, 17 May, the late King's body was taken in procession from Buckingham Palace to Westminster. Behind the gun-carriage walked the new King, alone, with his two eldest sons, Prince Edward and Prince Albert, in the uniform of naval cadets behind him. They were followed by the Kings of Denmark and Norway and eighteen other princes, British and foreign. Queen Alexandra rode in a closed carriage with her sister, the Dowager Empress of Russia and her daughters and ten-year-old Prince Henry, later Duke of Gloucester. This was essentially a family procession but, as the gun-carriage left Buckingham Palace, history was seen at its most poignant as the Royal Standard, which since the King's death had been at half mast, suddenly rose to its full height – The King is dead. God save the King!

At Westminster Hall the coffin was placed on a catafalque in the centre of the place which for nine hundred years had seen so much of the history of England, from the trial of Charles I to George IV's splendid coronation banquet. Round it stood, heads bowed over their arms reversed, four gentlemen-at-arms and four officers of the Brigade of Guards or of the Indian Army in relays of silent change.

For three days the late King's subjects, 'all sorts and conditions of men', shuffled silently past the bier; a slow-moving river of people flowing down the steps and dividing to pass on either side of the catafalque. Not a sound was heard but the soft tidal wash of thousands of feet on the ancient paving stones. Even outside, the hush was almost tangible, a thick blanket of sorrow over the waiting throng snaking back along the river beyond Chelsea Bridge. In those three days over a quarter of a million people filed through Westminster Hall.

One afternoon King George brought the Kaiser; they stood for a while, gazing at the coffin of their father and uncle, then the Kaiser laid a handsome wreath he had brought with him, knelt for a moment or two, then rose and clasped his cousin by the hand.

All this time, the royalty of Europe and beyond had been gathering in London and, on the night before the funeral, Thursday, 19 May, King George held a dinner at Windsor Castle attended by fifty-eight royal men and two presidents (President Pichon of France and ex-President Theodore Roosevelt of the United States). It is doubtful if so many princes have ever sat down at one table before or since.

The next morning, Friday, 20 May, they were all in London again for the state procession from Westminster to Paddington. This was modelled on Queen Victoria's funeral procession but, if anything, even more troops had been assembled. Through the night Edward's sorrowing subjects all over the country were woken by the tramp of soldiers marching to railway stations for the journey to London. From the late King's own army there were Highlanders and Hussars, Royal Engineers, Marines and line regiments, Artillery Regiments rumbling by with their guns, four regiments of Foot Guards, the Household Cavalry, seven detachments of Territorials and ten of the Special Reserve. There were five bands, those of the Household Cavalry, the Foot Guards, the Royal Marines, the Royal Engineers and the Royal Artillery. At the time of Queen Victoria's death, Britain was fighting a war in South Africa; now there were many more troops at home.

Then came the military attachés from all the foreign embassies and legations, followed by groups of officers from the armies and navies of Austria-Hungary, Bulgaria, Denmark, Germany, Norway, Portugal, Russia, Spain and Sweden in a dazzling array of uniforms. Sixteen lieutenant-generals preceded the Commander-in-Chief, still Field Marshal Earl Roberts VC. The headquarters staff, the Army Council, the Board of Admiralty and then, after another band, the Earl Marshal and all the most important officers of the court. Last of all, before the gun-carriage, two sombre black-coated figures among all the glittering uniforms, King Edward's two valets.

The gun-carriage was flanked by the bearer party from the King's Company, Grenadier Guards, equerries and Gentlemen at Arms, but Fritz Ponsonby, who was one of the equerries, recounts that 'as the extra equerries were afterwards added and all sorts of officials thought they had the right to walk at the side of the gun-carriage, there was a crowd-jostling effect which was undignified.'[13]

After the coffin walked alone the impressive figure of Admiral of the Fleet, HSH Prince Louis of Battenberg, personal ADC to the King, and then the King's favourite charger, Kildare, with her master's boots reversed in the stirrups and, behind her, led by a Highlander, the tiny figure, trotting along, of Caesar, King Edward's rough-haired terrier. Caesar caught the imagination of the crowd and the press and became something of a cult figure. He 'wrote his memoirs' entitled *Where's Master?* and children all over the country were given it for Christmas that year. He is buried in the garden of Marlborough House, but this was his hour of glory.

Then came the Kings, nine of them; first King George with the Kaiser and the old Duke of Connaught, then the Kings of Norway, the Hellenes, Spain, Bulgaria, Denmark, Portugal and the King of the Belgians. Never had so many kings been seen together and all but one were relations. The exception, the King of Bulgaria, earned the scorn of all the rest by having to have his horse led. But Fritz Ponsonby wrote that '[he] had a strong but evil personality, and gave one the impression that he could be capable of any crime; and history bore this out.'[14] After forty other

Opposite: The funeral procession of King Edward VII passing along Piccadilly. In the London procession the gun carriage was drawn by horses of the Royal Horse Artillery, the sailors taking over at Windsor. Since then the Navy has performed this duty for the sovereign in both places.

foreign princes and their suites, came a long line of twelve carriages, in the first of which sat Queen Alexandra, her sister and daughters and, after them, the households of His late Majesty, of his Queen and of the new King and Queen, walking. The procession closed with a detachment of the Police and of the Fire Brigade.

At Windsor, Ponsonby was again in charge. This time he had taken no chances with the arrangements and everything went off beautifully. Having made such an impression on the King last time, sailors once more pulled the gun-carriage from the station to the Castle, but this time by prior arrangement. As before, this procession on foot was full of heralds, Pursuivants, the Kings-of-Arms of the various orders, Black Rod, all in full dress which gave it a somewhat medieval look, but closer inspection would have shown it to be quite unlike the funerals of earlier kings and queens. Except for the two valets and the Yeomen of the Guard, there were none of the lesser ranks of the King's servants there. Gone were the Children of the Scalding House, the Clerk of the Scullery, the Wine Porters, the Yeomen of the Buttery. Indeed, these titles had long since disappeared, and not since Stuart times had such persons been seen in a funeral procession. But whereas in Stuart and Hanoverian times, such processions had largely been made up of the dead King's own subjects, this one was truly international with representatives from as far afield as Japan and Mexico, Persia, Siam, Argentina, China, Egypt, Haiti, the United States and Turkey as well as princes from Russia, Austria-Hungary, Sweden, Luxembourg, Monaco and the Balkan and German states.

As the cortège came down through the Castle, a four-year-old girl was watching from the roof of the Henry III Tower. This was May, daughter of Princess Alice and Prince Alexander of Teck. When it was explained to her what this colourful, but, at the same time, mournful parade was all about and the significance of the gun-carriage and its burden, she exclaimed, 'What! Uncle Bertie in a box?!'[15] And Lord Kinnoull's small daughter, who had also witnessed the procession, refused to say her prayers that night, explaining, 'It won't be any use, God will be too busy unpacking King Edward'.[16]

The King was this time followed by the Princes Edward and Albert, and further back came a single carriage, that of Queen Alexandra. The Queen Mother, as she was now to be known, the first to be so styled since Queen Henrietta Maria, was giving a good deal of trouble to the new King and Queen by insisting on the first place in royal precedence which by right belonged to Queen Mary. Queen Alexandra was supported by her sister the Dowager Tzarina Marie Feodorovna, née Princess Dagmar of Denmark, who told her that it was the practice in Russia, and when 'Motherdear' dug her toes in she was the most stubborn woman alive.

Queen Mary capitulated at once.

At the Chapel, the officers of the General Staff and the late King's ADCs fanned out to line the steps, while Garter King-of-Arms hurried up the aisle to be ready to read out the style and titles. The coffin was received by the Archbishops of Canterbury and York, the Bishops of Winchester and Oxford, the Dean of Windsor and his canons, minor canons and choristers, and the cortège moved slowly up into the choir, the new King going to stand at the head of the coffin and the Lord Chamberlain at the foot.

This time there were hymns for everyone to sing:

My God, my Father, while I stray,
Far from my home, on life's rough way,
O teach me from my heart to say,
  Thy Will be done.

and

Now the labourer's task is o'er;
Now the battle day is past ...

At the end of the service, after the late King's style had been proclaimed, 'God Save the King' was rousingly sung and then the coffin was lowered into the vault below, there to await the building of the handsome tomb to the right of the altar which houses both King Edward and Queen Alexandra. The tomb is by Sir Bertram Mackennal and on it, in marble, Caesar is immortalized, lying at his master's feet.

After the service, the royal family and the foreign representatives repaired to the Castle and there sat down to asparagus and poached salmon at round tables whence some of them carried home souvenirs of menu cards signed by those at their table.

As usual, eulogies and memorial sermons were widely given and a selection of three sermons by the Archbishop of Canterbury, Cannon Henry Scott-Holland of St Paul's Cathedral, and C. Silvester Horne, Chairman of the Congregational Union, were bound together and sold for 1d. They all thanked God for a ruler devoted to his people, but it is Canon Scott-Holland who gives us the most human view of the late King. He speaks of Him '... touching all hearts by his genial good-nature, his irresistible bonhomie, his delightful smile and his benignant kindness ...' He recalled

A range of mourning and commemorative jewellery.
Upper left: a cameo ring of George IV. *Upper centre:* a brooch commemorating the death of Princess Charlotte. *Upper right:* a cheap tin badge in memory of Edward VII. *Lower row:* Momento mori pendants commemorating the deaths of William III, Queen Anne and Mary II.

the sight of him, young and slight and uniformed, carrying home his beautiful bride to Windsor, as we Eton boys crowded cheering round the carriage . . . It is a wonderful thing to have gone through life, carrying everywhere, into each festal opportunity, this gay and sunny radiance . . . Our playfellow, our friend . . .[17]

Surely that is how King Edward VII would have wished to be remembered.

King George and Queen Mary were just getting used to their new roles as King and Queen when May's eldest brother Frank, Duke Francis of Teck, died in the summer of 1910. Frank was as feckless and irresponsible as his mother and had been a sore trial to his sister but they had had a happy holiday together at Balmoral following a sinus operation, and it was a terrible shock to her when he suddenly contracted pleurisy and died. He was buried with his mother, Princess Mary Adelaide, and his father in the vault below St George's and, for once his sister's iron self discipline broke and she wept bitterly in the privacy of her veil.

Before long all King Edward's peace-making was set at nought and, after a series of crises in the summer of 1914, Britain found herself at war with Germany. Possibly even 'Edward the Peacemaker' could not have averted it, for he had never got on with Kaiser Willie.

Only one member of the royal family was killed in action, Prince Maurice of Battenberg, second son of Princess Beatrice, in the first months of the war. He was buried with his companions in France. Princes Edward and Albert also saw action in the Army and Navy respectively. All the same, it must have been a terrible time for the royal family, divided as they were between the two opposing forces and all the animosity and anti-German hysteria that the war engendered. German members of the British royal family were subjected to much abuse, particularly in the press; Prince Louis of Battenberg was forced to resign as First Sea Lord although he had given his whole life to the British Navy, and the King felt impelled to rob his relatives of their German titles, replacing them with English peerages. Even the King himself was suspected of German sympathies and a rising tide of republicanism at the time of the Russian Revolution was possibly only rolled back by victory in 1918.

In 1917 two members of the royal family died and were buried at St George's and both were, by birth, German. Indeed, the first to die, the Duchess of Connaught, was that worst of all things German, a Prussian and a close relation of the Kaiser. She had, however, as wife of the Governor-General of Canada, proved her loyalty to Britain and no one begrudged her the small party of soldiers who attended her to the grave. Her funeral was a private family affair attended by most of the royal family, with everyone in khaki or naval uniform. A cross of purple and white flowers lay on the coffin, but there were no other flowers at the request of the Duke. The service was conducted by Archbishop Davidson of Canterbury.

Seven months later another German prince, but one even longer resident in England, was buried at St George's. This was Prince Christian of Schleswig-Holstein, husband of Princess Helena, or 'Lenchen' as she was known in Queen Victoria's family. He had no cause to love the German Empire, having been turned out of his state in the Prussian takeover of Germany in the last century, and had lived in England ever since. Again it was a quiet family funeral with a small procession of clarences and pony landaus carrying the mourners, in service dress or plain dark suits, from Cumberland Lodge, the Prince's home, to the Chapel. The coffin, drawn on a gun-carriage, was covered with a Union Jack and bore only the Prince's plumed hat and a wreath of laurels. Possibly it was judged that coronets and orders did not accord well with workaday khaki out of doors, but, once inside the Chapel, these were laid upon the coffin. Some rousing hymns were

[221]

sung; 'Last Post' and, at the late Prince's special request, 'Reveille', were played; and the mourners left the Chapel to the jaunty strains of 'John Peel' played in the Horseshoe Cloister in recognition of Prince Christian's interest in sport and country life.

In the case of both of these deaths, Court mourning passed virtually unnoticed in the general gloom of the war. After the war the British people were so sated with death and mourning that the old Victorian celebrations of death were largely abandoned. There had been so many deaths that, with a war to be won, there simply was not the time to give way to grief, nor the clothing to be had for elaborate mourning. It is from then and from the period after the war when everyone wanted to turn away from thoughts of death and get on with life, that the tradition, at any rate in Britain, of keeping a stiff upper lip and displaying no more grief than necessary in behaviour and dress emanates. Death was pushed firmly under the carpet where it remained for over fifty years. Only today are we beginning to emerge from this clamp-down on death, to see it as an acceptable, indeed, a necessary subject for conversation and the expression of grief as healthy and healing. But the formal life of the royal family and the Court is always a little behind the fashions and habits of the outside world and Court and family mourning continues to this day. For a family so much in the public eye, this has the merit of giving them some privacy for their grief, though today even this is very much curtailed.

Hardly had peace been declared and the King and Queen emerging from the strain of four years of war and getting back to peacetime duties, than a tragedy occurred in their immediate family. Though an attractive and normal-looking boy, their youngest son, Prince John, had been an epileptic since he was four years old. Lately these fits had grown worse and he had been installed with his devoted nurse, Mrs Bill, at Wood Farm, on the Sandringham estate. Such segregation may seem odd today, but it must be remembered that Queen Alexandra was still in possession of the vast Sandringham House, alone but for her unmarried daughter, Princess Victoria. This meant that the King, his family and household were crammed into York Cottage, a house no larger than the average manor house, where space was at a premium and privacy impossible. On 18 January 1919, Queen Mary wrote in her diary:

At 5.30 Lalla Bill telephoned me from Wood Farm, Wolferton, that our poor darling little Johnnie [then aged thirteen] had passed away suddenly after one of his attacks. The news gave me a great shock, tho' for the poor little boy's restless soul, death came as a great release. I broke the news to George and we motored down to Wood Farm. Found poor Lalla very resigned but heartbroken. Little Johnnie looked very peaceful lying there.[18]

Nowadays people do not die of epilepsy; it is largely controlled by drugs and a near normal life can be led. It is impossible to discover why Prince John died. He had fallen asleep after a bad fit and Mrs Bill, going in to wake him at teatime, had found him dead. Had he had another fit while alone and swallowed his tongue or vomited and drowned? And was Mrs Bill in any way to blame? Since, given contemporary medicine, he could never have lived a normal life, Queen Mary was perhaps right in looking upon his death as a release. On 21 January, Prince John was buried very privately in Sandringham churchyard beside that other Johnnie, his uncle, Prince Alexander John Charles Albert, who had died in 1871.

In 1922 haemophilia struck again. Princess Beatrice's second son, Lord Leopold Mountbatten, died suddenly following a minor operation. His mother was touring abroad when the disaster she had dreaded through all his thirty-two years occurred. There was to be one more death from haemophilia and since then the cruel disease seems to have died out in the British royal family though it continued in various foreign branches. In April 1928, Princess Alice and her husband, now known as the Earl of Athlone, were in South Africa where the Earl was Governor-General, when they received the tragic news of the death of their only son, Rupert, Viscount Trematon, at the age of twenty-one. Following a motor accident in France, young Rupert appeared to be making good progress in hospital when he dislodged the bandages in his sleep and the bleeding began all over again. His parents 'spent agonising days, owing to the vague and scanty reports [they] received',[19] and then he was dead. King George and Queen Mary arranged everything. The body was brought back by destroyer from France and, after a small family funeral in St George's Chapel, was buried in the Royal Burial Ground at Frogmore. His parents, who at the time could only attend a memorial service in Cape Town Cathedral, now lie with him there.

Throughout the Great War and the years of peace that followed, Queen Alexandra lived on at Sandringham and Marlborough House in the company of Princess Victoria and her devoted lady-in-waiting, Charlotte Knollys, who had been with her ever since, as a ravishing eighteen-year-old, Alexandra had taken Britain by storm in 1863 – over sixty years. In December 1924 the Queen Mother was eighty and still bearing traces of her legendary beauty, but she was failing in body and mind and querulous with it. Like all great beauties, she minded terribly her vanishing beauty: 'Think of me as I used to be, now I am breaking up,'[20] she wrote to an old friend. Her hearing was now completely gone and her eyesight

Queen Alexandra lying in state in Westminster Abbey.

going. Most trying she must have been to the King with her constant complaints and demands to be kept informed and consulted on state as well as family matters. Not usually a patient man, King George V was unfailingly kind and solicitous to 'Motherdear', writing to her regularly, however busy he was and visiting her whenever he could. The visits of her grandchildren always delighted her but gradually the Queen's old friends and servants died and she felt more and more lonely without them. Only dear Charlotte remained.

On 19 November 1925, Queen Alexandra had a sudden heart-attack at Sandringham. The King and Queen were already on the spot at York Cottage, and their sons were sent for but arrived too late. Poor Charlotte failed in her last duty, too; she was herself ill in bed with 'flu. Through the night and the next day the Queen Mother lingered, sometimes conscious. 'Saw darling Mama who knew us and I kissed her hand and her forehead,'[21] wrote Queen Mary in her journal. And then in the early evening of 20 November Queen Alexandra passed quietly away.

The following day, when the Princes arrived, a short service was held in the bedroom of the late Queen. 'Motherdear looked so lovely and young with pink draperies and flowers round her,'[22] wrote Queen Mary. How pleased the great beauty would have been that at least she did justice to herself in death. Then, carried by some of her servants and estate workers, old friends all of them, she left Sandringham for the last time. 'Although the afternoon was cold and cheerless,' writes Georgina Battiscombe, 'Charlotte Knollys had flung a window wide open, the better to watch the little procession. As the bearers crossed the wintry lawns they heard her crying aloud, like a little child.'[23] Poor Charlotte – a lost soul – her life's work was at an end.

For four days the coffin rested in the little church at Sandringham where Queen Alexandra had brought her children and grandchildren to church and had worshipped for sixty years. She was watched over by relays of Sandringham men in their sober Sunday suits. Then, on 26 November, in Queen Mary's economical phraseology:

> Some snow showers then fine. Lunched at 1 and at 1.45 drove to the Church where a short service was held after which Mama's coffin was carried by 10 Grenadiers of the King's Company to the gun carriage, and George, the boys and Olav, and the gentlemen walked after it down to Wolferton station, we ladies following in carriages and the people of the estate on foot and people lining the roads. All most touching.[24]

That night the Queen's body lay in the Chapel Royal, St James's Palace, watched over through the night by gentlemen-at-arms and Yeomen of the Guard, and next day she was carried in procession to Westminster Abbey. It was a military cortège as befitted a queen consort but a smaller one than that of her husband, and the coffin was drawn on a gun-carriage provided and manned by the Royal Horse Artillery. By now the gun-carriage had taken the place of the hearse even at the funerals of royal ladies. Behind the coffin walked the King, the Prince of Wales, the King of the Belgians, the King of Denmark (nephew), the King of Norway (son-in-law) and seventeen assorted British and foreign princes. For the first time at such an event, the King's Principal Air ADC was seen with those of the Army and Navy.

The royal ladies were driven straight to the Abbey: 'Crowds in streets. Wonderfully nice feeling shown,' recorded Queen Mary, while the service was 'Most beautiful and impressive.'[25] The 23rd Psalm was sung and the hymns, 'Now

'Piccadilly Flower Girls' Tribute to The Late Queen Alexandra'. Four Piccadilly flower sellers arriving at Marlborough House with their wreath for the Queen Mother.

the labourer's task is o'er' and 'On the Resurrection morning', both old favourites, while the anthem was the more unusual Contakion of the Faithful Departed from the Russian liturgy. Possibly through the influence of her sister, the Dowager Empress of Russia, Queen Alexandra had come to love Russian Church music.

After the service, the coffin remained under the lantern in the Abbey until the following day when it was taken privately to the Albert Memorial Chapel at Windsor where a service 'of a private character' was held. Here Queen Alexandra's body remained until King Edward's tomb had been made ready to receive it.

At New Year 1931, the Princess Royal, Duchess of Fife, King George V's sister, Louise, died. 'A bad beginning for a New Year,' the King wrote in his diary, 'I feel very depressed.'[26] Then in December 1935, his favourite sister, the unmarried Princess Victoria, died and the King was so distressed that, using the excuse of family mourning, he cancelled the State Opening of Parliament. This time his diary records, 'How I shall miss her and our daily talks on the telephone. No one ever had a sister like her.'[27] Except for the Queen, she was his nearest and dearest.

It was sad that the King should have been subjected to such a lowering of the spirits so soon after the Jubilee celebrations of that summer. Nothing had done more to raise his morale and make him feel genuinely loved and wanted for his own sake than the touching demonstrations of the Silver Jubilee and at the end of it all he was in better health than he had been since his long and dangerous illness of 1928–29. His convalescence at Bognor on that occasion is the origin of the Regis added to the name of the town.

On 21 December the King and Queen left London to spend Christmas at Sandringham, low in spirits from the King's sister's death and from worry over the international situation. On Christmas Day the King made his fourth Christmas broadcast and some noticed a slight huskiness and weakness in his voice but the speech was well received and listened to all over the country and the Empire. It will later be noticed that King George V was the first sovereign at whose passing both radio and the aeroplane had roles to play and that, in keeping with the now worldwide rule of the King Emperor, radio was to prove very important.

After Christmas the King and Queen spent a quiet three weeks at Sandringham with small jobs to be done in and out of the house and small pleasures like an amusing film after tea and a visit to his little grandson, Prince Edward of Kent, in his bath. On 5 January, he had a short ride on his fat grey pony, Jock, Queen Mary walking beside him, but he felt miserably ill and breathless and went early to bed.

The next day, Thursday, the King stayed in his room, tucked up in an armchair by the fire, and the following evening made his last entry in the diary he had kept daily since 1880: 'A little snow and wind. Dawson arrived this evening. I saw him and feel rotten.'[28] Lord Dawson of Penn was his doctor, summoned by the ever watchful Sister Black who had looked after him since 1928. That same evening the public first heard from the evening papers that the King was confined to his room with a cold, and late that night the BBC put out the first bulletin from Sandringham: 'The bronchial catarrh from which His Majesty the King is suffering is not severe, but there have appeared signs of cardiac weakness which must be regarded with some disquiet.'[29] It was signed by Lord Dawson together with Drs Frederic Willans and Stanley Hewett. Instantly the news flashed round the world and in England all light music was faded out and music of a solemn nature took its place.

The King's heart had taken a considerable pounding when he had septicaemia seven years before and at seventy it seemed less likely that it would take the strain. Lord Dawson summoned Sir Maurice Cassidy, the heart specialist, and on

Saturday the Prince of Wales arrived and also the Archbishop of Canterbury, Dr Cosmo Lang.

By now listeners world-wide were standing by their radios and waited with baited breath for the bulletins from Sandringham which were mainly to the effect of 'restful sleep', 'slight increase in anxiety', 'no change'. A crowd had also gathered at the gates of Sandringham and waited patiently in the cold and the snow showers for any news that was brought out to them.

On Sunday, the whole nation went to church and prayed fervently, but with diminishing hope, for the King's recovery. In Westminster Abbey and in many other churches a minute's silence was observed for the people's private prayers that he would be given the strength to struggle on.

Now the King was drifting in and out of consciousness. Sometimes his mind was as clear as ever and then he would become confused. Once he recognized his daughter Mary at his bedside, smiled at her and asked her if she had been skating, recalling long ago parties on the frozen lake, and then dozed off again. Then there is the, probably apocryphal, story of one of his doctors trying to soothe him in a fractious moment: '"Cheer up Your Majesty, you will soon be at Bognor again." "Bugger Bognor",'[30] came the trenchant reply. It is said to be not untypical of his language which Kenneth Rose describes as 'emphatic'.

On Monday the King was very weak but still able to go through the motions of reading *The Times* and, struggling to take in the news of his far-flung subjects, he turned to Lord Wigram, his Private Secretary, and asked, 'How is the Empire?' 'All is well, Sir, with the Empire,'[31] came the reassuring reply and the old King Emperor drifted away again into unconsciousness. That morning the Prince of Wales flew down from London, wishing to be with his father at the end.

All this time, the dreaded 'Red boxes' of papers for the King's attention had been piling up on his desk and it now became clear that something must be done so that the work of the realm could go on. Therefore on Monday morning it was decided to call a Privy Council meeting at Sandringham to appoint a Council of State to act on behalf of the King. This was to consist only of the Queen and the four Princes. Three Privy Councillors, Ramsay Macdonald, the Lord President of the Council, Lord Hailsham, the Lord Chancellor, and Sir John Simon, the Home Secretary were summoned. Lord Dawson, Lord Wigram and the Archbishop who were already in the house were also Privy Councillors and together they made a quorum. Sir Maurice Hankey, Clerk to the Privy Council, was in attendance. They gathered in the sitting room next to the King's bedroom with the door open to reveal the King sitting in his old Tibetan dressing-gown in front of the fire, looking, the Archbishop thought, 'pathetically weak and frail', a bed-table across his knees. As his visitors entered, they saw their Sovereign's face light up with a bright smile of welcome.

The Archbishop describes the scene:

> The President read the Order in Council. With a clear voice the King gave the reply so familiar to him, 'Approved'. Then Dawson, kneeling at his feet and watching his face, said, 'Sir, do you wish to sign yourself?' 'Yes', said the King, rallying for the last time to the old call of duty. 'I have always signed in my own hand.' Dawson tried to put the pen in his fingers, but owing to the failure of circulation, they could not hold it. Then the hands moved most pathetically over the paper in the effort to sign. This took some minutes. Then the King turned to his Councillors and said, 'I am very sorry to keep you waiting so long,' adding shortly after, 'You see, I can't concentrate.' Once again the hands moved impotently up and down. Then, with great adroitness, Dawson put the pen in his hand and guided it, saying, 'Make a mark, Sir, and you may sign it afterwards.' So two marks, X X, were made. Then the King turned again to his Councillors and dismissed them with the old kingly smile. It was his last official act: we were all deeply moved ...[32]

With her wonderful graciousness and self-control, the Queen then entertained the Councillors to lunch and they returned to London by air in the aeroplane in which the Prince of Wales had flown down shortly before. There was not room, however, for poor Hankey, the Clerk, who had to return by train.

Through the long afternoon and evening, the Queen was 'amazingly calm and strong'[33], indeed she seemed to be supporting her sons. The soft enveloping silence seemed to cover the whole house as people went quietly and sadly about their accustomed tasks. The family dined alone and, about 9 o'clock, in the household dining room, Dawson sighed, turned over a menu card and wrote his famous bulletin: 'The King's life is moving peacefully to its close.' Across the world people who had been sitting close to their silent wirelesses all evening groaned as the sombre tones of the announcer gave them the news they dreaded to hear.

At 11.15 the Archbishop was called to the King's room where he found the Queen and Princess Mary.

> Then after some time of quiet waiting, as the King's breathing grew more slow, I read the Twenty-third Psalm, some passages from the Scriptures such as St Paul's great 'I am persuaded ...' and some prayers at quiet intervals, and then,

The body of King George V arrives at King's Cross from Sandringham. The Royal Family
are lined up in the foreground, the Cabinet and Household in the background.

going to the King's side, I said the Commendatory Prayers – 'Go forth,
Christian Soul' – with a final benediction . . . Finally within a few minutes, the
breathing ceased and, in the words of the last bulletin, 'Death came peacefully
to the King at 11.55 p.m.' (with his wife and five children at his bedside).
Within five minutes a new day, a new King, a new reign. So passed my King,
my friend of all these long years. God grant him rest and peace and light!³⁴

In that first moment of the new reign, Queen Mary stepped forward and, with
impeccable dignity, kissed her eldest son's hand. It was the time-honoured
homage which was now his due, but he was profoundly embarrassed.

However, before even his father was dead, Edward had taken it upon himself to
order all the clocks at Sandringham to be put back, which by long custom, and for
reasons of punctuality, had been kept half an hour ahead of Greenwich mean time.

'I wonder what other customs will be put back also,'[35] wryly commented Archbishop Lang. This was a needlessly insensitive act which deeply shocked a number of people in the house.

Within moments the news had flashed out to the world and Englishmen turned sadly to their beds.

In Canada they were at their dinner when the great bell in the Peace Tower at Ottawa began to toll, and all business ceased for the day. Far away in India it was early morning and the bazaars were just opening: they closed at once, and the mosques and churches filled with sad worshippers. At Singapore an RAF aeroplane flew low over the city trailing a long black streamer, and a minute gun sounded for each year of that long and invaluable life. In Hong-Kong newspapers with black borders greeted the citizens as they went to their offices, and the sound of drums carried the news through startled African villages.[36]

'Words commemorating King George V death – "The sunset of his death tinged the whole world's sky",' wrote the Queen in her diary on a different page to her simple 'Am *heartbroken*' which was her immediate response, adding '... my children were angelic'.[37] The final entry in King George's diary is also in Queen Mary's handwriting: 'My dearest husband, King George V was much distressed at the bad writing above and begged me to write his diary for him next day. He passed away on January 20th at 5 minutes before midnight.'[38]

The following morning King Edward travelled to London for his accession in his private aeroplane and became, thereby, the first British sovereign to fly. The Proclamation of his Accession at St James's was watched from a window by Wallis Simpson. 'It was all very moving,' she said, 'But it has made me realise how different life is going to be.'[39]

Queen Mary, dreading the fortnight of obsequies she had experienced at the death of Edward VII, asked that her husband's body should not be left unburied for more than a week. Since King George's illness in 1928 much of the ceremonial had been planned in advance and so it was with confidence that the funeral was fixed for Tuesday, 28 January.

On the very evening after his death, the King's body, in his coffin of oak felled on the estate, was wheeled across the darkened park to Sandringham Church, led by a lone piper and lit by a single torch. And here, in the church where he had worshipped all his life, he lay for thirty-six hours. 'The coffin rested before the altar, watched over by gamekeepers, gardeners and other faithful retainers who, in this way, were able to pay a last tribute not only to their King but to a beloved squire.'[40] Then, on a bright, sunny morning, Thursday, 23 January, a bearer party of the King's Company, Grenadier Guards, carried him out to a gun-carriage of the Royal Horse Artillery and he was drawn away towards Wolferton Station. The coffin was covered with the Royal Standard and the family flowers that might have bedecked the coffin of any country gentleman. Behind the gun-carriage walked the new King and his brothers, hatless and in plain dark coats, and the Queen and Princess Mary riding in a carriage. And, in a carriage to herself, Charlotte, the late King's parrot in her cage. Then came Jock, the old grey pony, led by a groom and then a long tail of neighbours, tenants and workpeople. The King's old piper, Forsyth, played 'The Flowers of the Forest' as they tramped the three miles to the station. 'Just as we topped the last hill above the station,' wrote King Edward later, 'the stillness of the morning was broken by a wild, familiar sound – the crow of a cock pheasant':[39] a fitting farewell to the great shot!

At King's Cross, the imperial crown, brought from the Tower, was fastened to the lid of the coffin over the Royal Standard, and so it was as a King that he entered his capital for the last time. The procession to Westminster was a short, dark-coated one, moving in its stark simplicity: the King, his brothers and brother-in-law followed by the late King's household and an escort of household troops, the Queen and other royal ladies going by another route straight to Westminster.

As they tramped through the streets of London, King Edward's eye suddenly caught a flicker of something bright 'dancing along the pavement'. It was the jewelled Maltese cross from the top of the crown. It was retrieved by the NCO of the bearer party who put it in his pocket. It was a tiny incident noticed by almost no one, but the King 'wondered if it was a bad omen',[42] and so did others.

At Westminster Hall the cortège was met by the Archbishop of Canterbury. King Edward, not caring much for church attendance himself, had not wanted any kind of service, being 'anxious to spare the Queen', but Lang insisted that 'the whole ceremony would have been, as it were, blank without it'[43] and won the day, making the ceremony as simple and beautiful as possible but at the same time rich and historic by wearing a purple cope worn at the funeral of Charles II.

For four days the King lay in state in Westminster Hall and nearly a million of his subjects shuffled silently past the catafalque. On the last evening, King Edward and his three brothers decided to pay a last tribute to their father. In full-dress uniform they

Opposite: King George V's funeral procession winding down through Lower Ward, Windsor Castle to reach the west door of St George's Chapel.

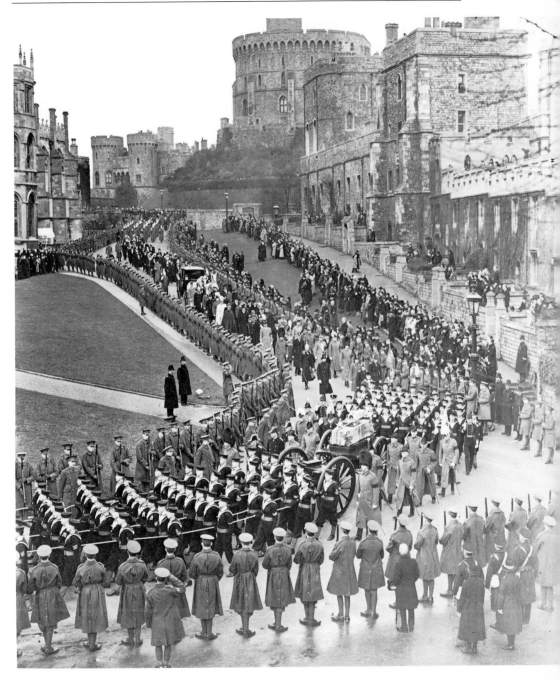

[233]

motored to Westminster, arriving shortly after midnight. Without the public being aware of our presence, we descended the staircase into the Hall and stationed ourselves round the catafalque between the officers already on vigil. Even at so late an hour the river of people still flowed past the coffin. But I doubt whether many recognised the King's four sons among the motionless uniformed figures bent over swords reversed. We stood there for twenty minutes in the dim candlelight and the great silence. I felt close to my father and all that he stood for.[44]

The following day, 28 January, the 'Sailor King' was fittingly drawn by sailors through the damp and misty streets of London. There had been casualties in the royal houses of Europe since 1910 and soon there would be more, and a world war had distanced Great Britain from the German heartland of its royal dynasty. All the same, five monarchs followed the coffin (Denmark, Norway, Rumania, Bulgaria and Belgium) and a host of foreign princes and representatives. It took two and a half hours to reach Paddington and the new King wrote that, 'Days afterwards the wail of the massed pipe bands echoed in my ears.'[45]

The crowds were the greatest that London had ever seen. In several places, swollen by more people coming up out of the underground stations, they swayed and broke through the cordons, delaying the cortège and providing the ambulance men with over ten thousand cases of fainting.

Waiting at Paddington, in a little black coat and beret, was the nine-year-old Princess Elizabeth with her governess. It was a long wait and they passed the time by playing noughts and crosses in the station-master's office but were in the forecourt by the time the coffin, with its massed sailors before and behind, was inched slowly down the long ramp into the station. Miss Crawford feared tears at this first sight of her grandfather's coffin but, she recalls, the Princess's attention was distracted by a sailor fainting just in front of the gun-carriage and the clever way in which his companions closed ranks and marched him along with them. The difficult moment had passed and then the Princess suddenly saw her mother, among the black-veiled ladies on the platform, and ran across to take her hand.

Microphones had been placed at vantage points all along the processional routes in London and Windsor and the world listened to the tramp of feet and the thump of muffled drums. The service in St George's Chapel, which began forty minutes late, owing to the crowds in London, was also relayed by radio to countries as far away as Japan, Morocco and the Dutch East Indies as well as the entire Empire. Archbishop Lang describes how, as the gun-carriage with its crew of bluejackets, reached the bottom of the steps to St George's, there 'followed two most poignant sounds, the bus'n's whistle, "Admiral on board" and "Admiral over the side", and then the pipes playing "The Flowers of the Forest" – it was this sound that went straight to my Scottish heart.'[46]

They sang the 23rd Psalm, 'Abide with me', and 'God be in my head' as Queen Mary, heavily veiled, stood at the foot of the coffin and then, as it was lowered into the vault and the Archbishop intoned the committal, 'Earth to earth, dust to dust ...', King Edward stepped forward and sprinkled on some earth from a silver bowl. 'We left him sadly, lying for the present with his ancestors in the Vault,'[47] wrote Queen Mary. Later a tomb designed by Sir Edwin Lutyens with effigies by Sir William Reid Dick was erected in the north aisle of the nave, and there the King and Queen now lie.

Cosmo Lang, who was in on all the family problems, had a long talk with King Edward and was not reassured as to his moral fibre. 'Well, we shall see,' he wrote. 'There is not only a new reign, but a new regime. I can only be most thankful for what has been, and for what is to be, hope for the best. God guide the King'![48] Sadly his hopes were not fulfilled. Less than a year later, King Edward abdicated in order to marry Mrs Wallis Simpson, and the throne devolved upon his brother Bertie, King George VI who, with the wonderful support of Queen Elizabeth, was to take Great Britain through another world war.

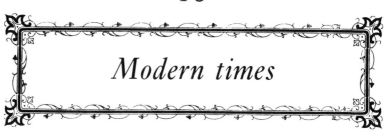

IO

Modern times

As the twentieth century progressed through the 1930s and into the 1940s, change was everywhere, not least in royal deaths and funeral traditions. We have seen before that the wireless played an important part in the funeral of King George V; his death was the first death of a sovereign upon which there had not been the usual spate of eulogies and funeral sermons delivered in all the great churches and universities and circulated afterwards. This time, not only did the whole world hear the Archbishop of Canterbury preach at the funeral service but, the day after the King's death, the Prime Minister, Stanley Baldwin, broadcast to the nation. On the following Sunday evening, the BBC held their own memorial service which was broadcast to the nation and beyond from the concert hall at Broadcasting House, the Archbishop giving the address. The eulogies were fewer in number but were much more widely heard.

Minor changes included members of the royal family being admitted to hospital for operations and occasionally dying there; in 1938 Prince Arthur of Connaught died in the Middlesex Hospital and King George V's only remaining sister, Queen Maud of Norway, in a private nursing home in London while on a visit to England. After a service in the Chapel at Marlborough House where she had been christened sixty-nine years before, the King sent HMS Royal Oak to carry her back to Oslo.

Motor hearses came into use for private royal funerals and these came to be used more and more as funeral processions, for all but military members of the royal family, went out of fashion. Instead of the coffin being brought down from London by train and then taken in procession to St George's, it became usual for it to be brought straight by motor hearse to the Chapel where it would lie in the Albert Memorial Chapel until the start of the service, when the men of the royal family would follow it into the choir. This made funerals easier to arrange in the war, requiring many fewer military personnel.

This was the pattern followed even for the Duke of Kent in 1942 who, had it not been for the war then at its height, would definitely have had a military funeral, such as had his brother, the Duke of Gloucester in 1974. The funeral of the old Duke of Connaught, son of Queen Victoria and one-time Commander-in-Chief of the Army who died also in 1942, was of the same type.

The death of Princess Louise, Duchess of Argyll, Queen Victoria's artist daughter, three months after the start of the Second World War, was the occasion for another royal innovation. At her own wish, the Princess's body was cremated. The ashes were then put into an ordinary-sized coffin for the funeral at St George's Chapel. Since the opening of the Royal Cemetery at Frogmore in 1904, the custom had been for the coffin to descend through the floor of the Chapel, as in former times, and to remain in the Royal Tomb House until a grave had been prepared for it at Frogmore, when it was privately transferred. This was done in the case of Princess Louise and others of that period.

In spite of the fact that Buckingham Palace was bombed in September 1940 ('I'm glad,' said the Queen, 'it makes me feel I can look the East End in the face.'),[1] the royal family sustained only one fatal casualty during the war and that one not directly as a result of enemy action.

In 1942 Prince George, Duke of Kent, was serving in the Royal Air Force but, much to his disgust, in a non-combative role. The old traditon of fighting princes had died and now they were considered an embarrassment on the battlefield and kept firmly away. A job on a headquarters staff was now the best they could hope for. However, in August 1942 the Duke of Kent was to fly to Iceland to inspect RAF and American air bases there. On 25 August, in 'vile weather', he and his party left Invergordon in a Sunderland flying boat and half an hour later crashed into the side of a mountain in Caithness. There were no survivors.

Queen Mary was at Badminton where she spent the entire war. She received the news of the death of her youngest son with 'heroic courage and unselfish thought for others' recalls her lady-in-waiting, Lady Cynthia Colville. 'I must go to Marina tomorrow,'[2] was her first thought, though the shock to herself was 'catastrophic'. Accordingly, next morning she was driven to Coppins to share her grief with the widowed Duchess of Kent who was thus left alone to bring up her three children, Prince Edward, aged seven, now Duke of Kent, Princess Alexandra, aged five, and the new baby, Prince Michael, who was only six weeks old.

Four weeks' Court mourning was ordered which, for most men in the royal circle meant nothing more than a black armband as they were constantly in uniform. The women mostly looked out something pre-war or calculated whether they could spare any coupons. Black was unpopular in the war when everyone wanted to keep their spirits up with bright clothing.

The Duke's body was brought south by train and the funeral was held in St George's on 29 August, the coffin having lain overnight in the Albert Memorial Chapel. It was a small, intimate gathering which included the Duke's chauffeur and old nanny as well as the Kings of Norway, Yugoslavia and Greece, the King and Queen of England and most of the royal family. 'I was greatly moved by the Service, short and explicit . . .,' recorded the King in his diary. 'Everybody there I knew but I did not dare to look at any of them for fear of breaking down.'[3] The King also noted that 'The RAF detailed the Bearer Party, all NCO Fighter Pilots, and Air Marshals and Air Vice Marshals acted as Pall Bearers.'[4] The Royal Air Force had come into its own as far as royal ceremonial was concerned. The Duke of Kent and his Duchess both now lie at Frogmore.

In October 1944, as allied troops stormed up through northern France and Belgium, an old lady of eighty-four died at her wartime home in Sussex. This was Princess Beatrice, youngest and last remaining daughter of Queen Victoria. It will be remembered that she had been widowed in 1895, her husband dying of malaria off West Africa, being brought home for burial at Whippingham Church, near Osborne, in a cask of Navy rum. But in 1944 the Isle of Wight was a prohibited zone and so the Princess's funeral was at St George's, brightened up for the occasion by the replacing of the banners of the Garter Knights, removed for safety earlier in the war. The King and Queen and young Princess Elizabeth attended the ceremony as well as Princess Beatrice's daughter, Queen Ena of Spain, and her son, the Marquis of Carisbrooke. As the coffin descended through the floor of the Chapel, the two Queens stepped forward and curtsied. Two months after the end of the war the Princess's remains were moved to the Isle of Wight, of which she had been Governor until her death. A naval guard of honour met the hearse at the quay at Cowes and the occasion was marked by all flags on the island flying at half mast. The Princess, who had been married in St Mildred's Church, Whippingham, and loved it and lavished gifts upon it, came at last to rest there with the husband who had lain there for fifty years.

Peace returned to Britain but, for the King, the strain which had all but exhausted him during the war, though lessened, was without end. There were continuing economic and Parliamentary crises, the Cold War, the Malayan emergency, and then in 1950 the trauma of the Korean War, and the King's physique was not weathering it well. In 1948 he developed thrombosis in his right leg and there were fears that amputation would be necessary. Rest and conventional treatment averted this fear but a major visit to Australia and New Zealand had to be postponed and, in March 1949, he underwent a right lumbar sympathectomy. This was highly successful; by June he was able to attend the Trooping of the Colour in an open landau and for the next two years his health seemed much improved.

By the early summer of 1951, however, the strain of continuing crises on the King was showing. He looked tired and worried and it was clear that he was in declining health. On 24 May he looked ill and had a temperature at the Ceremony of the Order of the Bath and that night retired to bed with ''flu'. When he seemed 'not...able to chuck out the bug',[5] an X-ray discovered a patch of inflammation in the left lung. After a course of penicillin he seemed much better, but almost all his engagements for the rest of the summer were cancelled. This author was to have been presented at an afternoon Court at Holyroodhouse in June and great was her disappointment on learning that the royal visit to Edinburgh was off.

The King rested at Royal Lodge and Sandringham from where he wrote to a friend, 'I am growing stronger every day.'[6] At Balmoral in August he was able to shoot all day but the weather was cold and wet; he caught a chill and the old trouble brewed up again.

In early September the King returned to London for X-rays. As a result of these a bronchoscopy was carried out on 15 September and a malignant tumour on the left lung was found. Surgery was obviously the only hope, although there was a grave risk of cardiac complications. 'If it's going to help me to get well again I don't mind but the very idea of the surgeon's knife again is hell,'[7] wrote the King to a friend. As far as is known, neither then nor later did he know that he had cancer. His concern was chiefly for his family, his doctors and his subjects, for the anxiety they would undergo.

The operation, performed by Sir Clement Price Thomas in the Drawing Room at Buckingham Palace, in which the whole of the left lung was removed, was completely successful but his surgeons were on a knife-edge of worry for days lest coronary thrombosis should take their patient from them. They were also anxious as to whether the removal of certain nerves of the larynx would deprive the King of his voice.

Day after day, through the autumn, King George's subjects waited outside the gates of Buckingham Palace for bulletins on his state of health, the wording of which was carefully monitored by the King himself to avoid undue anxiety. He was beautifully looked after at Buckingham Palace by a team of eight nurses and, not least, by the Queen herself who spent hours amusing and reading to him.

Within three weeks he was able to be up for some time each day and to walk about his rooms but, though he gained strength steadily, it was soon obvious that the tour of Australia and New Zealand, now planned for early the following year, was out of the question. Disappointment 'down under' was to a great extent allayed by the news that Princess Elizabeth and her husband would go in his place.

On 5 October, a meeting of the Privy Council was held at Buckingham Palace at which the King signed the documents dissolving Mr Attlee's second Labour government. There was no one present who had attended that last meeting of King George V's reign in his bedroom at Sandringham. Had there been so they would have had a very strong feeling of *déjà-vu*.

> The Councillors stood in the doorway which separated the Audience Chamber from his bedroom and listened while the orders of business were read by the Lord President. The King, with difficulty, uttered the word 'Approved'; then Sir Alan Lascelles [Private Secretary] carried to the bedside the three documents requiring signature and held them while the King affixed his name.[8]

But fortunately this was not the last act of King George VI. He lived to see Winston Churchill once more at the head of government.

Princess Elizabeth and the Duke of Edinburgh undertook in October and November a long-standing engagement to tour Canada and the United States. Her father was by now well on the road to recovery, but, all the same, the Princess 'took with her a sealed envelope containing, *inter alia*, the draft Accession Declaration and a message to both Houses of Parliament, to be opened only in the event of the King's death.'[9] The tour, the Princess's first 'imperial mission', was a huge success and made her father very happy and proud.

At the end of November, the King was able to go to Royal Lodge at Windsor, much more home to him than Buckingham Palace. There he was able to go for walks in the grounds of Windsor Castle and seemed much stronger, although a tiresome cough in early December made another bronchoscopy necessary.

The Christmas broadcast was recorded piecemeal over a period before Christmas as the King's voice was not yet strong enough for a long continuous speech. Even so, his listeners detected a certain hoarseness in his voice, but they were touched at being thanked for their prayers and support during his illness: 'I trust that you yourselves realised how greatly your prayers and good wishes have helped and are helping me in my recovery.'[10]

Christmas was celebrated very happily at Sandringham and the King was delighted to find that he could shoot again. He was looking forward to spending the spring in South Africa where the Prime Minister, Dr Malan, had put a house at their disposal. He and the Queen were to leave England on 10 March.

At the end of January the King and Queen were back in London and on 29 March made a family outing with their daughters to see *South Pacific* at Drury Lane. Next morning they were at London Airport to see Princess Elizabeth and the Duke of Edinburgh off on the long-awaited tour of Australia and New Zealand via Kenya. The King stood bareheaded on the tarmac and waved as their aircraft taxied down the runway. The next day, taking their two little grandchildren with them, he and the Queen returned to Sandringham.

On 5 February, a cloudless day of crisp sunshine, the King took part in a hare shoot – 'Keepers' Day' at Sandringham. He was in excellent form and shot well and at the end planned the next day's sport with the keepers. After dinner he sat relaxed for some time and then retired to work on some papers, leaving the Queen and her guests to watch a film. About midnight a policeman on duty in the garden noticed him fixing the latch of his bedroom window. Next morning, when his valet took in his tea, he found him lying peacefully, but dead.

It is now openly admitted that King George VI, like his father and his grandfather, King Edward VII, died of a smoking-related disease. Both arteriosclerosis and lung cancer are caused by smoking, yet, at the time, no direct connection seems to have been made and the royal patients were allowed to smoke again quite soon after major illness and surgery.

'The King is dead. God save The Queen.' But the new Queen was in Kenya, enjoying a day or two watching wildlife at Treetops, when the dreaded news was brought to her. It is assumed that, as on the Canadian tour, she carried with her the draft Accession Declaration but she had not dreamt of having to use it so soon after that cheerful farewell at the airport. The poignancy of the small, black-clad figure descending the steps of the aircraft that brought her home as Queen, to face a line of black-coated ministers, is familiar to many.

The King's illness had given all those concerned, the Lord Chamberlain's Office, the Earl Marshal, the Military, the Police etc., plenty of time to contemplate the eventuality of his obsequies, to the extent that, in response to the Queen's commands, they were able to arrange the funeral for 15 February, only nine days after his death. The plans, which must have been minutely laid, were put into action immediately. Within twenty-four hours, officers of the Brigade of Guards were practising the drill for keeping vigil round the catafalque in Westminster Hall for the lying-in-state which was by now a firm tradition, while the men practised street lining, reversing arms and the drill for Royal Guards of Honour.

[241]

First, the King, like his father and grandmother, lay for two days in Sandringham Church attended by estate workers and then, on 11 February, was brought to London and driven through the rainy streets, followed by a tiny, silent, black-coated procession; the gun-carriage of the Royal Horse Artillery was followed by the late King's son-in-law, his brother, the Duke of Gloucester and eight senior members of his household. No sound was heard by the watching crowds but the slow clop of horses' hooves.

A group of black-coated ladies waited at Westminster – the late King's widow, his mother, Queen Mary, in a peaked black velvet cap and a coat reaching to her feet, his daughters, the new Queen and Princess Margaret, and his sister, the Princess Royal. They looked small and vulnerable and all hearts went out to them. In New Palace Yard was a Guard of Honour of the Scots Guards and four of their officers took up their places round the coffin as soon as it was installed in the centre of the catafalque. This author's husband recalls seamstresses crouched on the steps, putting the last stitches to the purple drapery of the catafalque moments before the first of the public were admitted to the hall. Throughout the ninety hours that the late King's remains lay at Westminster, four officers of the Household Brigade stood, each at a corner of the top step of the dais, while four Yeomen of the Guard stood at the bottom. Two gentlemen-at-arms stood at the head of the coffin which was surmounted by the imperial state crown and regalia and by the Queen Mother's wreath of flowers. Every twenty minutes the guards were relieved, one by one, and no sound was heard by the shuffling multitudes but the steely clink of sword in scabbard.

Through three days and four nights the people came, queuing in the cold and snow flurries of a London February, all along the Embankment, over Lambeth Bridge, along past St Thomas's Hospital and doubling back by Lambeth Palace and over the bridge again. All who could wore dark coats and hats, for the Earl Marshal had ordered general mourning, that '... all persons do put themselves into mourning until after His late Majesty's funeral',[11] and anyway, the people mourned like a beloved relation this shy man who had stood with them through the long years of the war. But a sprinkling of the caps of off-duty nurses from the nearby hospitals could be seen throughout the queue. Inside the Hall the

Opposite: The Squire of Sandringham lies in St Mary Magdelene's Church on the estate, watched over by his own gamekeepers. The coffin is draped with the Royal Standard and surmounted only by his Queen's flowers.

Mysterious veiled figures – The Queen Mother and Princess Margaret leaving Westminster Hall for the funeral procession to Paddington station. In the background are Earl Mountbatten and the Duke of Windsor.

mourners divided into two lines at the top of the great steps and passed on each side of the coffin. Officers on vigil were warned not to look at the steadily shuffling feet for fear of feeling giddy.

On the last evening, 14 February, the young Queen and her sister came and stood watching for some minutes, unnoticed in the shadows, and later came the Queen Mother and, on another occasion, Queen Mary with the Duke of Windsor who had sailed from New York immediately upon hearing the news of his brother's death. The doors remained open until six o'clock on the morning of Friday, 15 February, the day of the funeral, but the numbers of mourners were not as great as at the lying-in-state of King George V. Many people were beginning to be accustomed to seeing state events on their television screens, or at least on a newsreel at the cinema.

Once more the streets were lined with troops though they were not this time hung with purple, and at 9.30 in the morning the funeral procession set out as 'the Abbey bells scattered their muffled peals over the roofs of Westminster'.[12] It was all very like the funeral of George V: the coffin, drawn as always since the funeral of Queen Victoria, by sailors, a hundred and fifty of them this time, was preceded by detachments of soldiers, sailors and airmen, four bands, senior officers of all three services, including some famous names from the war. As before, four royal dukes followed the coffin, though this time only two of them were brothers – the Dukes of Windsor and Gloucester – son-in-law, the Duke of Edinburgh, and the sixteen-year-old Duke of Kent in a black overcoat and top hat. But immediately behind the sovereign's standard bearer, this time mounted and following immediately behind the gun-carriage, came the Irish State Coach carrying the Queen, her mother and sister and the Princess Royal, all veiled but visible to the sympathetic watching crowds.

Three Kings – of Sweden, Greece and Denmark – headed the royal representatives, together with the President of France, while the old King of Norway rode in a carriage, and this time there was a considerable band of Commonwealth heads of government. After the Second World War, the European ties were weakening as the Commonwealth ones grew and strengthened. Group Captain Peter Townsend, as one of the King's equerries, walked beside the coffin, that 'crisp winter's morning'. 'Never had I known a walk so long, so slow, so sad,'[13] he wrote later. 'To the measured and mournful beat of the funeral airs of Handel and Chopin,'[14] the procession proceeded along Whitehall and the Mall. In the window of Marlborough House, sat Queen Mary, too frail to attend the funeral, with her old friend and lady-in-waiting, Lady Airlie.

> As the cortège wound slowly along the Queen whispered in a broken voice, 'Here *he* is,' and I knew that her dry eyes were seeing beyond the coffin a little boy in a sailor suit. She was past weeping, wrapped in the ineffable solitude of grief. I could not speak to comfort her. My tears choked me. The words I wanted to say would not come. We held each other's hand in silence.[15]

At Hyde Park Corner they passed the house where the late King, as Duke of York, had once lived. It was a sad sight now, bombed and partly demolished, draped in purple and black and with the Union Flag flying at half mast.

The crowds were immense but very orderly this time and subdued, with women openly weeping. Their unlikely hero, pushed unexpectedly on to the throne, shy and awkward of manner, had yet, by his simplicity, sincerity and devotion to his country and his people won in return the love and devotion of those people. Two minutes' silence was observed in many places, notably in South Wales where miners knelt at the coalface, heads bowed, their helmets on their knees.

Memorial services were held in St Paul's and in English churches of all denominations throughout London and the world, even in countries of the Communist bloc. *The Times* was full of tributes from the great and the good, and all spoke of the King's simplicity and devotion. An Australian cabinet minister summed it up for many: 'He was a good bloke.'[16]

At Paddington the mourners embarked at noon on a train pulled by the Eastnor Castle, and travelled behind drawn blinds to Windsor, followed by the Windsor Castle, adorned with purple shields and a crown, the modern equivalent of escutcheons, drawing the vans in which travelled the coffin and the bearer party. Along the route, people who had been unable to come to London stood bareheaded in the cold to watch it pass.

Meanwhile, at St George's Chapel, the invited congregation was being entertained by a wonderful programme of organ music arranged by Dr Harris, the organist. Suitable funeral pieces included the prelude to Stanford's opera, *The Travelling Companion*, and a funeral march by the Master of the King's Musick, Sir Arnold Bax, for the film *Malta GC*.

The procession from Windsor station followed the now established tradition of heralds, households, doctors, chaplains, terminating with the Yeomen of the Guard. There was just one carriage carrying the Queen and the other chief lady mourners. Other royal ladies were taken straight to the Chapel by car.

St George's was, said *The Times*, 'bathed in the light of the winter sun, symbol of the lux perpetua to which the dead are called.'[17] The 23rd Psalm was sung and, most suitably, the joyful Easter hymn, 'The Strife is o'er, the battle done; Now is the Victor's triumph won'. The anthem 'I heard a voice from Heaven' was in a new setting by Dr Harris himself instead of the more usual setting by Goss. At the committal, the slender black-veiled figure of the young Queen stepped forward to scatter earth on the coffin as it descended into the vault and then the organ burst forth with Parry's prelude, 'Ye boundless realms of Joy', which *The Times* described as 'not sombre but radiant',[18] a hopeful ending which lifted everyone's

Opposite: The moment of committal: as the King's coffin sinks into the vault, his daughter, Queen Elizabeth II, sprinkles the earth of the last rite upon the coffin.

spirits. The musical hand of the Queen Mother is surely seen in this beautiful service.

Eventually the body of King George VI was buried in his own beautiful little chantry on the north side of the Chapel. Raised tombs and effigies had by now gone out of fashion and his grave is marked only by an inscription in the floor and a plaque showing the King's head of the wall to the chantry.

Queen Mary was now into her sixth reign but the blow of her son's death had been too much for even her iron constitution to bear and she aged rapidly. She was, however, still able to see friends and relations at Marlborough House and her interest in art continued to the end. Indeed, within a week of her death she was writing to a friend: 'I feel weary and unwell but your charming catalogue has given me great pleasure. I particularly like the portrait of Marianito Goya with the silk hat – as one sees it was painted with great love.'[19]

Through the summer and autumn of 1952 Queen Mary carried on visiting exhibitions and antique shops, and read and wrote letters but, as the winter came on, she was too tired to go out and even to receive any but the oldest friends. One of these was Mabel, Lady Airlie who visited her in her bedroom and 'chatted away about trivial things' to avoid tiring her by having to talk.

All the while I was conscious of the perfection of everything around her; the exquisitely embroidered soft lawn nightgown . . . the nails delicately shaped and polished a pale pink; the immaculately arranged grey hair. Her face had still a gentle beauty of expression; no trace of hardness as so many faces have in old age, only resignation. As I kissed her hand before leaving her I noticed the extreme softness of her skin.[20]

Queen Mary's last outing was in February 1953 when she drove out to view the preparations, the stands and crush barriers, for the coronation. She let it be known that, in the eventuality of her death, nothing must prevent this from taking place and so when on 24 March Queen Mary did die 'peacefully while sleeping',[21] the preparations went on unabated.

The Duke of Windsor had been in London anyway when his mother was taken ill and he visited her to the end. The wound inflicted on Queen Mary by Edward VIII's abdication had never been healed and she had never received the Duchess, yet a tenderness between mother and eldest son remained and he had visited her a number of times through the years. Now he took his place behind her coffin as it was borne to Westminster, and remained for the funeral.

On a darkening afternoon, five days after her death, Queen Mary's body was carried out of the Queen's Chapel, Marlborough House, and then drawn on a gun-carriage down the Mall and along Whitehall to Westminster Hall where she lay in state under the magnificent pall made for Queen Alexandra, for thirty-six hours. For the second time in just over a year, long lines of people queued day and night to pay their last respects to one who had been a living monument before most of them were born.

After the lying-in-state, the proceedings became private. On the morning of 31 March, the coffin was privately collected by motor hearse and driven to Windsor where a private family funeral was held, the young Queen, so soon to be crowned, once again scattering earth as the coffin was wound down into the vault. Some time later Queen Mary joined her husband in the tomb in the north aisle which had seemed so lopsided without her, and her effigy was laid beside that of King George V.

Tributes to Queen Mary filled every newspaper and came from all round the world. All stressed her devotion to duty and the high standards by which she lived. The closing words of her biography by James Pope-Hennessy say it better and more neatly than most: 'It was Queen Mary's crowning reward, as it is the lesson to be drawn from any contemplation of her life, that, by undeviating service to her own highest ideals, she had ended by becoming, for millions, an ideal in herself.'[22]

During the years that followed, a number of members of the royal family died and were buried according to the now established form of private royal funeral, and were buried at Frogmore. The arrangements for such funerals are as follows: the coffin, which has rested either in the Albert Memorial Chapel or in the Nave, is carried by a bearer party into the choir and placed on a catafalque to be watched over by the Governor of the Castle and four Military Knights. The congregation arrives and takes their places in the choir, the royal family entering via the Galilee Porch. The immediate family of the deceased, the Queen, the Duke of Edinburgh and the Queen Mother assemble at the Deanery next door, and are conducted to their seats from there. The service is taken by the Dean and at the end a procession is formed to follow the coffin out of the Chapel. The Dean and the Lord Chamberlain precede the coffin and after it come the close family mourners, followed by the Queen and the royal family. Some, though not all, of the royal family then proceed to Frogmore for the brief committal in the Royal Burial Ground. At one early spring funeral, an elderly member of the family was overheard in a loud aside to his wife as they waited for the service in the Chapel to begin: 'I hope we don't have to go to Frogmore. Beastly cold place, Frogmore.'

Among those whose funerals followed these lines were Princess Helena Victoria (1948) and Princess Marie Louise (1956), elderly daughters of Princess Christian,

Princess Marina (1968), Lady Patricia Ramsay, formerly Princess Patricia of Connaught (1974), and her husband, Admiral Sir Alexander Ramsay, in 1972.

The Princess Royal, sister of George VI, who died in 1965 following a stroke at her home, Harewood House, near Leeds, was buried completely privately at Harewood, where her husband already lay, and the Lord Chamberlain's Office, which normally arranges all funerals of Royal Highnesses, was in no way involved.

One younger member of the royal family whose funeral also followed this pattern was Prince William of Gloucester, elder son of the Duke and Duchess of Gloucester. The dashing and glamorous young Prince was mad on polo and flying and it was the latter that led to his tragic death at the age of thirty-one in 1972. Prince William was taking part in an air race at Halfpenny Green in Staffordshire on August Bank Holiday. Fiercely competitive by nature, William was determined to win this one for he had decided to give up racing. On take-off he turned rather too quickly, lost height, sliced the top off a tree and crashed into a road. Both he and his passenger were killed. All his young friends, visibly shaken, attended the funeral, at St George's, four days later.

Written into the modern-day arrangements for royal funerals, there is provision for varying degrees of ceremonial. This depends upon the rank of the deceased as well as the wishes of the family, and includes queen consorts. We have already seen examples of this in Queen Alexandra's funeral and that of Queen Mary. Mostly those who receive ceremonial funerals are men, sons of the sovereign and military men.

An example of this last category was the Earl of Athlone (1957), brother of Queen Mary. Once His Serene Highness Prince Alexander of Teck but deprived of his German title during the First World War, the Earl was a Major General and had been Gold Stick. As such, he rated something of a military funeral with a procession from Windsor station, a thirteen-gun salute in the Long Walk and a bearer party from the Household Cavalry. His widow, Princess Alice, last surviving granddaughter of Queen Victoria, survived him by twenty-four years, dying, aged ninety-seven, in 1981. Her funeral was a private one as previously described and then she and her husband were both interred together in a double grave at Frogmore.

In May 1972, the Queen paid a state visit to France and, in the course of the few days she spent in Paris, she called on her uncle, the Duke of Windsor, once King Edward VIII, who was by then in an advanced state of cancer. Indeed, it was not known until the very day if he would be able to receive her. With a last valiant effort, he was determined to be up and dressed to see his niece and had all the tubes and needles through which he was now fed removed. It took his doctor and nurse nearly four hours to get him ready. The Queen was met at the front door of their home in the Bois de Boulogne by the Duchess who was seen, by the massed reporters, to curtsy deeply, and conducted upstairs to the Duke's sitting room. Here she found the Duke looking relaxed but emaciated in an armchair, dressed in a jaunty blue boating-jacket, his doctor hovering nearby. The meeting was short but cordial, the Queen doing most of the talking as the Duke could barely speak, and it was to be their last for, little more than a week later, just short of his seventy-eighth birthday, he was dead.

On 27 May the Duke asked his nurse, 'Am I dying?' 'You're quite intelligent enough to decide that for yourself,'[23] was her brisk but evasive reply. By evening he had sunk into a coma and his favourite pug, Black Diamond, who always lay on the foot of his bed, had forsaken his post and lay on the floor, his head turned away. 'See? The dog knows what's happening,'[24] remarked Doctor Thin to the nurse. In the early hours of the next morning, 28 May, the Duke of Windsor died quietly in his sleep.

For thirty-five years the Duke had been a 'weary, wayward, wandering ghost',[25] perpetually travelling with the Duchess between America and France with short visits to England and the war years in the Bahamas. Now he was to come home. It was announced that, at his own request, he was to be buried at Frogmore and that, one day, his Duchess would join him there. Meanwhile, the Queen sent an aircraft of the Queen's Flight to fetch his body and another for the Duchess who was to stay at Buckingham Palace.

At his final homecoming, the Duke of Windsor was treated like a king. He was met at RAF Benson by a Royal Guard of Honour, by the Duke and Duchess of Kent, members of the government and the French Ambassador. After a night in the chapel at Benson, the coffin draped in the Duke's personal standard and loaded with the Duchess's flowers, was driven to Windsor. At his arrival at the Castle, the flag on the Round Tower which flies night and day was lowered, and flags in the town and all over England flew at half mast until the funeral.

At the Queen's command, the Duke's body lay in state in the nave of the chapel and the public were admitted for four days. And the public came – in their thousands they came. There had always been a substantial body of feeling in the country that the Duke had been treated shabbily and now at last they had a chance to treat him like a king.

By now, the Duchess was installed at Buckingham Palace where she was kindly received by the Queen and the royal family but left largely alone. There is a rather pathetic photograph of her, caught by an alert photographer outside the Palace, peering from a window as the Queen rode out to the Trooping of the Colour.

There a lament was played on the pipes in honour of the one-time sovereign and a few moments of silence observed before the parade began.

On Monday, 5 June, the funeral, carefully planned by the Duke himself, took place at St George's and was attended by all the royal family and the King of Norway. It was called a private royal funeral and certainly it was without outside ceremonial but, as a King's son, even if not as an ex-king himself, he was entitled to certain honours in addition to the service as described above. As the congregation arrived, they heard the sombre tones of the Curfew Bell of the Castle which tolled for an hour before the service. This bell is now rung only for the birth of a prince, a royal marriage or the death of a sovereign. On the other hand, a salute of twenty-one guns was fired, as for a Royal Highness rather than that which is fired for a sovereign – the number of years of his life. The service was conducted by the Dean but the Archbishops of Canterbury and York were present and the Moderator of the Church of Scotland. The Duchess, in a short black veil, sat leaning forward between the Queen and the Duke of Edinburgh and at the end of the service the coffin did not descend into the vault. After the final hymn, 'Lead us Heavenly Father, Lead us', Garter King-of-Arms stepped forward and, as his predecessors had done for hundreds of years, proclaimed the Duke's style and titles. Slipped in at the end of the list of Knight of the Garter and Knight Grand Cross of this and that, Privy Councillor, Admiral of the Fleet, Field Marshal and Marshal of the Royal Air Force, came 'Sometime the Most High, Most Mighty and Most Excellent Monarch Edward the Eighth, By the Grace of God, of Great Britain, Ireland and the British Dominions beyond the Seas, King, Defender of the Faith, Emperor of India . . .', hurrying on to finish with 'Uncle of the Most High, Most Mighty and Most Excellent Monarch, Our Sovereign Lady Elizabeth the Second . . .'.[26] The Archbishop pronounced the blessing and then the 'Last Post' and 'Reveille' were sounded by the State Trumpeters of the Household Cavalry.

On this occasion the coffin was not taken straight to Frogmore but the royal family and congregation retired leaving it in the choir, watched over by four Military Knights. Later the Duke's body was interred very privately beside a spreading beech tree at Frogmore. The plate on his coffin reads, in English:

HRH The Prince Edward Albert Christian George
Andrew Patrick David, Duke of Windsor
Born 1894 Died 1972
King Edward VIII
20 January – 11 December 1936

'The Duke of Windsor comes home'. The body of the man who was once King Edward VIII arrived by VC10 at RAF Benson, Oxfordshire from Paris and was driven to the station church where it lay before being taken to Windsor for the laying-in-state and funeral.

Two years later the last of King George V's children died – his third son, Prince Henry, Duke of Gloucester. At the age of seventy-four, the Duke had been an invalid, confined by a series of strokes to his home, Barnwell Manor, in Northamptonshire for a number of years. In June 1974, he died peacefully, surrounded by his remaining family and devoted servants.

In line with the, by now, normal custom, the Duke's funeral had been carefully planned some years before and approved by the family. As the son of a monarch and also a Royal Field Marshal, his funeral was to be a ceremonial one. But, first, a personal, homely touch; for the last several decades, Prince Henry had been squire of the little village of Barnwell and it was as such that his coffin lay in Barnwell Church, surrounded by the Duchess's flowers, and villagers, estate workers and local friends came to pay their last respects.

On 14 June the funeral took place at Windsor with a military procession consisting of detachments of all the Duke's regiments, the Navy and the Royal Air Force, marching with two bands playing from Victoria Barracks to the Castle. His insignia were carried before the coffin on its gun-carriage, flanked by Field Marshals, Admirals and Air Marshals as pall bearers. A twenty-one gun salute was fired in the Long Walk and behind the coffin marched the new Duke, a sober civilian figure in top hat and tail coat, with the Prince of Wales, the Duke of Edinburgh, other men of the royal family and His Royal Highness's household. This included, all resplendent in top hats, his two butlers, his chauffeur, groom and valet, most of whom had been with him for many years.

Ceremonial in the Chapel followed closely that for the Duke of Windsor. As on that occasion, the coffin was accompanied up the aisle by both Archbishops and the Moderator of the Church of Scotland, Dr Steel, father of the Liberal leader. The service was short and moving with plenty of singing, hymns specially chosen by the Duchess including the beautiful 'O Love that wilt not let me go', and 'Fight the good fight with all thy might'. It ended with the Duke's style and titles and 'Last Post' and 'Reveille,' before the body of the Duke was taken to Frogmore and interred beside that of his son, William, on the other side of the same shady tree as his brother.

Today mourning is also divided into types – four of them. At the death of the sovereign, general mourning until the funeral is ordered by the Earl Marshal and is, it is hoped, observed by the general public. On this occasion the Court would be in mourning for six months, and there are very pretty photographs of the Queen and Princess Margaret at Ascot the summer after the King's death, dressed variously in black and white, grey and lavender. Court mourning, as the sovereign commands, is observed by all members of the royal family, their households, the household troops and Her Majesty's representatives at home and abroad. It consists of a black armband for those in uniform, dark suit and black tie for men, and black dress for ladies, and those in mourning are not expected to be seen in a public place – a theatre or restaurant, or at a dance – during the period of mourning, which is generally until after the funeral. Service mourning covers all the armed forces and entails a black armband in uniform and a black tie in plain clothes. Family mourning, again at the sovereign's discretion, is observed by members of the royal family and their household only when in attendance. The use of black-edged writing paper, once so rigidly observed by many sections of society, lingers on but is now much reduced even in the Queen's own household.

Of course, almost the grandest funeral of the century was that of Sir Winston Churchill in 1962. A full state funeral, under the auspices of the Earl Marshal, is a very rare occurrence, generally limited to sovereigns, but there have been three state funerals of eminent commoners since such distinctions have been formulated: Nelson in 1806, the Duke of Wellington in 1852, and Churchill in 1962. No one who was there or who saw it on television, will forget the grandeur of the occasion, the lying-in-state at Westminster, the vast procession to St Paul's, the service with the 'Battle Hymn of the Republic' thundered out by thousands of voices, the progress up the river with the elegant giraffe heads of the cranes dipping in salute and the unforgettably stately figure of the Earl Marshal, the late Duke of Norfolk, pacing at the head of the coffin.

We have not seen another such, but in 1979 there was one which, though not a state funeral, was a royal ceremonial occasion *par excellence* and a great tribute to a hero of our time.

Admiral of the Fleet Earl Mountbatten of Burma came right at the bottom of the hierarchy of the royal family. He was a great-grandson of Queen Victoria, but it was more as a great man – a hero to thousands of old sailors, survivors with him of the sinking of the Kelly in 1942, veterans of the Burma campaign in the Second World War – and as a victim of the troubles in Northern Ireland that he was honoured that September day in 1979.

At seventy-nine, Mountbatten had had a long and varied life: last Viceroy of India, First Sea Lord, Chief of the Defence Staff and, after retirement and widowhood, still active as Gold Stick, Commandant of the Royal Marines, Governor of the Isle of Wight, successful writer and television personality and latterly, stately home operator. He was also uncle, friend and self appointed adviser of the royal family. So his was still a busy life when he set off with some of his family for what was to be his last holiday at Classiebawn, his castle on the west coast of Ireland.

On August Bank Holiday Monday 1979 a family party consisting of Lord Mountbatten, his elder daughter, Lady Brabourne, Lord Brabourne, Doreen, Lady Brabourne, mother of Lord Brabourne, and their fourteen-year-old twins, Timothy and Nicholas, set off from Classiebawn in Lord Mountbatten's motor cruiser, Shadow V. It was a glorious morning and they were going to lift the lobster pots they had set the day before.

When the party arrived at the little harbour of Mullaghmore, young Paul Maxwell, at fifteen only a little older than the twins, had Shadow V's engine already turning over. The regular boatman had failed to turn up this year and Paul from Enniskillen, just over the Northern Ireland border, had taken it on as a holiday job. Granny was helped aboard by the twins, their parents took their seats and Lord Mountbatten his place at the wheel, and Shadow V eased out of the little harbour while the two Garda protection officers assigned to Mountbatten settled down to watch with binoculars from their car.

There were several other pleasure boats out that day and a number of people watching from the shore as Shadow V reached her destination a few hundred yards from the shore. Mountbatten eased back the throttle and Lord Brabourne was leaning over to bring up the first lobster pot when five pounds of gelignite exploded under Lord Mountbatten's seat. The boat disintegrated with a tearing crack and everyone in the boat was flung high into the air along with a random shower of wood and metal, seats, ropes and pieces of clothing. War had once more closed in on the Admiral and this time there was no escape.

Neighbouring boats were on the scene within seconds and the rescue operation began. Lord and Lady Brabourne were badly injured, though alive, and so was Timothy. But Nicholas was dead as was their young friend, Paul Maxwell, and Admiral of the Fleet Earl Mountbatten of Burma floated face down in the shreds of his Kelly jersey. The IRA had claimed their most famous victim.

Within minutes the news had flashed all round the world. The royal family at Balmoral were told, and so was the Lord Chamberlain and his staff. As it was a bank holiday, the officers of the Lord Chamberlain's Office were on leave, but by the end of the day they had reassembled at St James's Palace and the well-oiled wheels were already turning to arrange the grandest funeral since that of Sir Winston Churchill seventeen years before.

While the rest of the Mountbatten family rallied round to comfort and look after the survivors of the tragedy, in London the staff of the Lord Chamberlain's Office, officers at Headquarters, London District, the Metropolitan Police and Westminster Abbey were working almost literally night and day in order to bring to fruition in less than ten days the master plan which had been worked out down to the smallest detail by Mountbatten himself many months before.

Some years before his death, Lord Mountbatten went to the Lord Chamberlain's Office and told them exactly what he wanted. It was to be a ceremonial funeral at Westminster Abbey with full military honours. It was taken for granted that the royal family would be there to a man (and woman) and that there would be a splendid and international procession reflecting all the various phases of his life. The endless list of those to take part and to be invited to the Abbey was discussed. It was to include representatives of every organization he had ever been involved with. And then there was to be the journey from London to Romsey Abbey and the final resting place. The service was discussed with the Dean of Westminster, the hymns and readings decided upon.

All the same there was much to be done in a short time, and the thing which loomed largest on the scene was the necessity for a security operation on a scale never seen before. The fact of the murder by the IRA made it quite possible that there would be some attempt at a follow-up during the funeral procession. And all the men of the royal family would be marching in the procession scarcely more than an arm's length from the crowd lining the route and separated from them only by a widely spaced line of streetliners with heads bowed and backs turned to the crowd. The Metropolitan Police had to swamp the processional route with officers on rooftops and vantage points and with others mingling with the crowd and, such is the way of things in Britain, it had all to be done so unobtrusively that no one would be aware of the heavy police presence.

The Foreign Office was busy too, arranging the reception and accommodation of distinguished representatives from all over the world. The services, centred on Horse Guards, were arranging for contingents of troops from India, America, Canada, Burma and France to be flown in, accommodated and drilled as well as detachments from all of the British services. And all those organizing the funeral must be in touch with the Mountbatten family who were gradually making their wishes known. The Abbey staff rehearsed their different processions again and again with the organ playing and surrogate royals stepping off on a given note, while anyone who was abroad in the Mall or Whitehall at 4.30 one morning early that week would have seen a ghostly army padding silently through the streets. This was the only full rehearsal of the outdoor procession.

The Mountbatten family, with immense strength of will, were bracing themselves for the ordeal of the funeral. It was obvious from the start that Lord and Lady Brabourne would be unable to leave hospital in time, nor would Timothy, but all the others would be there. Lady Pamela Hicks had rushed out to Ireland to be with her sister, taking twelve year-old India to cheer Timothy, but now they returned and were joined by Lady Pamela's husband, David Hicks and their other children, Edwina and Ashley. The remaining Brabourne children also foregathered: Norton Knatchbull, now Lord Romsey, and his fiancée, Penelope Eastwood, Michael John, Philip, Joanna and Amanda. And some days before the funeral Mountbatten himself was brought home and lay in Romsey Abbey which had for so long been his local church.

The evening before the funeral, from all parts of the country and abroad, a crowd began to gather, preparing to spend the night in the Mall or Parliament Square to pay their last respects to their hero as he passed on his way to the grave.

Fortunately the weather was fine and warm, for as well as late summer tourists and the usual Londoners who turn out for every great spectacle, there were many who were in their seventies and eighties. These were men and women whose paths had crossed those of Lord Louis, as they still liked to call him, in a war which had started forty years ago almost to the day. Many wore their medals and Burma Star berets to honour the man who had led them to victory. And while this crowd was gathering, unknown to them, the body of Lord Mountbatten was being brought from Romsey and placed, a stone's throw from where they stood, in the Queen's Chapel at St James's where it was to lie overnight.

The next morning all was subdued bustle. The crowd gathered themselves together after the night in the open and stood quietly, munching sandwiches and telling the young among them stories of the great man. In St James's Palace the men of the royal family were foregathering with the Mountbatten men and other high ranking officers who were to walk in the procession, and the royal ladies and foreign royal visitors were gathering to drive to the Abbey by another route. Streetliners took up their places with heads bowed and hands folded over their arms reversed and in the roadway all round St James's Palace the procession was forming up. Only the echoing sound of orders shouted in several different languages broke in on the rustle of the trees and the quiet murmur of the crowd.

Now the mourners moved silently over the road and into the Queen's Chapel. A few short prayers were said and the coffin, on the shoulders of eight proud sailors, was borne out into the sunlight and placed on the gun-carriage.

The crowd fell silent and the first round of a nineteen-gun salute boomed out across the park, the Central Band of the Royal Air Force, their drums muffled and trimmed with black bows, struck up a mournful funeral march, and the procession moved slowly out into the Mall.

There were detachments of troops from the United States, matelots with red pom-poms from France, turbanned Indians, Canadians and Gurkhas with green pillboxes at a jaunty angle. These were followed by men and women from all the British services, tramping in slow time with set faces. And as the sound of one band died away in the distance another took up the sombre theme. Now came the Household Cavalry looking strange without their horses and marching stiffly in their high boots. And on and on they came. The head of the procession was already crossing Horse Guards when the gun-carriage left St James's, and it is tempting to

Opposite: Earl Mountbatten's charger, Dolly, with her master's boots reversed in the stirrups is led ahead of the coffin in the procession to Westminster Abbey.

wonder whether Mountbatten had thought of the funeral of Nelson, one of the great spectacles of all time, when he planned his own. On that occasion the head of the procession had reached St Paul's before the tail had left the Admiralty.

Now the nucleus of the cortège was under way. Officers of London District were followed by the insignia. Mountbatten loved orders and decorations and it took six men to carry his on velvet cushions: his Garter, his Bath, his Star of India and all the rest. And then came Dolly. Lord Mountbatten's old black charger, led by her groom, had the honour of walking immediately in front of the gun-carriage drawn by its gun crew of sailors. As one reporter put it: 'Dolly picked her feet up and put them down precisely. Her head nodded. The empty saddle on her gleaming back moved slowly with the rhythm of her walk. Her dead rider's boots, reversed in the stirrups, were polished brilliantly and they gleamed in the sun too.'[27] She made a deep impression on the watching crowd.

A hundred and thirty-one sailors made up the proud crew which drew the gun-carriage on which rested the coffin draped with the Union Flag and bearing Mountbatten's Gold Stick, his sword of honour and his admiral's cocked hat. These were all young men, too young to have served with Mountbatten, but he was still the hero of the Navy and there had been fierce competition for the honour of drawing his funeral car. Together with the pall bearers, high-ranking officers of several nations, they surrounded the coffin as though to protect it from any evil that might befall. No one seemed to protect the ten men who walked behind the coffin: the four grandsons looking very young and vulnerable in their black coats, followed by the Prince of Wales and the Duke of Edinburgh with David Hicks, and then the Dukes of Gloucester and Kent and Prince Michael – uniformed figures moving to the doleful rhythm as though unaware of any possible danger. This danger had been threatened but many in the crowd were aware of tall men with neat haircuts unobtrusively keeping pace with the marching figures from behind the front rank of spectators, and were reassured.

What were the thoughts of those ten men as they paced along? Three of the young grandsons were mourning the little brother they were to bury next day, and their grandmother, as well as a grandfather who had joined in all the games of their childhood, allowing himself to be buried up to the neck in sand at Classiebawn. Besides, they were all worried about their parents, still very ill in an Irish hospital. Prince Philip had loved Mountbatten more as a father than an uncle and had sought his help and advice in all the problems of his life. Now he was gone and where would he turn for that help now? Prince Charles had adored him as a hero as well as the nearest he had ever known to a grandfather. Royal persons do not have many confidants and his loss would leave an aching void which might never be

The coffin of Admiral of the Fleet Earl Mountbatten of Burma is borne through the streets of London on a naval gun carriage. The four young men immediately behind the gun crew are his grandsons and they are followed by the men of the Royal Family.

filled. These thoughts were reflected in their faces as they passed down the Mall.

Then came several more ranks of senior officers, Burmese, American and British, and the closing detachments of the procession – veterans of the Burma Star Association, the Kelly Reunion and the British Legion marching proudly to the massed bands of the Brigade of Guards, following the leader who had led them to victory so long ago. As one newspaper put it next day, 'princes, admirals, common

[261]

soldiers and sailors who had sweated in jungles and shivered at sea with him, marched together behind his coffin, united in grief.'[28]

As is often the case with our great ceremonial funerals, this was a scene of striking contradictions: the sun shone on scarlet uniforms and glinted on helmets and medals and a busy little breeze frisked among the trees and the plumes of the soldiers, yet there was no feeling of carnival here; the bands played, but the crowds did not cheer, and there was none of the usual dash and swing of a grand military parade, just the slow, heavy tread of sorrow. There was all the colour of hundreds of full-dress uniforms of several different countries and in the midst of them five slim figures, bareheaded in plainest black, the chief mourners.

Slowly the procession wound on its way to the muffled thump of Chopin's 'Funeral March' and the 'Dead March in Saul', those sombre accompaniments to so many of our grand occasions. Across Horse Guards they moved and into Whitehall, and now they were approaching the Abbey to the tolling of a single muffled bell. They passed the silent crowds in Parliament Square, and at last the gun-carriage drew up at the great west door. Here it was met by the Archbishop of Canterbury, Dr Coggan, and representatives of all the major denominations, and the coffin, once more on the shoulders of the eight bareheaded sailors, was borne into the Abbey and started up the long aisle. Except for the rich vestments of the clergy, the scene here might almost have been cut from a black and white film. Row upon row of mourners in deepest black filled the nave. Beyond it was the choir and then on one side of the catafalque the distant black figures of Lady Pamela Hicks and her daughters and nieces, the youngest, twelve-year-old India, clutching a posy of violets.

On the other side was the Queen and all the rest of the royal family from the Queen Mother, with a gentle smile for the young, to bouncy Marina Ogilvy looking uncomfortable in her unaccustomed sombre dress.

Royal ladies do not weep in public and no one did. The Queen hid her thoughts behind spectacles and a severe expresion. Was she thinking that Uncle Dickie had been the dominant influence on the lives of her husband and her son, or was she remembering Malta with Dickie and Edwina in the gay old days of her youth, or honeymooning at Broadlands and many later visits?

Earl Mountbatten had been related to almost every royal family in Europe and so there were two kings present and a score or more of princes and representatives of the governments of most of the world. One country, however, was not represented. Lord Mountbatten could not forgive the Japanese for the horrors he had seen in the Far East at the end of the war. He would not have them invited and they were deeply hurt.

The coffin of Earl Mountbatten is carried out of Westminster Abbey after the service, followed by members of his own and the Royal Family.

Inch by inch, as the organ played softly, the long procession moved up the aisle bearing the coffin to its place on the catafalque in the lantern. Prince Philip kept stretching his neck as though to dislodge a lump, and the Prince of Wales, looking pinched and stricken, had tears in his eyes as the service began. His voice, however, was firm as he read from Psalm 107, 'They that go down to the sea in ships and occupy their business in great waters, these men see the works of the Lord'. It might have been written for Lord Mountbatten.

It was all good rousing stuff, as he had intended: 'The tumult and the shouting dies; the captains and the kings depart' from Kipling's 'God of our fathers known of old', 'I vow to thee, my country', 'Jerusalem'. Ten buglers from the Royal Marines sounded the 'Last Post' and 'Reveille' on silver bugles and then the congregation sang the sailors' hymn, 'Eternal Father strong to save'. The *Daily Mail* reporter wrote next day, 'the great roaring chorus "... for those in peril on the sea" rushed out of the building and then the singing of the crowd came back in through the door'.[29] It was Mountbatten's favourite hymn for he had been in peril on the sea, but even he did not guess what peril there would be at the last.

Out into the sunshine once more, but the pageantry was ended. The coffin was placed on an army Landrover, plain and functional, and driven to Waterloo Station for Lord Mountbatten's last journey to Romsey. The royal family, the Mountbattens, and all who were to attend the interment followed and boarded the special train where black bordered menus proclaimed that luncheon would be served on the journey. British Rail, with unusual imagination, had found a guard who had served under Mountbatten. 'I'll look after him. I owe him that much,'[30] he said.

At Romsey it was a simpler, family affair. At the old stone Abbey the surrounding grass was ablaze with the massed wreaths sent by people of every kind from the Queen to the three Broadlands stable girls who had each sent a red rose. Prince Charles's wreath bore the coded message, 'To my HGF & GU from his loving and devoted HGS & GN' – Honorary Grandfather and Great Uncle, Honorary Grandson and Great Nephew.

The people of Romsey paid their respects to their squire in almost Victorian style. All the shops were shut that day and the whole town turned out and joined the Broadlands staff in and around the Abbey, while standing quietly in the invited congregation was John Maxwell who had buried his son Paul in Ireland the day before. And it should not be forgotten that this was not the only military funeral in Britain that day. In five churches all over the country the soldier victims of the IRA at Warrenpoint in Ulster, killed on the same day as Lord Mountbatten, were buried with full military honours.

[264]

And so, at last, after a short committal service, the sailors carried their admiral to his last resting place in the Broadlands Chapel in the sunlit Abbey. He had wanted it to be a 'happy occasion' and no one could make it that, but it had been an unforgettable one – a brilliant parade carried out just as he had planned it. It did justice to a great man and perhaps he would have said it was the best parade of his long life.

Royal funerals have passed through many stages since Tudor and Stuart times when they were comparatively impromptu and were yet rigidly controlled by sumptuary laws and by the fact that everyone knew his place and kept it, through the rather chaotic Georgian days when society was in a state of flux and the royal family was not held in high esteem, and the Victorian high noon of mourning, to today's beautifully planned and executed ceremonial, the envy of the world.

As we have seen, today's royal funerals fall into three categories. The state funeral is generally limited to sovereigns but may, by order of the sovereign, be extended to exceptionally distinguished persons. This is the responsibility of the Earl Marshal and the College of Arms, with the Lord Chamberlain's Office only involved in getting the royal family to the funeral. The ceremonial royal funeral is for those of the royal family who hold high military rank and consorts of the sovereign, and are under the auspices of the Lord Chamberlain, who would also expect to be involved in the third category – private royal funerals, particularly in the case of those of the rank of Royal Highness. Lying-in-state is again by order of the sovereign but is, in practice, limited to sovereigns and queen consorts, though it might include a prince of Wales or consort of a queen.

Stemming from King Edward VII's determination that the uncertainties of Queen Victoria's funeral should never be repeated, all royal obsequies today are carefully planned in advance from a proforma. Elderly members of the family are consulted and some find the planning of their funeral quite diverting, juggling with hymns and crossing people off the list to be invited as they die or fall from favour, and making their wishes known. This, and the wishes of the close family who are consulted throughout, helps to bring something personal to each funeral. The privacy of the mourners is preserved and yet, the public who, in this country, identify closely with the royal family are able to feel that this is a real family event in which they are invited to take some part and share the grief of the mourners. There is the ingredient of pathos and an undertone of the chivalry of bygone days about a great funeral procession which makes the casual bystander want to take off his hat, and which makes it an unforgettable experience and the greatest of all the many ceremonial occasions for which Britain is rightly famous.

Sources and References

Chapter 1 – A RIPE APPLE FROM THE TREE

1. Camden, *The Historie of the Most Renowned Princess Elizabeth, later Queene of England*, p221
2. Quoted in Johnson, *Elizabeth I: A Study in Power*, p432
3. Harington, *Letters and Epigrams*, p97
4. Quoted in Williams, *Elizabeth, Queen of England*, p350
5. Camden op. cit. p222
6. Ibid
7. Harington op. cit. p96
8. Quoted in Williams op. cit. p351
9. Carey, *Memoirs of the Life of Robert*, pp136–8
10. Carey op. cit. p138
11. Carey op. cit. p140
12. Camden op. cit. p223
13. Weston, *The Autobiography of an Elizabethan*, p222
14. Carey op. cit. pp140/1
15. Carey op. cit. pp141/2
16. Manningham, *Diary of John Manningham*, p146
17. Carey op. cit. pp143/4
18. Manningham op. cit. pp146/7
19. Manningham op. cit. p147
20. Chamberlain, *The Letters of John*, ed. N.E. McClure, p189
21. Clapham, *Elizabeth of England*, ed. E.P. & C. Read, p110 (footnote)
22. Manningham op. cit. p159
23. Sheppard, *The Old Palace of Whitehall*, pp297/8
24. Chamberlain op. cit. p190
25. Chamberlain op. cit. p189
26. Stow, *Annales or a General Chronicle of England*, p815

27. Ibid
28. Stanley, *Memorials of Westminster Abbey*, p182
29. Ibid

Chapter 2 – EARLY STUARTS

1. Calendar of Treasury Papers, Scottish. Quoted in Cunnington & Lucas, *Costume for Births, Marriages and Deaths*, p225
2. Inscription on memorial in Westminster Abbey (trans. from Latin)
3. Fuller, *Worthies of England*, vol ii, p129
4. Green, M.A.E., *Princesses of England*, vol vii, p95
5. Ibid
6. British Museum, Harleian MSS 642 ff 246–8
7. Cornwallis in Somers, *A Collection of Scarce & Valuable Tracts*, ed. Walter Scott, p231
8. Ibid
9. Cornwallis op. cit. p235
10. Ibid
11. Cornwallis op. cit. p243
12. Ibid
13. Cornwallis op. cit. p241
14. Chamberlain, *The Letters of John*, ed. N.E. McClure, no. 153
15. Cornwallis op. cit. p243
16. Cornwallis op. cit. p251
17. Chamberlain op. cit. no. 154
18. Ibid
19. Ibid
20. Ibid
21. Cornwallis op. cit. p211
22. Ibid
23. Ibid
24. Public Record Office – LC 2/4
25. Aikin, *Memoirs of the Court of James I*, p414
26. Cornwallis, Private Correspondence of Jane Lady, no. XLI
27. Broadsheet, National Portrait Gallery
28. Cornwallis op. cit. no. XLIII
29. Chamberlain op. cit. no. 327
30. Ibid
31. Chamberlain op. cit. no. 470
32. Cornwallis op. cit. no. LXXXIII

33. Chamberlain op. cit. no. 473
34. Ibid
35. Ibid
36. Fuller op. cit. vol i p108
37. Herbert, *Memoirs of the Last Two Years of the Reign of Charles I*, p168
38. Herbert op. cit. p179
39. Ibid
40. Quoted in Morrah, *A Royal Family*, pp114/15
41. Herbert op. cit. p180
42. Herbert op. cit. p184/5
43. Herbert op. cit. p188/9
44. Ibid
45. Coit, *The Royal Martyr*, p360
46. Herbert op. cit. p193
47. Quoted in Disraeli, *Commentaries on the Life & Reign of Charles I*, p454
48. Coit op. cit. p362
49. Coit op. cit. p363
50. Ibid
51. Coit op. cit. p364
52. Ibid
53. Ibid
54. Coit op. cit. p365
55. Henry, *Diaries & Letters 1631*, ed. M.H. Lee, 96 p12
56. Coit op. cit. p366
57. Herbert op. cit. p195
58. Ibid
59. Ibid
60. Herbert op. cit. p199
61. Herbert op. cit. p201
62. Herbert op. cit. p203
63. Herbert op. cit. p206
64. Fuller op. cit. vol iii, p504

Chapter 3 – LATER STUARTS

1. Evelyn, *The Diary of John*, ed. E.S. de Beer, vol III, p246
2. Burnet, *History of My Own Time*, vol i, p299
3. Pepys, *The Diary of Samuel*, ed. R.C. Latham & W. Matthews, vol i, p244
4. Burnet op. cit. vol i, p300
5. Pepys op. cit. vol i, p245

6. Green, *Princesses of England* vol vi, p322
7. State Papers Venetian 7 Jan 1661
8. Green op. cit. vol vi, pp323/4
9. Green op. cit. p325
10. Ibid
11. Quoted in Green, *Princesses* vol vi, p328
12. Burnet op. cit. vol i, p300
13. SP Ven 7 Jan 1661
14. Quoted in Oman, *Elizabeth of Bohemia*
15. Quoted in Green, *Princesses* vol vi, p329
16. Ibid
17. Wills from Doctors Commons – Camden Soc. 83.109
18. Evelyn op. cit. vol III, p316
19. Sheppard, *Memorials of St James's Palace*, p173
20. SP Ven 10 April 1671
21. Burnet op. cit. vol i, p346
22. SP Ven 6 April 1671
23. SP Dom. 6 April 1671
24. SP Ven 17 April 1671
25. Sheppard op. cit. p175
26. SP Dom. 1682, p560
27. Eliot, *Warburton*, p555
28. Fowler/Cornforth, *English Decoration in the 18th century*, pp170/1
29. SP Dom. 1682, p556
30. Evelyn op. cit. vol III, pp413/14
31. Bruce in Crawfurd, *The Last Days of Charles II*, p27
32. Mason, Anne Margaret, Lady in *Household Words*, p278
33. Ibid
34. Ibid
35. Fraser, *Charles II*, p446
36. Crawfurd op. cit. p40
37. Ibid
38. Fraser op. cit. p454
39. Crawfurd op. cit. p42
40. Crawfurd op. cit. p44
41. Crawfurd op. cit. p45
42. *Household Words*, p279
43. Ibid
44. Bulstrode, *Memoirs & Reflections upon the Reign & Government of King Charles I & King Charles II*, p428
45. *London Gazette* 9 Feb 1685

46. Evelyn op. cit. p415
47. Fowler/Cornforth op. cit. p172
48. Evelyn op. cit. p415
49. PRO – LC 2/11 f561
50. Ibid
51. Burnet op. cit. vol iii, p151
52. Burnet op. cit. p151/2
53. Burnet op. cit. p152
54. Ibid
55. Tenison in van der Zee, *William & Mary*, p386
56. Macaulay, *The History of England*, vol IV, p434
57. Fiennes, *The Journeys of Celia*, ed. C. Morris, pp294/5
58. Burnet op. cit. vol iii, p154
59. Evelyn op. cit. 5 March 1695, p204
60. Burnet op. cit. vol iii, p335
61. Quoted in van der Zee op. cit. p475
62. Thomson, *Memoirs of Sarah, Duchess of Marlborough*, vol ii, p156
63. Ibid
64. Ibid
65. Luttrell, *Brief Historical Relation of Affairs of State*, p367
66. Swift, *Journal to Stella* I, p324
67. Wortley Montagu, *Letters & Works of Lady Mary* vol I, pCXXXVIV
68. *London Gazette* quoted in *Correspondence of Jonathan Swift* vol II, footnote to p103
69. Wentworth Papers 416 quoted in Green op. cit. p324
70. PRO – LC 2/18

Chapter 4 – EARLY GEORGIANS

1. *Gentleman's Magazine* Nov 1737 (Historical Chronicle)
2. Hervey, *Memoirs of the Reign of George II*, vol iii, p295
3. Hervey op. cit. p340
4. Hervey op. cit. p319
5. Hervey op. cit. p304
6. Hervey op. cit. pp307/8
7. Hervey op. cit. p312
8. Hervey op. cit. p318
9. Hervey op. cit. p319
10. Hervey op. cit. footnote to p333
11. Ibid
12. Hervey op. cit. p344

13. Hervey op. cit. p346
14. Quoted in Wilkins, *Caroline the Illustrious*, p365
15. Ibid
16. PRO – SP 36/44 f 42
17. PRO – LC 2/24
18. Wilkins op. cit. p366
19. Ibid
20. Hervey op. cit. vol iii, p351
21. Walpole, *Memoirs of King George II*, vol iii, p83
22. Walpole, *Letters*, vol iii, p39
23. Ibid
24. *Gentleman's Magazine*, vol xxi March 1751
25. Ibid
26. Walpole, *Memoirs*, vol i, p436 (footnote)
27. Walpole, *Letters*, vol iii, p43
28. *Gentleman's Magazine*, vol xxi April 1751
29. PRO – LC 2/26
30. Ibid
31. PRO – LC 2/25(1)
32. PRO – LC 2/26
33. PRO – LC 2/36
34. Walpole, *Letters*, vol iv, p439
35. Walpole op. cit. vol iv, p446
36. Walpole op. cit. vol iv, p449
37. Walpole op. cit. vol iv, pp445–7

Chapter 5 – LATER GEORGIANS

1. Delany, *Autobiography & Correspondence of Mary Granville, Mrs Delany* ser. 2, vol 3, p107
2. Ibid
3. Ibid
4. *Gentleman's Magazine* Nov 1810
5. Ibid
6. Belsham, *Memoirs of the Reign of George III*, vol I, p394
7. *New Monthly Magazine*, vol 8, p531
8. Creevey, *The Creevey Papers*, ed. Sir H. Maxwell, p266
9. Hamilton, *A Record of the Life & Death of H.R.H. The Princess Charlotte*, p66
10. Ibid
11. *Gentleman's Magazine*, vol 87, p449

12. Hamilton op. cit. p68
13. Quoted in Stuart, *Daughter of England*, p307
14. Quoted in Stuart op. cit. p309
15. Ibid
16. Stuart op. cit. p311
17. Arblay, *Diary & Letters of Madame d'Arblay (Fanny Burney)* L1134, p749 (quoting from *Macbeth*)
18. Ibid
19. *New Monthly Magazine*, vol VIII, p527
20. Ibid
21. *New Monthly Magazine*, vol VIII, p528
22. *Lady's Magazine*, vol 48, p569
23. Hamilton op. cit. p147/8
24. Hamilton op. cit. p150
25. Hamilton op. cit. p149
26. Hamilton op. cit. p150
27. *New Monthly Magazine*, vol VIII p531
28. Ibid
29. Ibid
30. Ibid
31. Ibid
32. *Lady's Magazine*, vol 49, p389
33. Ibid
34. Duchess of Gloucester to Mme d'Arblay quoted in Hedley, *Queen Charlotte*, p297
35. Arblay op. cit. p298
36. Ibid
37. *Lady's Magazine*, vol 49, p495
38. *Ackermann's Repository 1818*, p365
39. Harcourt Papers quoted in Hedley op. cit. p325
40. *Lady's Magazine*, vol 49, p279
41. *Lady's Magazine*, vol 49, p282
42. Ibid
43. *Lady's Magazine*, vol 52, p50
44. Percy Fitzgerald quoted in Duff, *Edward of Kent*, p286
45. *Gentleman's Magazine*, vol 90, p177
46. Brooke, *King George III* (foreword), pix
47. *George III, His Court & Family*, vol II, p442
48. RA 44331. Quoted in Brooke, *George III*, p386
49. Creevey op. cit. pp297/8
50. *Gentleman's Magazine* vol 90(1), p172
51. Ibid

52. Op. cit. p173
53. Ibid
54. Op. cit. p176
55. Ibid

Chapter 6 – THE END OF THE HANOVERIANS

1. Adolphus, *Memoirs of Queen Caroline*, vol IV, pp61/2
2. Adolphus op. cit. vol IV, pp70–149
3. PRO – LC 2/48
4. Greville, *Journals of the Reign of George IV*, p89
5. Ibid
6. Ibid
7. Ibid
8. Hibbert, *George IV*, p712
9. Pückler-Muskau, *A Regency Visitor (The Letters of Prince Pückler-Muskau)*, ed. E.M. Butler, pp148/9
10. Creevey, *The Creevey Papers*, ed. Sir H. Maxwell, p553
11. Croker, *Correspondence & Diaries*, vol ii, pp64/5
12. Sir Wathen Waller quoted in Hibbert op. cit. p335
13. Ibid
14. Huish, *Memoirs of George IV*, vol II, p411
15. Huish op. cit. vol II, p409
16. Ibid
17. Huish op. cit. vol II, p411
18. Huish op. cit. p412
19. Huish op. cit. p413
20. Ibid
21. Jekyll, *Correspondence of Mr Joseph Jekyll . . . 1818–1838*, p242/3
22. Huish op. cit. vol II, p405
23. Agar Ellis quoted in Hibbert op. cit. p337
24. Lord Dover's papers quoted in Hibbert op. cit. p337/8
25. Ellenborough, Lord, *A Political Diary*, vol ii, pp310/11
26. Jekyll op. cit. p243
27. PRO – LC 2/62
28. Quoted in Ziegler, *King William IV*, p289
29. Ibid
30. Quoted in Somerset, *Ladies in Waiting*, p217
31. Esher (ed.), *Letters of Queen Victoria*, vol I, p75

32. Greville, *Journals of the Reign of Queen Victoria*, vol I, p8
33. *Illustrated London News* Sat 6 May 1843
34. Ibid
35. *Pictorial Times* Sat 6 May 1843
36. *Illustrated London News* Sat 6 May 1843
37. Ibid
38. *London Gazette* Nov 1849
39. Quoted in Stuart, *Daughters of George III*, p285
40. Quoted in Ashdown, *Ladies in Waiting*, p149
41. Mallet, *Life with Queen Victoria*, p18
42. *The Times*, 27 March 1861

Chapter 7 – LATE VICTORIANS

1. Bennett, *King Without a Crown*, p369
2. Esher (ed.), *Letters of Queen Victoria 1837–61*, p471
3. Esher op. cit.
4. Quoted in Fulford, *The Prince Consort*, p270
5. Quoted in Martin, *The Life of His Royal Highness The Prince Consort*, p433
6. Quoted in Martin op. cit. p439
7. Ibid
8. Quoted in Martin op. cit. p440
9. Ibid
10. Quoted in Martin op. cit. p442
11. *The Times* Monday 16 December 1861
12. Quoted in Fulford op. cit. p272
13. Beaconsfield, *Letters from Benjamin Disraeli to Frances Anne, Marchioness of Londonderry 1837–1861*, p189
14. Esher op. cit. pp372/3
15. Ibid
16. Bennett op. cit. p381
17. *The Observer* Sunday 15 December 1861
18. *The Observer* Monday 16 December 1861
19. Ibid
20. *Punch* 21 December 1861
21. *London Gazette* Monday 16 December 1861
22. *Daily Telegraph* 24 December 1861
23. Ibid
24. Ibid
25. Ibid

26. Ibid
27. Mallet, *Life with Queen Victoria*, p4
28. Ponsonby, A., *Life of Sir Henry Ponsonby*, p38
29. *The Times* 25 January 1878
30. *The Times* 29 March 1884
31. Ibid
32. Ibid
33. *The Gentlewoman* 2 January 1892
34. Madol, *The Private Life of Queen Alexandra*, p168
35. Esher (ed.), *Letters of Queen Victoria 1886–1901* (Journal), p25
36. Ibid
37. Ibid
38. Esher op. cit. (Journal) pp28/9
39. Esher op. cit. (Journal) p207
40. Ibid
41. Cooke, *Princess Mary Adelaide, Duchess of Teck*, vol II, p315

Chapter 8 – QUEEN VICTORIA

1. Esher (ed.), *Journals & Letters of Queen Victoria 1886–1901*, p642
2. PRO – LC 2/149
3. Bell, *Randall Davidson, Archbishop of Canterbury*, p352
4. Ibid
5. *London Gazette* 23 January 1901 – Bulletin from Osborne 7.8 p.m. 22 January 1901
6. Lant, *Insubstantial Pageant*, p247
7. Bell op. cit. p355
8. Ponsonby, F., *Recollections of Three Reigns*, p85
9. Ponsonby op. cit. p86
10. Ponsonby op. cit. p87
11. *The Daily Graphic* Monday 4 February 1901
12. Ibid
13. Princess Marie Louise, *My Memories of Six Reigns*, p116
14. *The Times* 4 February 1901
15. Ponsonby op. cit. p88
16. Ponsonby op. cit. pp88/9
17. Ibid
18. Ponsonby op. cit. pp93/4

Chapter 9 – THE HOUSE OF WINDSOR

1. Pope-Hennessy, *Queen Mary*, p388
2. Quoted in St Aubyn, *Edward VII, Prince & King*, p473
3. Maurois, *King Edward & His Times*, p275
4. St Aubyn op. cit. p474
5. Bell, *Randall Davidson, Archbishop of Canterbury*, p608
6. *The Times* 7 May 1910
7. St Aubyn op. cit. p475
8. Rose, *King George V*, p77
9. Esher, *Journals & Letters 1870–1930*, vol iii, p11
10. Ibid
11. Ponsonby, F., *Recollections of Three Reigns*, p271
12. *The Times* 11 May 1910
13. Ponsonby op. cit. p271
14. Ponsonby op. cit. p272
15. Princess Alice, *For My Grandchildren*, p126
16. Rose op. cit. p77
17. *Memorial Sermons*, p16
18. Quoted in Pope-Hennessy op. cit. p511
19. Princess Alice op. cit. p186
20. Battiscombe, *Queen Alexandra*, p302
21. Quoted in Pope-Hennessy op. cit. p538
22. Ibid
23. Battiscombe op. cit. p302
24. Pope-Hennessy op. cit. p538
25. Ibid
26. Quoted in Nicolson, *King George V*, 451
27. Quoted in Nicolson op. cit. p530
28. Ibid
29. The Times Publication, *Hail & Farewell*, p4
30. Rose op. cit. p360
31. Bryant, *George V*, p175
32. Quoted in Lockhart, *Cosmo Gordon Lang*, p391
33. Ibid
34. Lockhart op. cit. p392
35. Ibid
36. Bryant op. cit. p176
37. Quoted in Pope-Hennessy op. cit. p559
38. Ibid
39. Quoted in Windsor, *A King's Story*, p266
40. Windsor op. cit. p266

41. Ibid
42. Windsor op. cit. p267
43. Lockhart op. cit. p393
44. Windsor op. cit. p269
45. Ibid
46. Lockhart op. cit. p394
47. Quoted in Pope-Hennessy op. cit. p562
48. Lockhart op. cit. p395

Chapter 10 – MODERN TIMES

1. Wheeler Bennett, *King George VI*, p470
2. Colville, *Crowded Life*, p131
3. Wheeler Bennet op. cit. p548
4. Ibid
5. Wheeler Bennett op. cit. p787
6. Ibid
7. Wheeler Bennett op. cit. p788
8. Wheeler Bennett op. cit. p794
9. Wheeler Bennett op. cit. p799
10. Christmas Speech 1951 quoted in Wheeler Bennett op. cit. p802
11. *London Gazette* Tuesday 12 February 1952
12. *The Times* Saturday 16 February 1952
13. Townsend, *Time & Chance*, p193
14. Ibid
15. Airlie, *Thatched with Gold*, p235
16. *The Times* Saturday 16 February 1952
17. Ibid
18. Ibid
19. Queen Mary to Duke of Baena quoted in Pope-Hennessy, *Queen Mary*, p621
20. Airlie op. cit. p237
21. Bulletin, *The Times* 25 March 1953
22. Pope-Hennessy op. cit. p622
23. Bryan & Murphy, *The Windsor Story*, p677
24. Ibid
25. Sir Colin Coote in *Daily Telegraph* quoted in Donaldson, *Edward VIII*, p409
26. Quoted in Bryan & Murphy op. cit. p685
27. *Daily Mail* 6 September 1979
28. *Daily Express* 6 September 1979
29. *Daily Mail* 6 September 1979
30. *Daily Express* 6 September 1979

Bibliography

Ackermann's Repository 1817–27

ADOLPHUS, J.H. *Memoirs of Queen Caroline*, London 1821

AIKIN, LUCY *Memoirs of the Court of Queen Elizabeth*, London 1818
  Memoirs of the Court of Charles 1, London 1833

AIRLIE, MABELL, Countess of *Thatched with Gold*, London 1962

ALICE, H.R.H. PRINCESS, COUNTESS OF ATHLONE *For My Grandchildren*, London 1966

ARBLAY, *Diary and Letters of Madame d'Arblay (Fanny Burney) 1778–81*, London 1904
    (ed. Barrett, Charlotte)

ARKELL, R.L. *Caroline of Ansbach*, Oxford 1939

ASHDOWN, DULCIE *Queen Victoria's Mother, Ladies in Waiting*, London 1976

ASHLEY, MAURICE *James II*, London 1977

ASQUITH, MARGOT *Autobiography*, London 1922

ATTLEE, C.R. *As It Happened*, London 1954

BATE, DR GEORGE *Elenchus . . . Anglia*, 1685

BATTISCOMBE, GEORGINA *Queen Alexandra*, London 1969

BEACONSFIELD, 1ST VISCOUNT *Letters from Benjamin Disraeli to Frances Anne, Marchioness of Londonderry 1837–1861*, ed. The Marchioness of Londonderry, London 1938

DE BEER, E.S. (ed.) *The Diary of John Evelyn*, Oxford 1955

BEESLEY, E.S. *Queen Elizabeth*, London 1920

BELL, RT. REV G.K.A. *Randall Davidson (Archbishop of Canterbury)*, Oxford 1938

BELLOC, HILAIRE *Charles the First, King of England*, London 1933

BELSHAM, WILLIAM *Memoirs of the Reign of George III, 1802–1820*, London 1824

BENNETT, DAPHNE *King without a crown*, London 1977

BENTON, E.F. *King Edward VII*, London 1933

BINGHAM, CAROLINE *James I of England*, London 1982

BOND, MAURICE *The Romance of St George's Chapel, Windsor Castle*, Windsor 1983

BOWEN, MAJORIE *The Third Mary Stuart*, London 1929

BOWLE, JOHN *Charles I*, London 1975

BROOKE, JOHN *King George III*, London 1972

BROOKE SHEPHERD, GORDON *Uncle of Europe*, London 1975

BRYAN, J. III and MURPHY, CHARLES J.V. *The Windsor Story*, London 1979

BRYANT, ARTHUR *King Charles II*, London 1931
 George V, London 1936

BURNETT, GILBERT *History of my own time* (ed. O. Airy), London 1900

BULSTRODE, SIR RICHARD *Memoirs and reflections upon the Reign and Government of King Charles I and King Charles II*, London 1721

BUTLER, E.M. (ed.) *A Regency Visitor* (The letters of Prince Pückler-Muskau), London 1957

'CAESAR' *Where's Master?*,' London 1910

CAMDEN, WILLIAM *The Historie of the Most Renowned Princess Elizabeth, Late Queene of England . . .*, London 1630

CAREY, ROBERT *Memoirs of the Life of*, London 1759

CATHCART, HELEN *The Queen Mother*, London 1965

CHAMBERLAIN, JOHN *Letters . . . during the Reign of Queen Elizabeth*, Camden Society 1861

CHAMBERLIN, FREDERICK *The Private Character of Queen Elizabeth*, London 1921
 The Sayings of Queen Elizabeth, London 1923

Chemist and Druggist, The, Vol 101, August 16, 1924

CHETTLE, HENRY *The Order and Proceeding at the funeral of . . . Elizabeth*, London 1603

CLEUGH, JAMES *Prince Rupert*, London 1934

CLISSOLD, PETER 'Samuel Travers and the Naval Knights of Windsor' in *The Mariner's Mirror*, February 1974

COIT, C.W. *The Royal Martyr*, London 1924

COLVILLE, LADY CYNTHIA *Crowded Life*, London 1963

CONNELL, NEVILLE *Anne*, London 1937

COOKE, C. KINLOCH *Princess Mary Adelaide, Duchess of Teck*, London 1900

CORNWALLIS *The Private Correspondence of Jane, Lady C 1613–1644*, London 1842

CRAINZ, FRANCO *An Obstetrical Tragedy*, London 1977

CRANKSHAW, EDWARD *The Fall of the House of Habsburg*, London 1963

CRAWFORD, MARION *The Little Princesses*, London 1950

CRAWFURD, RAYMOND *The Last Days of Charles II*, Oxford 1909

CREIGHTON, MANDELL *Queen Elizabeth*, London 1899

CROKER, J.W. *Correspondence and Diaries*, London 1884

CUMMING, VALERIE *Royal Attributes, The Dress of Two Royal Cousins 1542–1587*, Royal Stuart Papers XXIV, 1984

CUNNINGTON, PHILLIS and LUCAS, CATHERINE *Costume for Births, Marriages and Deaths*, London 1972

CURL, JAMES STEVENS *A Celebration of Death*, London 1980

CURTIS BROWN, BEATRICE *The Letters of Queen Anne*, London 1935

Daily Telegraph, The 1861–1979

DELANY, M. *Autobiography and correspondence of Mary Granville, Mrs Delany*, London 1861

DICKENS, CHARLES (ed.) *Last Moments of an English king. Household Words*, Vol IX, 1854

D'ISRAELI, I *Commentaries on the Life and Reign of Charles I*, London 1831

DONALDSON, FRANCES *Edward VIII*, London 1974

DUFF, DAVID *Edward of Kent*, London 1938

 The Life Story of H.R.H. Princess Louise, Duchess of Argyll, London 1940

 The Shy Princess, London 1958

 Hessian Tapestry, London 1967

 Albert and Victoria, London 1972

DUTTON, RALPH *English Court Life*, London 1963

ELLENBOROUGH, E. LAW (Lord) *A Political Diary* (ed. Lord Colchester), London 1881

ESSAD-BEY, MOHAMMED *Nicholas II, Prisoner of the People*, London 1936

ESHER, LORD (ed.) *Letters of Queen Victoria*, 1886–1901

ESHER, REGINALD, Viscount (ed.) and OLIVER, V. *Journals and Letters* (of Queen Victoria), London 1938

ETHU, REGINALD, Viscount *Journals & Letters 1870–1930*, London 1938

FITZROY, SIR ALMERIC *Memoirs*, London 1926

FOWLER, JOHN and CORNFORTH, JOHN *English Decoration in the Eighteenth Century*, London 1974

FRANKLAND, NOBLE *Prince Henry, Duke of Gloucester*, London 1979

FRASER, ANTONIA *Oliver Cromwell, One Chief of Men*, London 1973

 Charles II, London 1979

FRITZ, PAUL *The Trade in Death* (in Eighteenth Century Studies), Spring 1982

Frogmore Gardens, Windsor Castle Short Guide

FULFORD, ROGER *The Prince Consort*, London 1949

 George IV, London 1949

FULLER, THOMAS *Worthies of England*, London 1811

Gentleman's Magazine, The 1737–1820

Gentlewomen, The 2 January 1892

George III, His Life and Family, London 1824

Graphic, The Daily 1901–1910

GREEN, DAVID *Queen Anne*, London 1970

GREEN, MARY ANNE EVERETT *Princesses of England*, London 1849–55

GREENWOOD, DOUGLAS *Who's Buried Where in England*, London 1982

GREGG, PAULINE *King Charles I*, London 1981

GREVILLE, C.C. *Journals of the Reigns of George IV, William IV and Queen Victoria, 1837–1852*, London 1885

GREW, E. and M.S. *The English Court in Exile, James II at St Germain*, London 1911

HAMILTON, E.B. *A Record of the Life and Death of H.R.H. the Princess Charlotte*, London 1817

HAMILTON, ELIZABETH *William's Mary*, London 1972

HARINGTON, SIR JOHN (ed. N.E. McClure) *Letters and Epigrams*, Philadelphia 1930 (ed. T. Peck) *Nugae Antiquae*, London 1769

HARRISON, MICHAEL *Clarence. The Life of H.R.H. the Duke of Clarence and Avondale*, London 1972

HARTNELL, NORMAN *Silver and Gold*, London 1955

HARRISON, G.B. *The Elizabethan Journals, Being a record of those things most talked of during the years 1591–1603*, London 1928

HEATH, JAMES *A Chronicle of the Late Intestine War in the Three Kingdoms . . . in Four Parts*, London 1676

HEATH, JAMES *Flagellum or the Life and Death, Birth and Burial of Oliver Cromwell*, London 1663

HEDLEY, OLWEN *Queen Charlotte*, London 1975

HENRY, PHILIP *Diaries and Letters 1631–96* ed. M.H. Lee, London 1882

HERBERT, SIR THOMAS *Memoirs of the Last Two Years of the Reign of Charles I*, London 1839

HERVEY, JOHN LORD *Memoirs of the Reign of George II* (ed. Croker, J.W.), London 1884

HIBBERT, CHRISTOPHER *George IV*, London 1973
The Court at Windsor, London 1964

HOLMES, SIR RICHARD *Edward VII His Life and Times*, London 1911

HOLMES, M.R. *A Carved Head of Elizabeth I* in The Antiquarian Journal, Vol 40, 1970

HOPKIRK, MARY *Queen Adelaide*, London 1946

HOUGH, RICHARD *Mountbatten, Hero of Our Time*, London 1980

HUISH, ROBERT *William IV*, London 1837
Memoirs of George IV, London 1831
Memoirs of H.R.H. Charlotte, Princess of Wales . . ., London 1818

HUME, MARTIN *The Wives of Henry VIII*, London 1905

Illustrated London News, The 1843–1979

JEKYLL, J. *Correspondence of Mr Joseph Jekyll with his sister-in-law, Lady Gertrude Sloane Allaby 1818–1838*, London 1894

JENKINS, ELIZABETH *Elizabeth the Great*, London 1958

JESSE, J.H. *Memoirs of the Life and Reign of King George III*, London 1901

JOHNSON, PAUL *Elizabeth I: A Study in Power*, London 1974

JONES, CHRISTOPHER *The Great Palace, The Story of Parliament*, London 1983
JUDD, DENIS *King George VI*, London 1982

KING, STELLA *Princess Marina, Her Life and Times*, London 1969

Lady's Magazine, The 1817–20
LANT, JEFFREY L. *Insubstantial Pageant*, London 1979
LEAVESLEY, J.H. *The Common Touch*, Sydney 1983
LEE, M.H. (ed.) *Diaries and Letters of Philip Henry 1631–96*, London 1882
LEE, SIDNEY *Queen Victoria*, London 1902
   King Edward VII, London 1927
LOCKHART, J.G. *Cosmo Gordon Lang*, London 1949
LOFTS, NORAH *Anne Boleyn*, London 1979
London Gazette
LONGFORD, ELIZABETH *Victoria RI*, London 1964
LUTTRELL, N. *Brief Historical Relation of Affairs of State*, Oxford 1857

MACAULAY, T.B.M. *The History of England, from the Accession of James I*, London 1855
MADOL, HANS ROGER *The Private Life of Queen Alexandra*, London/Melbourne 1940
MCCLURE, N.E. (ed.) *The Letters of John Chamberlain*, Philadelphia 1939
MAKIN, W.J. *The Life of George the Fifth*, London 1936
MALLET, VICTOR *Life with Queen Victoria. Marie Mallet's Letters from Court 1887–1901*, London 1968
MANNINGHAM, JOHN *Diary of John Manningham*, Camden Society 1868
MARIE LOUISE, H.H. PRINCESS *My Memories of Six Reigns*, London 1956
MARTIN, THEODORE *The Life of His Royal Highness The Prince Consort*, London 1880
MASSIE, R.K. *Nicholas and Alexandra*, New York 1967
MAUROIS, ANDRÉ *King Edward and his Times*, London 1933
MAXWELL, SIR HERBERT (ed.) *The Creevey Papers*, London 1903
Monthly Magazine, The 1820/21
MONTGOMERY-MASSINGBERD, HUGH *Burke's Guide to the British Monarchy*, London 1977
MORRAH, PATRICK *A Royal Family*, London 1982
MORRIS, C. (ed.) *The Journeys of Celia Fiennes*, London 1949

NALSON, JOHN A True Copy of the Journal of the High Court of Justice for the Trial of King Charles I (1648)
NEALE, REV E. *Life of Edward, Duke of Kent*, London 1850
NEVILLE, LADY DOROTHY *Under Five Reigns*, London 1910
NICOLSON, HAROLD *King George V*, London 1952
NOBLE, REV MARK *Memoirs of the Protectoral House of Cromwell*, Birmingham 1787

Observer, The 15/16 December 1861
OMAN, CAROLE *Elizabeth of Bohemia*, London 1938
OSBORN, E. (ed.) *Political and Social Letters of a Lady of the Eighteenth Century*, London
    1890

PEPYS, SAMUEL *The Diary of Samuel Pepys* (ed. Latham, R.C. and Matthews, W.), London
    1972
Pictorial Times Saturday, 6 May 1843
PONSONBY, SIR ARTHUR *Life of Sir Henry Ponsonby*, London 1942
PONSONBY, SIR FREDERICK (1st Lord Sysonby) *Recollections of Three Reigns*, London 1951
POPE-HENNESSY, JAMES *Queen Mary*, London 1959

READ, E.P. and C. JOHN CLAPHAM (ed.) *Elizabeth of England*, London 1951
ROBB, NESCA A. *William of Orange*, London 1966
ROSE, KENNETH *King George V*, London 1983
The Royal Mausoleum, Frogmore – Guide, Windsor 1964
Royal Mews, Buckingham Palace, The (Guide), London 1979
RUSH, B.R. (ed.) *Residence at the Court of St James*, London 1872

ST AUBYN, GILES *Edward VII, Prince and King*, New York 1979
SCOTT, WALTER (ed.) *A Collection of Scarce and Valuable Tracts*. Collected by J.S. Somers,
    London 1809
SCOTT STEVENSON, GERTRUDE (ed.) *The Letters of Madame The Correspondence of Elizabeth
    Charlotte of Bavaria, Princess Palatine, Duchess of Orleans 1661–1722*, London 1924
SHEPPARD, E. *The Old Palace of Whitehall*, London 1902
    Memorials of St James's Palace, London 1894
SOMERSET, ANNE *Ladies in Waiting*, London 1984
STANLEY, DEAN *Memorials of Westminster Abbey*, London 1869
State Papers Domestic, Calendar of
State Papers Venetian, Calendar of
STEERHOLM, CLARA and HARDY *James I of England*
STOW, JOHN *Annales or a General Chronicle of England*, London 1631
STRICKLAND, AGNES *Queen Elizabeth*, London 1907
STUART, D.M. *Daughters of George III*, London 1939
    Daughter of England, London 1951
SWIFT, JONATHAN *Journal to Stella*, London 1901

TANNER, J.R. *English Constitutional Conflicts*, London 1928
TAYLOR, LOU *Mourning Dress*, London 1983
THOMAS, W.M. *Letters and Works of Lady Mary Wortley Montagu*, London 1887

THOMSON, MRS A.T. *Memoirs of Sarah, Duchess of Marlborough and of the Court of Queen Anne*, London 1839

Times, The

Times, The *Hail and Farewell*, London 1936

TOOLEY, SARAH A. *The Life of Queen Alexandra*, London 1902

TOWNSEND, PETER *Time and Chance*, London 1978

TURNER, F.C. *James II*, London 1948

VARLEY, F.J. *Oliver Cromwell's Latter End*, London 1939

WAGNER, SIR ANTHONY *Heralds of England*, London 1967

WALLINGTON, NEHEMIAH *The Reign of Charles I*, London 1869

WALPOLE, HORACE *Memoirs of the Reign of George II* (ed. Lord Holland), London 1846
Letters (ed. Toynbee, Mrs P.), Oxford 1903

WARBURTON, ELIOT *Memoirs of Prince Rupert and the Cavaliers*, London 1849

WARWICK, SIR PHILIP *Memoirs of the Reign of Charles I*, London 1701

WEDGWOOD, C.V. *The Trial of Charles I*, London 1977

Westminster Abbey Official Guide, London 1977

WESTON, WILLIAM *The Autobiography of an Elizabethan* tr. from Latin by Philip Caraman, London 1955

WHEELER-BENNETT, J.W. *King George VI*, London 1958

WHITE, REV G.C. (ed.) *Glimpses of King William IV and Queen Adelaide* (from Clitherow Letters), London 1892

WILKINS, W.H. *Caroline the Illustrious*, London 1901

WILKINSON, CLENNELL *Prince Rupert the Cavalier*, London 1934

WILLIAM IV *Last Moment and Death of His Majesty*, London 1837

WILLIAMS, NEVILLE *Elizabeth, Queen of England*, London 1967

WILLSON, D. HARRIS *King James VI & I*, London 1956

WINDSOR, HRH THE DUKE OF *A King's Story*, London 1951

WOOTTON *Chronicles of Pharmacy*, London 1910

ZEE, HENRI and BARBARA VAN DER *William & Mary*, London 1973

ZIEGLER, PHILIP *King William IV*, London 1971

Index